Mustang

From Mess Decks to Wardroom

Leave safe haven and stand out to sea with an adventurer who lived thirty-two years of naval service to the fullest. From a boyhood desire to go to sea, spawned in landlocked Arkansas, coupled with determination and undying love for the Navy, this career Navy man "came up through the hawse pipe"—known as the path of a Mustang. As he navigates the sometimes-treacherous waters of ship life and shore leave, his exploits and escapades land him in hot water, while teaching him lessons that help him throughout his career. Life at sea, which can be hard and spare, offered late night interludes ashore. His colorful adventures in ports around the world will keep you wondering what happens next. Assignment to twelve ships meant deployment to waters off "hot spots" and war zones—the Caribbean, Cuba, and Vietnam in the 1960s, and the Middle East in the late 1980s. We're along for the cruise, as he masters amphibious landings, aircraft carrier operations, salvage operations, duty on the gunline off Vietnam, and support of a deep-diving submersible on a Top Secret-mission. Each serve to mature a headstrong young man through his rise from seaman recruit to Navy commander, and captain of a ship at sea. One hundred, seventy-nine photographs and maps help to put you in the action.

Mustang

From Mess Decks to Wardroom

Cdr. Lee M. Foley, USN (Retired)

HERITAGE BOOKS
2019

HERITAGE BOOKS
AN IMPRINT OF HERITAGE BOOKS, INC.

Books, CDs, and more—Worldwide

For our listing of thousands of titles see our website
at
www.HeritageBooks.com

Published 2019 by
HERITAGE BOOKS, INC.
Publishing Division
5810 Ruatan Street
Berwyn Heights, Md. 20740

Copyright © 2019 Cdr. Lee M. Foley, USN (Retired)

All rights reserved. No part of this book may be reproduced or transmitted in any form or by any means, electronic or mechanical, including photocopying, recording or by any information storage and retrieval system without written permission from the author, except for the inclusion of brief quotations in a review.

International Standard Book Number
Paperbound: 978-0-7884-5899-6

Dedication

This book is dedicated
to my mom Dorothy, who nurtured the dream and encouraged it, and was there when it was achieved,
to my wife Nida, who supported and assisted me in scaling the heights to bring the dream to fulfillment,
and to my son Bo, who made my life and dream complete and rewarding. My life's journey was more richly enhanced by his birth and I savor his companionship and love even as he has grown to manhood.

Last, but not least, *Mustang* is dedicated to the men and women whom I've known and served with for more than 32 years in my beloved Navy. Without them, nothing would have been possible and I salute and thank them, one and all.

Contents

Foreword by Rear Adm. Ernie Christensen, USN (Retired)	xiii
Acknowledgements	xv
Preface	xix
1. Boot Camp	1
2. Duty aboard *Lindenwald*	9
3. Short Stint aboard *Mountrail*	27
4. Assignment to a "Bird Farm"	33
5. Flagship Duty	41
6. Return to the Caribbean and "the Med"	49
7. Short Stint aboard *Raleigh*	59
8. "Destroyer man" at last	67
9. First Combat Tour aboard *Noa*	81
10. Second Combat Tour aboard *Noa*	89
11. Final Combat Duty aboard *Noa*	95
12. Naval Reserve Center Duty	105
13. Reporting aboard *Apache*	111
14. New Command Atmosphere	121
15. Duty aboard *Mount Vernon*	131
16. Naval Training Center, San Diego	159
17. Destroyer Tender *Samuel Gompers*	167
18. Degree Completion and Shore Duty	187
19. First Lieutenant aboard *Roanoke*	189
20. Pre-Command Training	199
21. Command of *Excel*	203
22. Replenishment ship *Kansas City*	231
23. Naval War College	248
24. Defense Nuclear Agency	252
25. Final Duty Station	258
Postscript	262

Photos

Foreword: Promotion to commander by Captain Christensen	xiv
Acknowledgements: Some Navy uniforms in 1961	xviii
Preface-1: Paddle-wheel frigate *Mississippi* riding out a typhoon	xix
Preface-2: Amphibious Ready Group in the Caribbean in 1968	xx
Preface-3: Well deck of the dock landing ship USS *Ashland*	xxi
Preface-4: Seaman Apprentice Foley and Commander Foley	xxiv
Preface-5: William S. Sims Jr. awaiting Adm. William S. Sims	xxvi
1-1: Navy recruits and the training ship USS *Recruit* (TDE-1)	1
1-2: A sailor shows off a well-travelled white seabag	3
1-3: USS *Recruit* (TDE-1) at San Diego, California	4
1-4: Boxing bout at Great Lakes Naval Training Station	5
1-5: Boot Camp photograph of Seaman Recruit Lee Foley	6
1-6: Company 118, Recruit Training Center, San Diego	7
2-1: Corry Field at Naval Air Station, Pensacola	9
2-2: A Boatswain's Mate Seaman pipes a command	11
2-3: Dock landing ship USS *Lindenwald* at sea	12
2-4: Berthing compartments aboard the carrier USS *Yorktown*	14
2-5: Painting of St. Thomas by Albert K. Murray, 1943	18
2-6: USS *Terrebonne Parish* anchored off Piraeus, Greece	21
2-7: A corner of the Port of Toulon, France	21
2-8: Admirals George W. Anderson Jr. and David L. McDonald	22
2-9: Signalman aboard the carrier USS *Yorktown*	25
2-10: Navy ships at anchor at Guantanamo Bay, Cuba	26
3-1: Attack transport USS *Mountrail* berthed pierside	27
3-2: Signalman Third Lee Foley aboard the *Mountrail*	29
3-3: Barcelona, Spain	30
3-4: Lisbon, Portugal, early 1900s	30
4-1: Training aircraft carrier USS *Lexington* under way	33
4-2: Navy Yard, Brooklyn, New York	34
4-3: Fleet at anchor in New York Harbor	36
4-4: U.S. Naval Air Station, Pensacola	37
4-5: Signalman Second Lee Foley aboard USS *Lexington*	38
5-1: Command ship USS *Taconic*'s signal bridge	41
5-2: Amphibious flagship USS *Taconic* at sea	42
5-3: Semaphore communications aboard USS *Enterprise*	43
5-4: Sailors on liberty ashore, during the early 1920s	46
5-5: Philadelphia Naval Shipyard, Pennsylvania	48
6-1: Aerial view of Naval Operating Base, Norfolk	49
6-2: Rear Adm. Raymond E. Peet, USN	50
6-3: "Flag plot" aboard an amphibious force command ship	51

6-4: Rear Adm. William P. Mack, USN	52
6-5: Entry gate to Naval Base, Rota, Spain	54
6-6: Attack submarine USS *Scorpion*	55
6-7: Soviet *Krupny*-class guided missile destroyer at sea	57
7-1: USS *Raleigh* off Guantanamo Bay, Cuba	59
7-2: Sailors walking down a city street in Colon, Panama	61
7-3: Destroyer escort USS *O'Callahan* at sea	62
7-4: Heavy cruiser USS *Houston* passing through the Gatun locks	63
7-5: Certificates of ship passage through the Panama Canal	64
7-6: Panama City, Panama	64
8-1: Destroyer USS *Noa* in heavy seas	67
8-2: USS *Noa* after her FRAM 1 conversion	68
8-3: Gooney birds on Midway Island	69
8-4: Subic Bay, gateway to the Philippine Islands	70
8-5: Olongapo City, Philippine Islands	71
8-6: Guidance for Sailors and Marines on liberty in Olongapo	72
8-7: Jeepney public transportation in the Philippines	73
8-8: Battleship USS *New Jersey* bombarding enemy targets	74
8-9: Old abandoned lighthouse tower on Grande Island	75
8-10: Five-inch shell casings aboard the oiler USS *Mattaponi*	76
8-11: Hospital ship USS *Sanctuary* at Wakayama Harbor	77
8-12: Vice Adm. Marc A. Mitscher, USN	79
8-13: Commander Horace D. Mann Jr., USN	80
9-1: Carrier USS *Bon Homme Richard* with destroyer USS *Noa*	81
9-2: Drone anti-submarine helicopter (DASH) in flight	82
9-3: Chiefs Quarters aboard the light cruiser USS *Brooklyn*	82
9-4: USS *Perkins'* (DD-877) DASH hangar and flight deck	84
9-5: USS *Oriskany* catapulting an A-4 attack aircraft	85
9-6: Grumman C-2A cargo plane	86
9-7: USS *Samuel Gompers* providing services to destroyers	87
9-8: Children in small boats begging for coins	88
10-1: Guided missile destroyer USS *King* under way	90
10-2: Bell UH-1 helicopter gunship firing a 2.75-inch rocket	91
10-3: Indigenous craft at Kaohsiung, Taiwan	93
11-1: Vietnamese junk used to intercept Viet Cong craft	95
11-2: Drawing of a "Swift boat" by Ensign John Roach	97
11-3: Destroyer USS *Frank E. Evans* (DD-754) under way	98
11-4: *Frank E. Evans'* after section alongside *Everett F. Larson*	99
11-5: Fleet oiler USS *Ponchatoula* at work in the South China Sea	100
11-6: Lockhart Road, Wan Chai, Hong Kong	102
13-1: Fleet ocean tug USS *Apache* under way	111
13-2: Newly commissioned Warrant Officer Lee Foley	112

13-3: Auxiliary repair dry dock USS *White Sands*	114
13-4: Portion of the wreckage of submarine USS *Thresher*	115
13-5: Bathyscaph *Trieste II* at sea	115
13-6: Naval Amphibious Base, Coronado	117
14-1: Fleet tug USS *Salinan* under way	126
14-2: Navy's deep submergence rescue vehicle (DSRV)	129
15-1: USS *Mount Vernon* off the Massachusetts coast	131
15-2: Attack transport USS *Pickaway* off Camp Pendleton	132
15-3: Capt. William F. Keller Jr., USN	133
15-4: Amphibious Squadron Five plaque	135
15-5: View from inside USS *Mount Vernon*'s wet well deck	135
15-6: Painting of USS *Ranger* at sea by R. G. Smith	138
15-7: *Mount Vernon* proceeding through typhoon-churned seas	140
15-8: Future wife Zenaida Antonio, and her mother	145
15-9: South Vietnamese refugees arrive aboard an aircraft carrier	150
15-10: Task Force 76 ships staged off Vung Tau, Vietnam	151
15-11: South Vietnamese UH-1s landing aboard USS *Midway*	152
15-12: Taking a break from flight quarters aboard *Mount Vernon*	152
15-13: Helicopter being pushed over the side of USS *Okinawa*	153
15-14: Former South Vietnamese Navy ships at Subic Bay	154
15-15: Mary Soo and assistants in Hong Kong	156
15-16: Mary Soo, a legend for over fifty years	156
15-17: CWO2 Foley, ship's Boatswain USS *Mount Vernon*	158
16-1: Panoramic view of Naval Training Station, San Diego	159
16-2: Aerial view of Naval Training Center San Diego	159
17-1: Destroyer tender USS *Samuel Gompers* under way	167
17-2: Hand drawn portrait of Capt. Robert J. O'Malia, USN	173
17-3: The Foley's Wedding Day, 8 July 1978	176
17-4: Passing under a traditional sword arch at wedding	177
17-5: Tai Chung, Taiwan	178
17-6: Promotion to lieutenant	185
17-7: Forty-two *Samuel Gompers*' crewmembers re-enlist	186
19-1: Fleet replenishment ship USS *Roanoke* off San Diego	189
19-2: Chief Engineer LTJG Ben Lindsey, USN	190
19-3: Capt. William H. Reed, USN	191
19-4: LTJG Mike Cameron wearing a few of his many ribbons	192
19-5: Being promoted to lieutenant commander aboard *Roanoke*	193
19-6: Rear Adm. Robert Toney aboard USS *Flint*	195
19-7: Vulcan Phalanx and Sea Sparrow weapons systems	196
19-8: Liberty ship SS *Henry Berg* wrecked in the Farallon Islands	198
20-1: Navy Surface Warfare Officers School building in Newport	199
20-2: YPs berthed near Luce Hall, Naval War College	200

21-1: U.S. Atlantic Fleet Change of Command Ceremony	203
21-2: Ocean minesweeper USS *Excel* under way	204
21-3: LCDR Foley reading an award citation	205
21-4: Light cargo ship USS *Hewell* at anchor	208
21-5: Aerial view of the town of Monterey and harbor	210
21-6: Drawing of Astoria on the Columbia River	211
21-7: Commander, Mine Group One, conference at Seattle	212
21-8: Heavy cruiser USS *Louisville* at Ketchikan, Alaska	215
21-9: Destroyer USS *Dallas* noses her bow toward Juneau	216
21-10: Painting *Kodiak Quarters* by William F. Draper	217
21-11: *Excel's* Combat Information Center during an exercise	220
21-12: Dan buoy being brought aboard *Excel*	221
21-13: *Excel* en route to Vancouver, British Columbia	222
21-14: Presentation of a plaque to a high school student	223
21-15: Member of the Navy's Marine Mammal Program	224
21-16: Heavy cruiser USS *Augusta* at Portland, Oregon	225
21-17: Hospital ship USS *Mercy* entering Vancouver Harbor	226
21-18: Excellence Awards displayed on *Excel's* deckhouse	228
21-19: "Red E" on *Excel's* stack	228
21-20: Secretary of the Navy Energy Conservation Award flag	229
22-1: Battleship Battlegroup Sierra	231
22-2: LT Ernie Christensen, #4 Slot Pilot, Blue Angels	232
22-3: CDR Christensen, Commanding Officer, "Top Gun"	233
22-4: CAPT Philip S. Anselmo, USN	234
22-5: CDR John Scott, USN	234
22-6: LT Jerry Spillers, LDO, USN	235
22-7: Heavy cruiser USS *San Francisco* entering San Francisco Bay	237
22-8: Battlegroups Echo and Sierra sailing together	238
22-9: USS *Kansas City* or *Wichita* refuels the battleship *Missouri*	239
22-10: *Kansas City* replenishing *Ranger* and *Long Beach*	240
22-11: *Oliver Hazard Perry*-class frigate escorting an oil tanker	241
22-12: SecNav James Webb and Captain Ernie Christensen	243
22-13: *Kansas City's* Executive Officer with SecNav	243
22-14: Shellback Initiation aboard *Kansas City*	244
22-15: Proof of being a trusty Shellback	245
22-16: Perth, Australia, on the banks of the Swan River	246
22-17: Sydney's famed opera house and harbor bridge	246
22-18: Picturesque eastern coast of Australia	247
23-1: Luce Hall of the U.S. Naval War College	248
23-2: Alfred Thayer Mahan	249
23-3: Salve Regina College, Newport, Rhode Island	249
23-4: Admiral William J. Crowe Jr., USN	250

24-1: Aerial view of Johnston Atoll and Sand Island — 252
24-2: Johnston Atoll Chemical Agent Disposal System Plant — 254
24-3: EP-X-U-2 patrol aircraft in flight — 255
25-1: Bo, Nida, and I cutting my retirement cake — 260
25-2: Shadow Box, hand-made by BMCS David Caro, USN — 260
25-3: LCDR Jim Taplett and LT Dave Bruhn — 261
25-4: BM1 Dutch "Buddah" Menke, USN, (Retired) — 261
Postscript-1: At age eight and on retirement day — 262
Postscript-2: Fancy knot board by BMC Manual Gomez — 263

Maps

2-1: Northern Caribbean basin — 19
10-1: Area of U.S. Naval Operations in North Vietnam, 1964-65 — 89
16-1: Rung Sat Special Zone — 161
22-1: Persian Gulf, Gulf of Oman, and surrounding countries — 241

Foreword

I challenge anyone to have the energy, drive and learned skills necessary to follow Commander Lee Foley's path and to have attained the quality of his stature among his peers and superiors as a naval officer. This book provides a glimpse into the intricacy of this exceptional man's life in our navy. He is 'Heart and Soul' a man who did literally everything over the course of his career and in doing so accomplished it with wonderful perspective and a never-ending sense of service and humor.

Lee is at once, a strongly directed successful man, a retired naval officer and, most of all, a friend. But to describe him in only those confining phrases takes away from what he has done and who he is. He is so much more. A dedicated and successful seafarer, he is representative of the great naval men, past and present, whose singular focus, direction, and dedication led to the expansive presence of the United States Navy on the seven seas and while "showing the flag," a reminder of democracy, to the seagoing nations of the world.

Lee represents the reasons why our sailors won the seas surrounding these great United States of America in the late 1700s, why our naval service prevailed in the Pacific during the latter parts of the last century, and why our men and women remain today, extraordinarily motivated, well-trained, and well-suited to continue this dominance of man and machine amidst the very forceful nature of the world's oceans.

Born in Chicago, raised in Mountain Home, Arkansas, and matured in the Atlantic, Mediterranean, and Pacific, Lee Foley was my executive officer when I took command of the fleet replenishment ship USS *Kansas City* (AOR-3) in April, 1987. As a Naval Aviator, my assignment to an AOR represented the confluence of knowledge of aircraft carrier operations and carrier group support operations. It is how the U.S. Navy blends air and surface operations and commands.

Lee was not only my principal communications channel to the officers and men of the *Kansas City*, he was my advisor, my sounding board and my confidant throughout my tour as commanding officer. In those capacities, I could not have searched for, nor hoped for, a better man to ease me into the "Surface Navy," and thrust me forward into the far reaches of the Pacific. Our duties included arduous, routine operations in difficult weather; crises operations; and extraordinarily long hours, days, and weeks on station in support of combat operations.

Operating the AOR in very close proximity to ships steaming alongside, ranging from destroyers to aircraft carriers, to receive "beans, oil, and bullets," requires great skill and a continuum of focused attention and actions to ensure the safety of the sailors aboard both the delivery and receiving ships. During such evolutions, Commander Lee Foley's consummate seamanship shone brightly; his expertise was hard-won on a long road from seaman recruit to master chief, and up through the chief warrant officer and limited duty officer ranks to lieutenant commander. Following his transfer to the unrestricted line officer community, the Navy immediately ordered him to the command of his own ship. He brought this invaluable perspective to my ship as well.

I am Lee's greatest admirer and fan!

Ernie Christensen
Rear Admiral, USN, retired

Photo Foreword

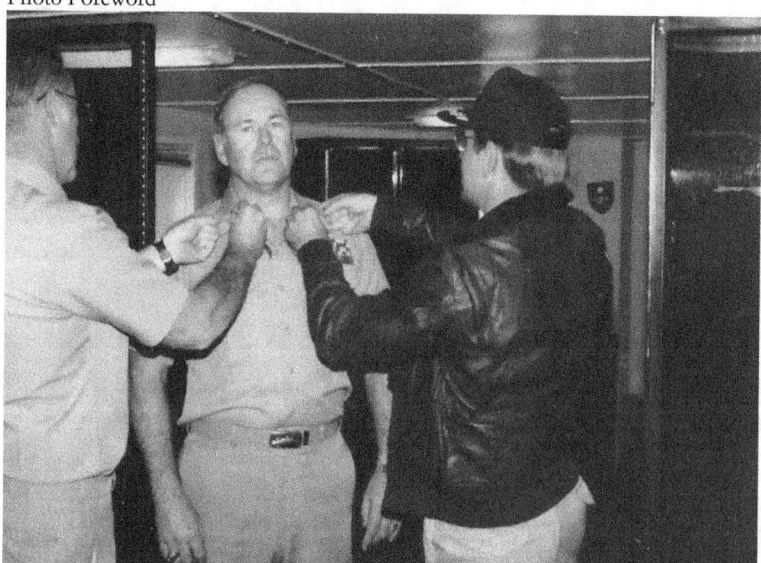

CAPT Ernie Christensen (at right), commanding officer, USS *Kansas City*, promoting his executive officer Lee M. Foley to commander by pinning silver oak leaves on his shirt collar points, assisted by LCDR Jerry Spillers, the ship's First Lieutenant. Author's collection

Acknowledgements

Ships are only as good as the men and women who serve on them. When stories like MUSTANG are told it is usually the story of a ship, or ships. The men and women seem to get lost in the overall picture. For this reason, I want to acknowledge the men and women who sailed with me. We will always be shipmates.

I would particularly like to thank Commander David Bruhn, USN, Ret. for his willingness to assist in bringing Mustang to life. Without his gift for words and phrases, and a keen knowledge of the Navy, my desire to write a memoir commemorating my career would never have reached fruition. He freely shared excerpts from other books he has authored and I'm grateful for those additions to this one.

I owe much of my success to officers I was fortunate enough to work for. These include Rear Admirals Ernie Christensen and Robert Toney; Commodores Mike Barker and Tom York; Captains Robert O'Malia, Phillip Mansell, and Bill Reed; Commanders Tony Coulapedis, George Howe, and Horace. D. Mann; and Lieutenants Bill Horne and George "Dusty" Rhodes, among others. These gentlemen saw the potential in a raw enlisted sailor, and later on in the officer I would become, and took the time and effort to guide and teach me as they assisted my career in moving forward. I am forever indebted and grateful that they believed in me.

The enlisted men and women I served with as one of them, and then later, as I was given the trust and responsibility as an officer to lead and take care of them, are an integral part of MUSTANG. I never forgot that I was a "white hat," that I cleaned compartments and heads, that I shined brightwork, handled lines, served as a mess cook, ran errands, chipped and painted, and swabbed decks. Without these sailors trusting me and believing in what I asked them to do, I would never have been given Command at Sea or been promoted to full Commander.

When I was eight years old, I told my mother Dorothy that I wanted to be a sailor. She nurtured and encouraged that idea for nine years until I joined the Navy. After I joined, she was always there to offer advice when I asked, to listen to some of my tales of woe, but always to help me keep focused on the next goal as my career unfolded, first as an enlisted sailor and later as an officer. She was there at the start and when I retired thirty-two plus years later. She passed some years ago, but I hope she was proud of me and knew that I loved and cherished her.

My wife Nida deserves a lot of credit. Navy wives who wait for us while we're deployed must have the patience of Job. They spend many months alone dealing with problems that sometimes are overwhelming and they can't turn to us because we're at sea. A Navy wife must be both parents rolled into one and raise our children, for the most part, alone while we're gone. Then, when we return home and look to be the head of the household again, she must relinquish control, and fall back into a more natural role, with a smile on her face. It is never easy to maintain a marriage when you're a sailor and your life is the sea. In almost 41 years of marriage, and 15 of those years as a Navy wife, Nida never complained and always looked to put a positive face on whatever situation came up.

When I felt that I had been treated unfairly and was passed over for promotion, I was strongly considering reverting to Master Chief Petty Officer. Nida's counsel was not to do that, to never go back. I was an officer so just keep trying to do my best and it would all work out. She was right. We made some major moves in the Navy. From San Diego to San Francisco; to Newport, Rhode Island; to Pearl Harbor, Hawaii; and finally to Albuquerque, New Mexico. When orders came, she was as excited as I was as we embarked on something new. Being a Navy wife is not easy, but Nida made it look like a walk in the park with a smile on her face. With support and encouragement like that, I was able to fully focus on furthering my Navy career.

Being a "Navy Brat" isn't easy either. Youngsters just get settled in a new community and new schools, and then they are pulled out as the Navy family picks up stakes and relocates. It is hard to lose friends it took time to make, and then have to start over somewhere new. Our son Bo was no different and really didn't like all the moving, although I don't think he minded Hawaii too much. When we finally got to Albuquerque we didn't move anymore, at least while he was growing up. He was able to keep the same friends through elementary school, middle school and high school, and at the University of New Mexico. I'm sure having both parents full-time and a stable environment did wonders for his peace of mind. He has been our pride and joy since the day he blessed us by coming into our lives.

I was blessed to have Lynn Marie Tosello editing the manuscript for *Mustang*. Her innate feel for what was grammatically correct and her knowledge of sentence structure and punctuation helped bring a sometimes-busy picture into crisp and perfect focus.

xviii   Acknowledgements

Photo Acknowledgements

Some uniforms of the Navy, when I joined in 1961. From left to right: Second Class Petty Officer, Yeoman; Lieutenant Commander, Navy Nurse Corps; Third Class Petty Officer, Hospital Corpsman; Captain, Navy Aide/Attaché; Master Chief Petty Officer, Utilitiesman.
Naval History and Heritage Command

Preface

Twenty years from now you will be more disappointed by the things that you didn't do than by the ones you did do. So throw off the bowlines. Sail away from the safe harbor. Catch the trade winds in your sails. Explore. Dream. Discover.

—Mark Twain

Photo Preface-1

Painting by Heine of the paddle-wheel frigate USS *Mississippi* riding out a typhoon in the Pacific, 7 October 1854.
Naval History and Heritage Command photograph #NH 46039

Today, ships at sea receive continuous up-to-the-moment weather information—including typhoon warnings—gleaned from satellites and other sources, and analyzed by meteorological centers ashore. Such was not the case in the early 1970s and for hundreds of years earlier, when the first warning of the approach of a typhoon or hurricane was a report, normally by a crewmember aboard ship, "Captain, the glass is falling." A significant decrease in atmospheric pressure in a very short time, as measured by a column of mercury in a glass barometer, signaled the approach of a storm. The ship would then typically try to run from the storm, or find shelter from approaching high winds and seas in the lee of an island, if such existed nearby, or batten down everything, and ride it out. Many ships were lost at sea due to extreme weather.

Photo Preface-2

Ships of an Amphibious Ready Group operating together in the Caribbean in 1968. From (l-r) are the attack cargo ship USS *Rankin* (AKA-103), dock landing ship USS *Fort Snelling* (LSD-30), amphibious assault ship USS *Boxer* (LPH-4), tank landing ship USS *Graham County* (LST-1176), and the high-speed transport USS *Kirwin* (APD-90). Naval History and Heritage Command photograph #NH 97284

In the early 1970s, a U.S. Navy amphibious ready group (ARG) on deployment in the Pacific was caught up in one of several typhoons, spawned in warm waters during typhoon season. An ARG consists of a naval element—a group of warships known as an amphibious task force—and a landing force of U.S. Marines. Together, the ships and their crews, and the embarked Marines, comprise a well-trained force of "sea soldiers" on patrol, ready to carry out amphibious landings, if necessary, on hostile shores in troubled areas of the world.

Super Typhoon Nora (fully discussed in Chapter 15) wrought much damage, including ripping the bow doors off a tank landing ship, and causing an estimated $130 million of damage/losses to Marine Corps equipment stowed aboard a dock landing ship. Subsequently, a Court of Inquiry—an Administrative fact-finding body comprised of two

Navy captains and one Marine Corps colonel, as well as one JAG (Judge Advocate General) officer to advise the court—found the ship's Bosun aboard the dock landing ship guilty of improperly securing the equipment, and issued him a Letter of Admonition.

Photo Preface-3

View of the well deck of the dock landing ship USS *Ashland* (LSD-1) in the Pacific during World War II. The photograph, from the collection of Adm. Harry W. Hill, USN, is annotated with a handwritten caption, "Even with the stern gate closed, the least amount of roll causes THIS." All but the latter word has been cropped above. Naval History and Heritage Command photograph #NH 65829

Marine Corps "top brass" insisted that someone be punished even though the facts supported correct securing of equipment. The court cited failure to follow guidance contained in a technical manual that delineated how the equipment was to be secured. However, the manual referenced was one in effect in the fleet after the incident, not the manual then in force. The officer found guilty was invited to submit a rebuttal of the findings, if he believed them unfair or if excessive punishment had been levied against him.

That officer was me, then a Chief Warrant Officer Second (CWO2) assigned to the ship as the ship's bosun, working under the First Lieutenant whose duties and responsibilities included ship's maintenance topside, and seamanship evolutions including the care and operation of the amphibious craft in the well deck. Apparently as a result of the punitive letter in my officer's record, I was passed over for promotion to CWO3 a short time later, but then good things began to happen. I was promoted to CWO3 the following year with promotion backdated, and the year after that, promoted to CWO4, two years early.

I had been told by a senior Navy captain, unofficially, many months after the Court of Inquiry, that the Navy only reluctantly endorsed the findings. Commander, Seventh Fleet, did not concur and felt I was a scapegoat, especially with the attempt to use a manual that wasn't in effect at the time of the incident. As the findings followed the chain of command upward into the Chief of Naval Operations' office, the Navy was evidently pleased that I merely wrote a strong rebuttal based on the manual and pictures, and attributed no blame to anyone senior to me in the Navy or the Marines. I was told that my response played a major role in my backdated promotion to CWO3, my early promotion to CWO4, and my later being one of only six warrant officers, Navy-wide, selected as a Deck Limited Duty Officer.

At this point, some readers might be wondering why I am relating details about an experience which was very painful for me. The answer is, because it illustrates the importance of not letting setbacks "beat one down," or unduly dictate the course of one's life. At one point or another, most people have been disadvantaged by another person or persons. In such cases, it's important to put such things behind you and continue to persevere in whatever undertakings are at hand. I was fortunate that promotion boards chose to make decisions based on the entirety of my record, and not simply use the "blot on my copybook" as a disqualifier to future upward mobility. Other than the initial pass over for CWO3, the Letter of Admonition did not appear to have hurt or hindered my career.

DECADES OF SERVICE IN A VARITY OF SHIPS

I decided to write this book in the hopes that lessons contained within it will help to inspire young people, whether they pursue military service, or other endeavors in life. On a percentage basis, few enlisted sailors earn an officer's commission. Such an accomplishment is termed "up though the hawse pipe" in the U.S. Merchant Marine, meaning up from the lower decks, a refence to the climb from spaces typically occupied by enlisted sailors lower in a ship to "officers country," higher up, near the main deck. Ex-enlisted officers are not always viewed favorable by "regular officers." In fact, in the Royal Navy, they were referred to as "rankers," occasionally "bloody rankers,"—meaning up from the ranks.

In the U.S. Navy, a certain number of senior enlisted are selected for warrant officer or limited duty officer. The applicants for warrant officer must be an E7 (chief petty officer) or higher; those successful are utilized by the Navy in particular tough division officer jobs, requiring specific expertise, not expected of a regular junior officer. Those applying for limited duty officer status may be a rank lower (E6), as they are being sought to ultimately move into department head jobs (above that of division officer) requiring specific knowledge and experience. The other means to obtain a commission is for an enlisted sailor to be selected for and graduate from the Naval Academy, graduate from a university or college with a Naval Reserve Officers Training Corps program, or be selected for and successfully complete Officers Candidate School. The latter programs require a college degree; CWO and LDO do not.

A few ex-enlisted sailors achieve senior officer status, the rank of commander or higher, and a very select few make it to flag rank (rear admiral and above). Most such senior officers have relatively little enlisted time (normally a single 4-year enlistment), before attending college and following a standard officer career path. My journey was longer. I progressed through every rung of the enlisted ranks (E1, seaman recruit; through E9, master chief petty officer), before doing the same for the chief warrant officer and limited duty officer hierarchies, up through lieutenant commander. I then applied for, and was selected for a transfer to regular line officer, following which I was selected for command at sea. I then had the great privilege and honor to command USS *Excel* (MSO-439), a wooden-hulled, ocean going minesweeper.

I first went to sea in 1961, after reporting aboard the dock landing ship USS *Lindenwald* (LSD-6), and completed my last tour at sea in 1987, as executive officer of the replenishment oiler USS *Kansas City* (AOR-3). When I joined the Navy, I was issued one of the last World War II vintage white sea bags, before a change was made to green sea bags. Sailors then still wore black flat hats as part of their dress blue uniforms, and the fleet still had snorkel-equipped diesel submarines. I witnessed the accession of nuclear-powered ships and submarines, the return of battleships to the fleet, and the introduction of the *Ticonderoga* (CG-47)-class cruisers. These powerful warships featured the Aegis combat system, which was later modified to allow the ships to shoot down enemy ballistic missiles—an extremely technologically challenging endeavor.

STAND OUT TO SEA

This book is intended to help former sailors recall with pleasure, sailing the deep, and good runs ashore with shipmates. Current sailors, seamen, and coastguardsmen will find information and lessons learned still applicable. For readers who have not trod the deck of a pitching ship at sea, prepare to (vicariously) cast off all lines, and stand out of harbor with the U.S. Navy, from the early 1960s through the late 1980s. This history is woven into my personal story of progressing from seaman recruit to Navy commander, which required hard work, passion, commitment, a zest for adventure, and some luck along the way. I needed some luck to emerge relatively unscathed from situations I either created, or which resulted from the inadvertent mistakes of a young sailor.

With age comes wisdom. The following two photographs are of the same individual: one a brash young sailor on top of the world, with no worries; the other a senior naval officer, many years older and much more measured, with many important responsibilities and duties.

Photo Preface-4

As a Seaman Apprentice, 1961
Author's collection

Upon promotion to Commander, 1987

EXPLANATION OF OFFICER AND ENLISTED RANKS

The following tables are intended to provide an overview of Navy officer and enlisted ranks. The bottom table is devoted to enlisted ranks; the one above it, warrant officer ranks; and the uppermost table, officer ranks. Chief Warrant Officers (CWOs) are technical specialists who possess knowledge and skills in specific occupational areas at a level beyond what is normally expected of a Master Chief Petty Officer.

Rank	Abbreviation	Pay Grade	Rank	Abbreviation	Pay Grade
Admiral	ADM	O-10	Commander	CDR	O-5
Vice Admiral	VADM	O-9	Lieutenant Commander	LCDR	O-4
Rear Admiral (upper half)	RADM	O-8	Lieutenant	LT	O-3
Rear Admiral (lower half)	RDML	O-7	Lieutenant Junior Grade	LTJG	O-2
Captain	CAPT	O-6	Ensign	ENS	O-1
Chief Warrant Officer	CWO5	W-5	Chief Warrant Officer	CWO2	W-2
Chief Warrant Officer	CWO4	W-4	Warrant Officer	WO1	W-1
Chief Warrant Officer	CWO3	W-3			
Master Chief Petty Officer	MCPO	E-9	Petty Officer Third Class	PO3	E-4
Senior Chief Petty Officer	SCPO	E-8	Seaman	SN	E-3
Chief Petty Officer	CPO	E-7	Seaman Apprentice	SA	E-2
Petty Officer First Class	PO1	E-6	Seaman Recruit	SR	E-1
Petty Officer Second Class	PO2	E-5			

The lowest Navy rank is Seaman Recruit (E-1), and the highest, Admiral (O-10). Absent is the Fleet Admiral rank of World War II. Fleet Admirals during that war were Chester W. Nimitz, William D. Leahy, Ernest J. King, and William F. Halsey. The Warrant Officer (W-1) rank is included in the associated table, but is no longer in use. W-5 was established in the Navy in 2002.

ENLISTED RANKS, RATES, AND RATINGS

Rank plus rate equals rating. For example, the rank of a Senior Chief Boatswain's Mate (BMCS) is senior chief petty officer (E-8), and their rate is boatswain's mate. A senior chief boatswain's mate would most often be called "Senior Chief" aboard ship, because everyone would know they were a boatswain's mate and, if not, Senior Chief would always be appropriate. Chiefs, Senior Chiefs, and Master Chiefs are addressed thus, out of respect for their high enlisted rank. Below these ranks, a First Class Boatswain's Mate, for example, would typically be referred to as "Boatswain's Mate First" or simply, "Boats." Even more confusing for those who have not trod the deckplates of a Navy ship, are the nicknames associated with different ratings. The fleet "shorthand" for boatswain's mates is "Boats;" signalmen, "Flags;" gunner's mates, "Guns;" quartermasters, "Wheels;" cooks, "Stew burners;" engineering ratings "snipes;" aviation ratings "Airedales," and so forth.

NAVAL AND NAUTICAL TERMS

Photo Preface-5

William S. Sims Jr., saluting 7 April 1919, while awaiting the arrival of his father, Adm. William S. Sims, USN. His small-scale sailor's suit, included a peacoat with a flat hat featuring a cap band from USS *Melville*, which had been Sims' flagship as commander, U.S. Naval Forces in European Waters during and shortly after the First World War. Naval History and Heritage Command photograph #NH 44922

- 1MC: The general announcing system on a ship
- Aft: Toward the stern of a ship
- Aye, aye: As in Yes, sir, I heard the order, I understand it, and I will comply

- Battle Group: A group of warships and supply ships centered around an aircraft carrier or, for a time, a battleship
- Bitts: Mostly found near the bow and the stern of a ship; used to secure lines with a hitch or a loop
- Black flat hat: Dark blue wool hat which the Navy officially retired on April 1, 1963
- Bos'n Locker (Boatswain's Locker): A room usually underneath the foc'sle for the storage of line and deck supplies, also a space for Boatswain's Mates to convene
- Bollards: Short thick posts on a wharf, to which a ship's lines may be secured
- Bulkheads: Walls
- Chocks: Hold a line rather than using it as a tie point
- Commodore: Honorary title given to an officer who is in harge of a squadron, almost always a captain in rank
- Cleats: Fixtures found on a ship used to secure lines
- Conn: One has the Conn when he or she is controlling the movement of a ship under way
- CPO (Chief Petty Officer of all grades, E-7, E-8, and E-9)
- Fantail: The after most part of a ship
- Fo'c'sle: Forecastle Deck leading to the bow of a ship
- Forward: Toward the bow of a ship
- Flag Rank: Officers who attain the rank of Rear Admiral and above
- Head: Bathroom
- Leave: Vacation time
- Liberty: Free time away from work of shorter duration than Leave
- MAA (Master-at-Arms): A Navy rate/rating similar in duties to a police officer
- Marlinspike: A metal tool often used in the arts of rope work
- Mast: A vertical upright pole on a ship where various pieces of equipment are mounted
- Mess Decks: An area aboard ship where sailors eat
- Mustang: Slang term for an officer who came from the enlisted ranks
- Non-Skid: A rough epoxy coating used for weather decks
- Passageway: Hallway

- Pilot House: Where the ship is controlled when under way, also called the Bridge
- Port: When standing on the bridge of a ship looking toward the bow, port refers to the left side
- Quarterdeck: Ceremonial area of the ship used while in port for either boarding, or disembarking the ship
- Quarters: A gathering of personnel to take daily muster, and to pass information; can be for the entire command, or just a department or division
- Sea and Anchor Detail: Set while entering or leaving port, requires the manning of multiple stations throughout the ship
- Starboard: When standing on the bridge of a ship looking toward the bow, starboard refers to the right side
- Stern: The after part of a ship
- SWO (Surface Warfare Officer): Shipboard officers
- UNREP (Underway Replenishment): Transferring fuel, munitions and stores between ships while under way
- Very Well: Expression of acknowledgement a senior gives a subordinate
- Wardroom: Officer's dining area and lounge, also a collective term for the officers aboard a ship
- WestPac: Western Pacific
- XO (Executive Officer): Second in command
- Yardarm: A horizontal bracing mounted on the ship's mast; usually holds blinker lights and light antennas

COMMANDING OFFICER TITLES

Finally, it is probably incumbent on me to explain the many forms of address commonly used regarding the commanding officer of a Navy ship. By long-established tradition, such an officer is "the Captain," no matter their rank. A Naval officer of the rank of captain commanding a powerful, sleek cruiser, aircraft carrier, or "big deck" amphibious or service force ship has the honor of being called "Captain." So also does an officer of the rank of commander in charge of a destroyer, and officers of lesser rank with smaller ships. They are all Captains. The formal title of each is "Commanding Officer," followed by the ship's name. Less formal monikers include "skipper," and "Old Man."

1

Boot Camp

In its basic elements the training of a Bluejacket [enlisted sailor] is the same as for men of the other branches of our Armed Forces. All are outfitted. All are toughened physically and mentally. All are practiced in discipline. All undergo the process that changes them from everyday civilians to the two-fisted fighters, able and willing to prove that men who live in freedom can protect that normal right.

Each service develops these qualities in terms of its own needs and in the Navy, of course, that means ships and everything that goes with them. Upon graduation from the training station some men go to the fleet at once. Others go on to further and more specialized training in accordance with their ability and the order of Navy needs. All eventually take their places in the complicated and efficient organization that protects the sea lanes for the United Nationals on all the oceans of the world.

—From a Naval History and Heritage Command document, titled "The Making of a US Blue Jacket," depicting recruit training.

Photo 1-1

Navy recruits receive instructions as they sit on bleachers sited at the bow of the training ship USS *Recruit* (TDE-1), San Diego, California, 11 December 1969. National Archives photograph #USN 1142049

As the TWA Constellation propeller-driven airliner descended in darkness to land in Los Angeles, the lights of the city spread as far as the eye could see in any direction. It was hard to imagine that I had been in Mountain Home, Arkansas, the previous day, excited about the prospect of joining the Navy. In high school, my only desire had been to graduate and join the Navy. Now I was on my way. The bus ride from Mountain Home, a small city and my home in the southern Ozark Mountains, to Little Rock, followed by a night at the YMCA, and then the plane flight, all attested to the fact that my life had changed forever.

From LA, a large group of prospective recruits were put on another plane for the short, 100-mile jaunt down the coast to San Diego. Arriving at midnight, we were ushered onto a bus, and taken less than a mile from the airport to Navy Recruit Training Command, which bordered Marine Recruit Training Command. There apparently being no place to sleep, we spent the night in a small gathering area. At 0530, a khaki-clad individual collected us, and marched the group in a very loose formation to the Mess Hall for breakfast.

What a shock – as long as you ate everything on your tray you could go back through the serving line as often as you wished. The only catch was that you had to finish eating and be back outside on the "grinder" within 15 minutes. (The grinder was an expansive, concrete covered-area, used to teach new "boots" the art of marching and "close order drill." Many, many hours would be spent there; on graduation day, it would be used as a parade deck.) For me, unlimited food was a bonus and I would have "seconds" every single meal.

After chow, we returned to the holding area, where we were given "fart sacks," a white mattress cover with a drawstring, and then marched to O&R. Outfitting and Receiving, and our barracks, were located on a small island separated from the rest of Boot Camp by a bridge. Our first four weeks of training were spent, by and large, on it (Nimitz Island), with only short trips to Main Side for classroom instruction.

After O&R we went to the Recruit Barber Shop, were shorn, and lined up on numbers painted on the cement outside. Our Recruit Company Commander (the Navy equivalent of a Marine Corps Drill Instructor), a chief machinist's mate named Howell, took control of us and supervised the issuance of our new Navy clothing. Along with the uniforms and a seabag, we were given a cardboard box in which to pack our civilian clothing for shipment home. I was the only recruit issued a white seabag like sailors in WWII, instead of one of the standard green ones then in use, for which I've always been glad. Eighty-five of us were formed into Company 118 and marched off to our barracks to begin Navy Life. (Unbeknown to me, I was to return fifteen years later as the battalion commander of the same battalion in which I had been a recruit).

Photo 1-2

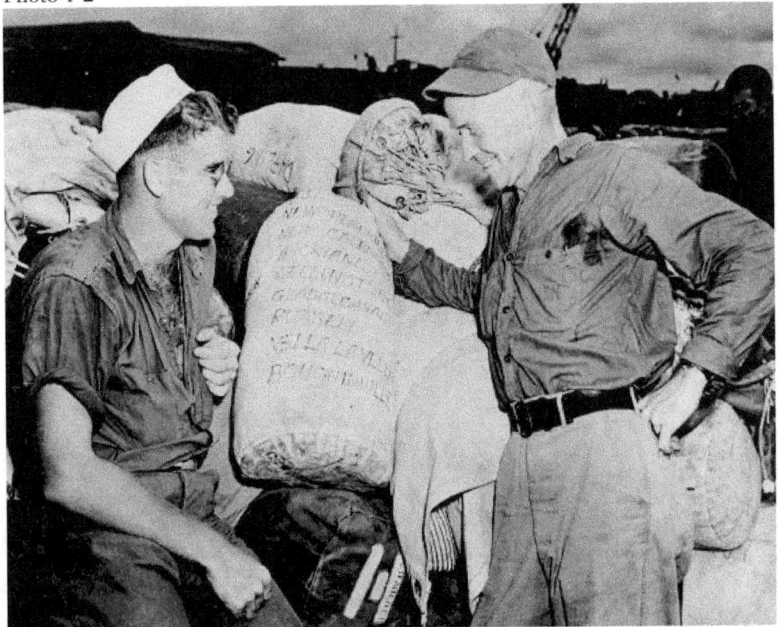

A sailor shows off a well-travelled white seabag, listing the places he had been during his recent service in the Solomons Campaign, in the South Pacific, in World War II. Naval History and Heritage Command photograph #80-G-490384

Our routine thereafter became a whirlwind of inspections of every conceivable type, classroom instruction, marching, physical fitness, small arms training, and close order drill with rifles. We were also given batteries of tests to ascertain our individual aptitudes and abilities, in order that we could be assigned to Navy ratings (jobs) for which we were deemed most suited. Interspersed with this were weekly haircuts and visits to doctors and dentists on a fairly regular basis. I saw more doctors during Boot Camp than I had in my entire 17 years before joining the Navy. We were ordered to stay healthy and, by God, we did.

From my youthful perspective, Recruit Classification left much to be desired. Following graduation, I wanted to immediately report to a destroyer sailing the Pacific as a new member of the deck force. The Navy had other ideas. Based on my test scores, a no-nonsense chief told me that he was assigning me to Communications Technician (R) "A" School and I was going whether I liked it or not. The duties of this rating (a precursor to cryptologic technician) involved the collection of communication intelligence; which meant I would likely be assigned to a shore command following completion of training. He ordered me to sign a form, volunteering to attend the school and discretion being the better part of valor, I did.

LANDBASED TRAINING SHIP USS *RECRUIT*

Photo 1-3

USS *Recruit* (TDE-1), a shipboard training mockup at San Diego, California, used to teach basic seamanship to recruits, circa the 1960s.
Naval History and Heritage Command photograph #NH 80759

The sixth week of training was Service Week, during which all recruits from the various companies in a particular class were pressed into service duties. These included working as servers and dishwashers in the Mess Hall, maintaining grounds around the base, and assignment to duties aboard USS *Recruit* (TDE-1), a mock-up of a WWII destroyer escort. For some unexplained reason, I ended up running errands for the boatswain's mates in charge, who conducted training in marlinspike and deck seamanship. When the BMs found out that I could tie knots and do limited fancy work with line, they drafted me to help in teaching other recruits how to tie knots. Service Week was very pleasant for me.

"SMOKERS"

One of the activities that all recruits had to participate in was boxing tournaments called Smokers. Each bout was three rounds in duration with opponents matched by height and weight. You only had to fight once, but it could be brutal. My opponent was a former northern California Golden Gloves Champion; while my experience had been gained in country brawls, where anything was acceptable in an attempt to win. Needless to say, it wasn't pretty. I spent most of the three rounds trying to get back on my feet while my opponent barely broke a sweat. I guess the best thing that could be said was that I didn't quit. However, I sure was glad when it was over and we only had to do it once.

Photo 1-4

Boxing bout at Great Lakes Naval Training Station, date unknown.
Naval History and Heritage Command #NH 122808

GRADUATION

> *The weeks of training in drill and ceremony are put to the test during Graduation/Pass and Review. Your dress uniform, specially tailored for you is donned, your shoulders are square and your head high. You have accomplished a task few in the U.S. will, and are now part of the world's finest naval force.*
>
> —Military Readiness Command guidance.

Navy Boot Camp during the 1960s was run on the demerit system. Each recruit could only accumulate a total of 20 demerits during the sixteen weeks of training. If you were awarded more demerits, it was grounds for discharge for inaptitude, or being set back to another class following yours, to redo portions of your training. Recruits making it to within one week of graduation with 20 or fewer demerits (a majority of them), were expected to graduate on time, as scheduled. The belief was that no one would even breathe wrong during the final week.

During graduation rehearsal the Friday before graduation, "all hands" were assembled in their respective companies and battalions on the parade field in dress uniform. As we practiced marching and saluting for the forthcoming Pass in Review, my nose started to bleed all over my uniform. I have fair skin and the California sun had played havoc with my face in general and my nose in particular. Chief Howell appeared from nowhere and ordered me to stop bleeding immediately. Try as I might, my nose refused to cooperate and he assessed me 5 demerits. As a result of this action, it appeared that my dream of being a sailor would end before it started, or I would be set back with a new company commander and recruits I didn't even know.

Photo 1-5

"Boot Camp" photograph, Seaman Recruit Foley attired in Dress Whites.
Author's collection

That night I approached Chief Howell and conveyed to him that I would accept any punishment, or perform any task, to keep from being discharged or set back. As I stood at attention in front of his desk, he contemplated my Hard Card, a summation of everything I was, or had accomplished, during training to that point. I stood first in my company academically, first in my battalion (comprised of six companies) in small arms shooting and marlinspike/deck seamanship skills, fourth in the battalion academically, and near the bottom of both my company and battalion in military behavior.

Photo 1-6

Company 118, Recruit Training Center, San Diego. Chief Machinist's Mate R. E. Howell is in the center of the formation, and Seaman Recruit Foley in the top row, second from the right, 12 April 1961.
Author's collection

Howell eventually looked up at me and ordered me to "field day" (clean) the barracks by myself and perform 400 deep knee bends while holding a rifle over my head. (These were done in sets of 25, followed by 3 minutes of rest and then 25 more. This cycle continued until the punishment was complete). Late that evening I completed everything and the 5 demerits were wiped out. Our last week of training went by in a blur, and graduation took place, complete with much pomp and ceremony, and crowds galore. I was awarded a trophy for my shooting skills. Graduated, we proceeded to Processing where we were handed a big manila envelope containing our personnel and medical records under seal and a smaller envelope with our orders. Mine directed me to report to Naval Training Center, Pensacola, Florida, for attendance at Communications Technician (R) "A" School.

Pertinent Advice
(from the *Bluejacket's Manual 1940*)

Everyone makes mistakes. This is human. That is why we have "erasers on our pencils." When you make mistakes do not try to bluff them through or make a lot of foolish excuses. Admit your mistakes frankly and take your medicine. But do not make the same mistake twice, and try not to make too many mistakes.

If you do not show respect to your officers or petty officers, you cannot expect them to show any respect for you.

Some men work without being told, some work when they are told, and some few only work when driven. The first class is easy to train, and from it will come our future leaders. The second class can be trained, and from it we get our followers. The last class cannot be trained, and in it are the ones whose discharge is to be hastened.

Yours is a profession, not a job. You do more than serve for pay alone.

The government educates and trains you, and then gives you a fine position for life, for which, in turn, you agree to do whatever the government demands.

Always boost. If you cannot boost, at least do not knock. "Any fool can criticize. Most fools do."

The efficiency of any ship depends upon the efficiency of the men aboard her. "Good men on poor ships are better than poor men on good ships."

2

Duty aboard *Lindenwald*

The U.S. Navy Boatswain's Mate rating was officially established in 1794. Boatswain's Mates train, direct, and supervise personnel in ship's maintenance duties in all activities relating to marlinspikes, decks, boat seamanship, painting, upkeep of ship's external structure, rigging, deck equipment, and life boats.

—U.S. Navy description of the Boatswain's Mate rating.

Photo 2-1

Flag raising ceremony at the dedication of Corry Field at Naval Air Station, Pensacola, Florida, December 8, 1934.
History and Heritage Command photograph #NH 113410

Following the completion of Boot Camp, I reported to Corry Field in Pensacola, Florida, and began Communication Technician (R) "A" School. Near the end of my course of instruction, I found myself at the top of my class, although the lead instructor and I had a personal conflict. About ten days before graduation it erupted into a physical confrontation. I went to Captain's Mast, was dropped from the school, and received a letter in my personnel jacket that recommended I never be allowed to be in any form of naval communications.

Captain's Mast (often called Mast by sailors) refers to non-judicial punishment (NJP) authorized by the Uniform Code of Military Justice. Article 15 permits commanders to administratively discipline personnel without a court-martial. Punishment can range from reprimand to reduction in rank, loss of pay, restriction to the command, and/or extra duties. Commanders may dismiss charges levied against those brought before them but, as might be expected, there is typically much of the former, and little of the latter.

As was common for sailors who attrite out of Navy schools, I was sent to the fleet as a non-rated seaman, to join other such individuals comprising a ship's deck force. However, one did not have to get in trouble to find themselves in the deck force. Many Navy recruiters, upon a potential recruit telling them they were unsure what they wanted to do (and therefore might fail to enlist), would attempt to "close the deal." This was done by telling the young person, "We have a great program in which you report directly to a ship without having chosen a rate (occupation). This allows you to look around before you decide what you would really like to do." What they did not disclose, was that sailors in the deck force did the hardest work aboard ship. They also did not tell potential recruits that it would not be easy to leave the deck force. This is because a seaman allowed to work elsewhere on board, still counted against the deck force, leaving it short-handed.

Sailors in the deck force tended to be tough. Many were from hardscrabble backgrounds, others had not been choir boys when a judge had told them to "join the military or go to jail." Others became hard as a result of the work environment aboard ship. The deck force put in longer hours than any other group, except perhaps for engineers, who were responsible for maintaining and repairing propulsion, electrical, and auxiliary machinery and equipment. But, while engineers worked in sheltered spaces deep within the ship (which, admittedly were often very hot and humid), the deck forces toiled topside, exposed to whatever the weather brought, for hours on end.

A relatively small number of rated Boatswain's Mates (BMs) ran the deck force. These were former non-rated seaman who chose to remain in the deck force and move up its ranks by "striking for" (declaring their desire to become) Boatswain's Mate and passing the requisite Navy rating examination. BMs, while small in number, had considerable power for their respective ranks, and led with "iron fists" as needed to control young toughs under them.

Photo 2-2

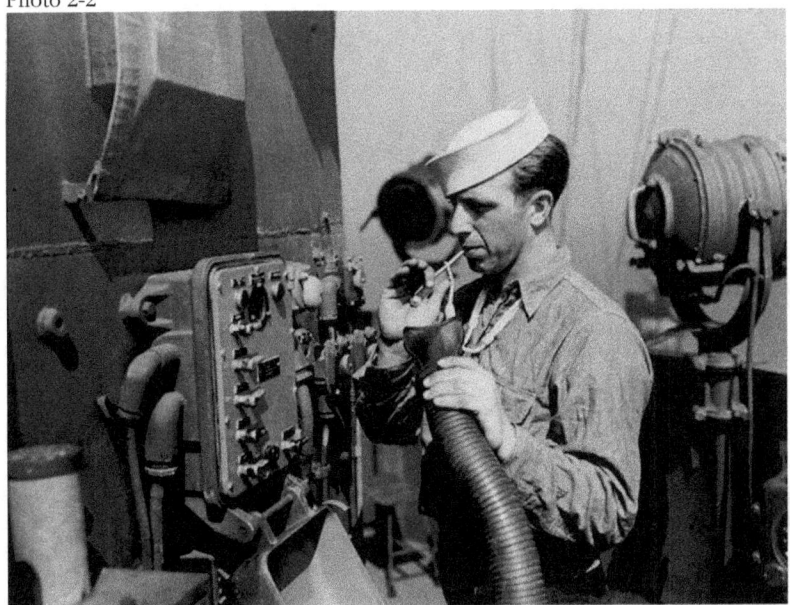

Boatswain's Mate Seaman pipes a command over the loudspeaker system and voice tube, circa 1943-1945. Note fancy lanyard on his "call."
National Archives photograph #80-G-K-2666

The ship's boatswain was a warrant officer who was in charge of the boatswain's mates and seamen, oversight of the ship's deck evolutions, work pertaining to the boats, rigging, anchoring, mooring and unmooring, etc. The chief or leading boatswain's mate worked under the ship's boatswain, or the first lieutenant (a regular officer) on ships without a warrant boatswain. "Bosun" is the correct pronunciation. Often the boatswain or his mates were called "Boats," and the seamen working under them, "Deck Apes."

Of course, none of this was known to me at the time. I had left Pensacola for Norfolk, Virginia, very excited, having received orders to the dock landing ship USS *Lindenwald* (LSD-6), home ported at Naval Amphibious Base, Little Creek. The "amphib base," located in Virginia Beach, adjacent to Norfolk, Virginia, was the major operating base for the amphibious forces in the U.S. Atlantic Fleet.

Dock landing ship USS *Lindenwald* (LSD-6) at sea, 18 January 1965.
Naval History and Heritage Command photograph #NH 107622

I didn't view my time in CT "A" School as a waste or a failure. Rather, I thought of it as an initial obstacle to be overcome in getting assigned to a ship. After arriving in Norfolk, I took a cab to the Naval Amphibious Base. Exiting the taxi, I hoisted my seabag to my shoulder and proceeded to the guard shack at the entry to the base and presented my orders. The guard took a perfunctory look at the papers, and waved me through the gate. I proceeded down the street to the Finger Piers where numerous ships were tied up. I counted three different ships with a single numeral 6 for a hull number.

Not knowing what my ship looked like, or which one it was, I asked an old petty officer walking by if he knew where the *Lindenwald* was parked. He stood there for a minute looking me up and down, then replied, "Ships ain't parked, Boy, you got that? As for the "Limping Lindy," you're practically standing beneath her starboard anchor." With that, he took his leave, calling back to me over his shoulder, "You'll be sorry." I heard him laughing as he continued on his way.

I walked down the pier and up the accommodation ladder to the *Lindenwald*'s quarterdeck. There I saluted the Ensign (American Flag), turned and saluted the OOD (Officer of the Deck), and requested permission to report aboard for duty. The OOD was a chief gunner's mate who looked at me, snorted, shook his head, and exclaimed, "Just what we need, another green recruit." He took my orders and logged me aboard. The POOW (Petty Officer of the Watch) then called the duty boatswain's mate and told him to come claim me.

About fifteen minutes later, an old BM2 with three "hashmarks" (red stripes, one for each four years of Naval service) on his undress blue jumper appeared on the quarterdeck. He told me his name was BM2 Sorrel and said "Fall in behind me, Boy, and follow me to the Deck Compartment. After we got to the berthing area, Sorrel showed me my assigned bunk and locker and told me to come see him in his stateroom when I was squared away. *Lindenwald* was unique. After WWII service in the Pacific she had been decommissioned and transferred to the Military Sea Transportation Service as USNS *Lindenwald* (T-LSD-6), operated by a civilian crew. Recommissioned USS *Lindenwald* on 1 July 1960, her deck seamen and engineering firemen slept in standard Navy berthing compartments, while more senior crewmembers were assigned to 2-man and 4-man staterooms.

My bunk was a piece of canvas laced to an aluminum frame. No bunk light, no privacy curtain or panel, and no divider—which sailors today enjoy. Sailors then slept in tiered racks with approximately two feet between each one. The ones at the very bottom had hinges on one side, allowing them to be "triced up" each morning to facilitate cleaning underneath. Aisles between the tiers were so narrow that only one person at a time could move through them. My locker was made from aluminum and measured three feet high by one and one-half feet wide by one foot deep. Since in those days, enlisted sailors were not allowed to have civilian clothes aboard ship, the contents of my seabag fit into the locker perfectly.

I had finished stowing my locker and was making up my rack when I heard grumbling and shuffling behind me. Turning around I found myself confronted by a group of hostile and upset non-rated sailors. A challenge, "What are you doing in our compartment "Boot"? was followed by, "We don't want no outsiders living with us; maybe we should cut you up a little!" Recognizing that an unavoidable fight was forthcoming, I punched the sailor closest to me as hard as I could and kicked another (displaying an opened boatswain's knife in his hand) in the kneecap. I was badly outnumbered, but fortunately, the restricted space limited access to me. BM2 Sorrel must have heard the fight because he arrived on the scene with another old BM2 named Davis, and the two of them waded into the fray and separated us by force.

Photo 2-4

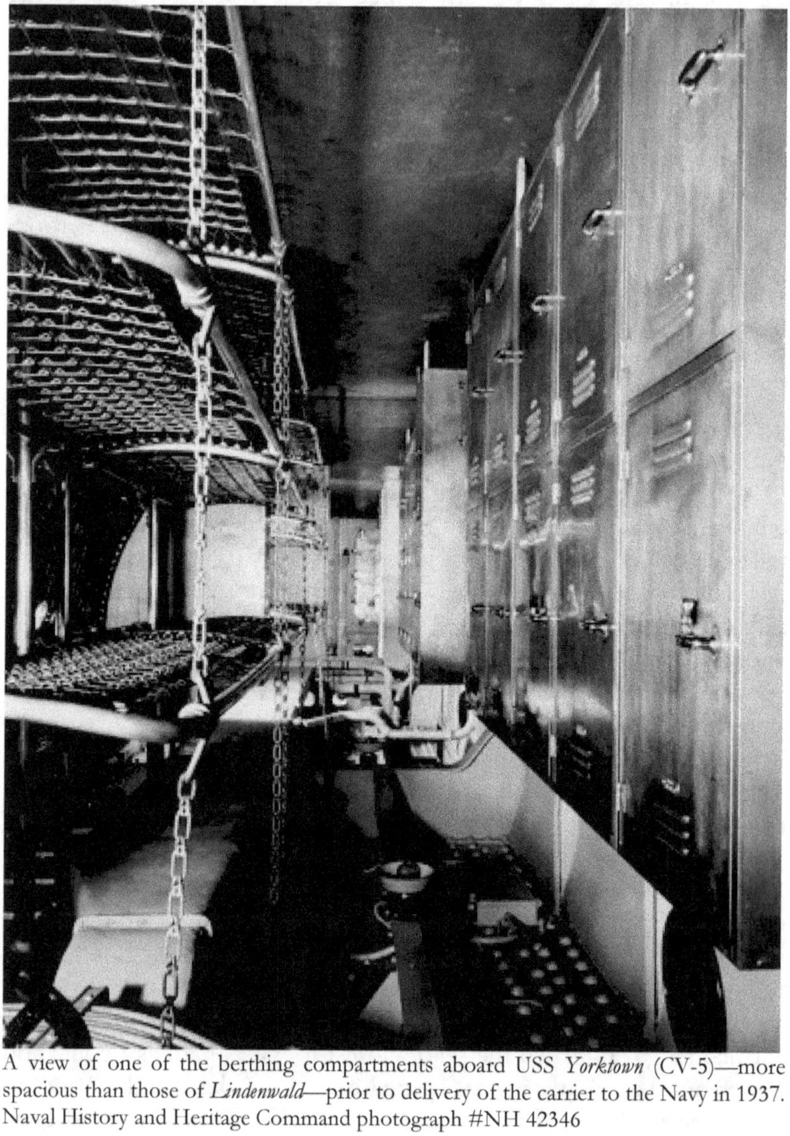

A view of one of the berthing compartments aboard USS *Yorktown* (CV-5)—more spacious than those of *Lindenwald*—prior to delivery of the carrier to the Navy in 1937. Naval History and Heritage Command photograph #NH 42346

Davis called "Sick Bay" and had a corpsman come down and check everyone out. The guy whose knee I kicked wasn't going to be moving around much for a while. Sorrel asked me if I wanted to place anyone on report. "No, Boats, I can take care of myself. I don't need a Report Chit or a rated boatswain's mate to protect me." Sorrel and Davis looked at each other, grinned, and then Davis said to me, "You'll do, kid. Come see me after you get cleaned up." I should explain that "Boot" was a derogatory term used universally throughout the fleet, directed at sailors newly arrived from recruit training.

As I washed my face in a sink, I heard someone behind me and turned with fists clenched. The sailor I faced was about my height and weight, but wasn't acting hostile. Smiling, he said, "We're not looking to fight any more. We just wanted to see if you had any guts." Sticking out his hand, he said, "I'm BMSN McJunkin, Leading Seaman. You and all these other apes work for me." As he left, he yelled to the others that the new kid better be left alone.

FIRST UNDER WAY

My first two months aboard ship went by in a blur. The boatswain's mates, finding out that I kept my mouth shut and did more than my share of the work, gradually accepted me as part of Deck Department. I was never bored, but always felt something was missing. When *Lindenwald* finally got under way for a deployment to the Caribbean, I found out what was missing – going to sea. Her four-month cruise in Autumn 1961 was in response to the Dominican Crisis. Earlier, on 30 May 1961, Rafael Leonidas Trujillo Molina, the president of the Dominican Republic, had been assassinated by elements of his army. *Lindenwald* was assigned patrol duties off the capital city Ciudad Trujillo (later renamed Santo Domingo), and her presence helped to stabilize the Caribbean area during the subsequent Dominican Republic revolt of November, 1961.

Lindenwald was an *Ashland*-class dock landing ship, one of the first of this type, built during World War II. Commissioned on 9 December 1943, she was designed to transport landing craft, amphibious vehicles and troops into an amphibious landing area. She had to ballast down to flood her well deck; lower the stern gate to the sea; and disembark her craft and vehicles for an assault on a hostile beach. Once a beachhead was established, she could then act as an offshore repair dock for damaged landing craft and vehicles. Characterized by an icebreaker bow, large, slow rotating propellers, and extended bridge-wings, she had earned five battle stars for service in World War II.

Being at sea was fantastic to me and I never lost that feeling. It was like a homecoming that I never wanted to end. There really is no way to describe the feeling of a ship rolling under your feet at sea, to smell the salt air, to see the sun setting over the ocean at night, and even more-beautiful, the sun rising over the horizon in the morning. When a ship takes in all lines, clears her berth and stands out to sea, everything becomes a little cleaner and you find yourself in the most wonderful of all worlds, "haze gray and under way."

STANDING WATCH

Aboard a Navy ship at sea, all but a handful of the officers and men stand eight hours of watch each day, in addition to many hours spent carrying out their normal duties. Because hours of watch, in addition to hours of work, result in sleep deprivation, watches are the bane of most sailors. Each watch is four hours long, with the exception of the one from 1600 to 2000, which is split into two 2-hour watches. Called "dog watches," these change the watch rotation each day. If such did not exist, the same sailors would continue to stand the same watches for days on end, until when next their ship entered port.

A normal three-section watch rotation involves standing a watch, and then having two watches off, before standing another watch. During normal work hours, sailors are expected to be working and not catching up on missed sleep. Those standing the midwatch are usually allowed an extra hour of sleep after getting off watch, rising at 0700, vice 0600, when the rest of the crew is awakened to begin a new day. The sailors that stood the midwatch, would work until noon, then be back on watch. If watches were not dogged, this would involve the afternoon watch, and then the midwatch once again. By dogging the watch, they would instead, get the evening watch, after which they could enjoy a night of uninterrupted sleep.

Three-section Under way Watch Rotation			
Midwatch	0000 to 0400	First dog watch	1600 to 1800
Morning watch	0400 to 0800	Second dog watch	1800 to 2000
Forenoon watch	0800 to 1200	Evening watch	2000 to 2400
Afternoon watch	1200 to 1600		

Of course, most sailors do not immediately fall asleep after a period of alertness, so the best one could hope for, was five-plus-hours of rest. The following two days would bring the morning watch and midwatch, with associated, broken periods of sleep. When a Navy ship is at sea, most of her crew are tired. When rough seas are encountered, many are also seasick. Interestingly, fatigue seems to vanish when a ship enters a liberty port. Given the choice to go ashore, if not in the duty section, or remain on board for some extra rest, few sailors choose the latter.

I enjoyed standing watches. I honestly loved them all. Even "port and starboard watches" were enjoyable to me. The latter practice (on watch for 4 hours, off for 4 hours and then back on again) is mandated when there are insufficient numbers of qualified watchstanders for the watch team on the bridge, in engineering spaces, radio central, or the combat information center. Of course, I got tired like everyone else, but I never wearied of the routine.

The biggest impediment to some was uniforms. Bridge watches were stood in the uniform of the day, either undress blues or undress whites. Eating the evening meal on the mess decks also required that you be in the uniform of the day and there were zero exceptions to these two rules. This was especially hard on those who worked in the engineering spaces, clad in working uniforms or coveralls because the very nature of the tasks they performed resulted in getting dirty. To come up from a hot fireroom or engine room, exhausted, and then have to shower and change to an undress uniform just to eat was not popular.

I stood topside watches. Following a "trick" (turn) as a lookout, non-rated seamen rotated through a series of different duties—which helped to prevent boredom and ensure attentive watch standing. These were: messenger-of-the-watch, carrying out the orders of the officer of the deck or junior officer of the deck; helmsman, steering the ship; lee helmsman, operating the engine order telegraph to transmit ordered speed changes to the throttleman in main control; and sound-powered phone talker, communicating with other watch stations throughout the ship and keeping the bridge status board updated with reference to ship and aircraft contacts, and the status of the ship's engineering plant.

The phone talker stood behind a clear Plexiglas status board and added or updated information as necessary. This was done by writing backwards with a grease pencil, enabling those in front of the board who needed the information, to read forward script. A rag was used to scrub annotations before updates were made.

I never became seasick and quickly qualified at all positions including helmsman, the most prestigious. *Lindenwald*'s wheel was made of wood and extremely large, closely resembling those of old sailing ships. Seaman Bill Francis taught me to steer and he was the best I've ever seen. Steering a ship, acted on by wind and wave, is not like driving a car. To maintain course, a helmsman might have to use a few degrees of rudder, or even tens of degrees in heavy storms. Swirling high winds and changing tidal currents presented additional challenges.

Not even the roughest weather was able to affect Francis's skill. Eventually I became a Master Helmsman, qualified to steer the ship during special evolutions, such as when making an approach to a pier, or when in close proximity to an oiler during underway replenishment, but I never reached the level of competence that Francis displayed. He was in a class by himself.

ESCAPADES ASHORE WHILE ON LIBERTY

During this, my first deployment, I prospered at sea, learning how to do the jobs I was given quickly and correctly. "Showing the flag" involved patrols off the Dominican Republic, amphibious landing exercises with our embarked Marines, group maneuvers with other ships, honing our gunnery skills, and visits to various Caribbean ports. When *Lindenwald* called at St. Thomas in the American Virgin Islands, Deck Department held a party at Bluebeard's Inn, which became quite wild. During the party, I drank sufficient quantities of alcohol to impair my admittedly youthful, not fully developed, judgement.

Photo 2-5

Painting of St. Thomas by Albert K. Murray, 1943.
Naval History and Heritage Command Accession #88-195-BX

I don't remember leaving Bluebeards, but I apparently liberated a fire truck and careened around the island roads at high speeds with the siren screaming and bell ringing until the local police ran the truck off the road and arrested me. I was still at the scene in the back of the police vehicle in handcuffs when BM2 Davis and several other shipmates showed up. Amid much gesturing and loud talking, sums of money changed hands, apologies were offered, my handcuffs were removed, and I was placed in Davis's custody.

I am not sure how Davis arrived there, but as soon as the police left with the fire truck, he hailed a cab and personally took me back to the ship. *Lindenwald*'s executive officer and several department heads were ashore at the time and had seen the out-of-control fire truck. Fortunately, they weren't close enough to visually identify the driver. Since no report ever came to the ship, I was off the hook except for reimbursing Davis and the other seamen $200. I was greatly relieved when we left St. Thomas the following morning.

Map 2-1

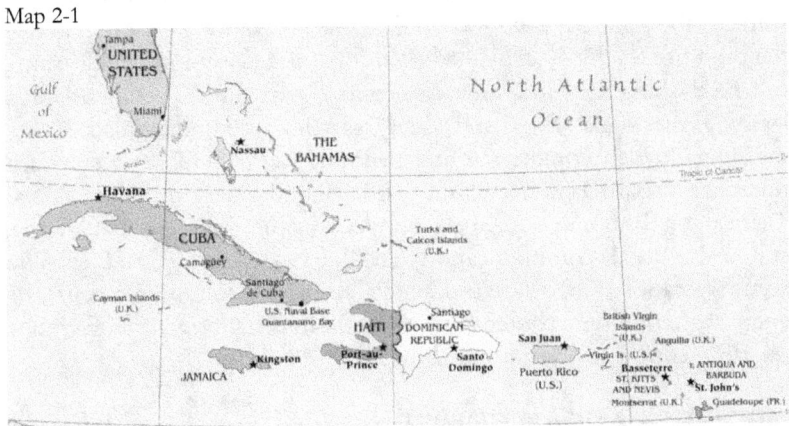

Northern Caribbean basin

Our last port of call was San Juan, Puerto Rico, and the casino at the Caribe Hilton Hotel is renowned. I drank and ran the streets and explored seedy bars. However, I did not over indulge, like I had in St. Thomas. Steaming back to Norfolk, the weather was rotten. Sea and anchor detail going into Hampton Roads in the dead of winter was a frozen nightmare. My station on the fo'c'sle was totally exposed and my shipmates and I were besieged by 20-25 knots of wind and 10-degree temperature, made worse by forward motion of the ship. By the time we berthed at Pier 4 and secured from sea and anchor detail, we resembled blue-clad snowmen.

Shortly after our return to Little Creek, I took the written and practical test for Seaman and passed. Moving up the enlisted ranks from lowly Seaman Recruit (E1) and Seaman Apprentice (E2), my job assignments didn't really change, but the small pay raise and new Seaman patch on my uniform was enough for me.

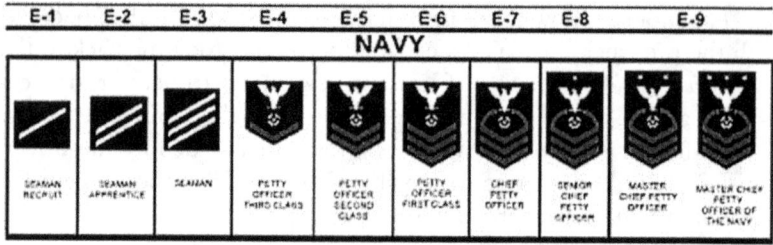

Although still in Deck Department, I had become acquainted with some of the signalmen who worked on the signal bridge, located above the pilot house. They explained their jobs to me and I started learning to read flashing light and semaphore in my spare time. I also worked at learning the signal flags and their complex International and U.S. meanings, which could be found in Publication HO-102 (a standard reference aboard U.S. Navy and Merchant Marine Ships) and Allied Tactical publications. Some may wonder why the Navy, then and today, still uses visual communications in the era of radio and satellite communications. It is because, unlike electronic communications, the enemy cannot intercept semaphore and flashing light signals unless they are close enough to see and read them.

MEDITERRANEAN CRUISE

Following the holidays, *Lindenwald* crossed the Atlantic with the tank landing ship USS *Terrebonne Parish* (LST-1156) for duty with the Sixth Fleet in the Mediterranean. Due to engineering problems, we could barely make 12 knots during the crossing, and experienced high winds and heavy seas for most of our transit. The seas became so bad, at one point, that lookouts were strapped to the bridge wings and the helmsman was secured to the wheel. Our first port of call was Toulon, France, where both ships had some much-needed work done in the machinery spaces. Toulon was a great liberty town that we all enjoyed and, while there, I was able to get three days of leave and visit Paris with a friend of mine from *Terrebonne Parish*. The travel brochures don't do it justice. The city of love and romance has some of the most fabulous sites to see anywhere in the world, and the food is exquisite. More than fifty years later, I still retain memories of Paris.

Photo 2-6

USS *Terrebonne Parish* (LST-1156) anchored off Piraeus, Greece.
National Archives photograph #USN 1047698

Photo 2-7

A corner of the Port of Toulon, France
Naval History and Heritage Command photograph #NH 121664

We next went to Genoa, Italy, for two days and, even though I got ashore only one day, it was still a great place to explore and buy souvenirs. We were in Genoa by ourselves, but when we left, we once again joined up with the *Terrebonne Parish* and went to Athens, Greece. The ships had to anchor and we rode liberty boats into Fleet Landing. We were there for three days. It was great. I had liberty two of them, and duty on the second day. It was still cold in the Med and we were over the side on stages (long planks held together with line and hoisted up and down from the main deck), painting the sides of the ship.

Anchored about a half mile away was the cruiser USS *Springfield* (CLG-7), flagship of Vice Adm. David L. McDonald, the commander of the United States Sixth Fleet. I guess my chain of command aboard ship didn't think the admiral knew we had dungarees, because they had us in undress blue uniforms with peacoats and white hats while we painted. If I had been the admiral, I probably would have been ashore, but I was just a seaman so I painted as my white hat blew off, my uniform became gray-splotched, and I became chilled to the bone.

Photo 2-8

Vice Adm. David L. McDonald, USN, commander, Sixth Fleet, discusses the fleet's recent activities with Adm. George W. Anderson Jr., USN, chief of Naval Operations, aboard his flagship, USS *Springfield* (CLG-7), 1 June 1962. The chart of the northwestern Mediterranean shows the location of many of the Sixth Fleet's ships.
Naval History and Heritage Command photograph #USN 711075

Athens was tawdry in the 1960s, even by sailor standards. Anything could be obtained for very little money. On the third and last day of liberty, I again went ashore with my friend from the *Terrebonne Parish*, and we enjoyed a Greek night to end all. My ship was due to leave harbor at 0800 and his to follow ours out at 0830. We both overslept and when I looked out a window, I could see the *Lindenwald* weighing anchor (bringing up the "hook"), preparing to get under way. We dashed out of our gratis lodgings—leaving two confused girls behind.

The only watercraft at Fleet Landing was *Terrebonne Parish*'s liberty boat. We jumped in, and I compelled the coxswain (seaman in charge) to pursue my ship. As he sped seaward in the harbor, I started yelling to get her attention. Luckily, someone heard me and called the bridge and she came to a stop. As *Lindenwald* lay to, one of the BMs dropped a Jacobs ladder (a hanging ladder consisting of vertical ropes supporting horizontal wooden rungs) over the side and I scrambled up it. As I was climbing the ladder, I saw the captain lean over the side of the bridge wing and ask the Bos'n, a deck below, if I belonged to him. The language he used, although respectful to the commanding officer, conveyed his displeasure with me. Commander George B. Howe Jr., who was then the commanding officer, would be relieved by CDR Frederick P. McDermott later in the cruise.

The Bos'n was solid and strong as an ox. He wore his hair cut short like a Marine, had numerous tattoos, and drank endless cups of coffee. Occasionally, he would look at one of us seaman and say, "Boy, get me some coffee." Now that order may seem autocratic and would be out of place in today's Navy, but back then it was a blessing in disguise. If the Bos'n singled you out to get his coffee that became your assignment for the rest of the day unless you had to go on watch. Instead of chipping paint, polishing "brightwork" (brass), or doing other routine work that needed doing, the anointed seaman followed around in the Bos'n's wake all day (trailed behind him), ready to grab his cup when he held it out and find more coffee.

When you were the Bos'n's messenger no one messed with you, not even the chiefs. There was also another plus side to this assignment. When not running coffee the "gofer" was the recipient of non-stop commentary in a gravelly, deep voice on all kinds of marlinspike and deck seamanship topics. It was a real sailor education and I hung on every word. The Bos'n taught us all, if we were willing to listen and learn, and I absorbed his hard-earned knowledge like a sponge.

CAPTAIN'S MAST

Two days out of Athens on a mirror-smooth sea under a deep blue and cloudless sky, Commander Howe held Captain's Mast on the starboard bridge wing and I was the guest of honor. The "Old Man" (respectful term for the skipper) was a Mustang, a former chief signalman. After listening to my pitiful tale of woe, he asked Sorrel and Davis about my performance. They both allowed as how I was an excellent worker, never quit until the job was done, and made a great deck hand. He then asked my Leading Petty Officer, and the Bos'n if I was worth saving. Both affirmed that I was, and they wanted me to remain in Deck. However, the Bos'n added a condition, suggesting that I probably should never be allowed to go on liberty.

The captain looked at me for a few minutes and then sentenced me to be restricted to the limits of the ship for two months. Days at sea did not count toward restriction time, which meant I would not be allowed to go ashore again until we returned to Little Creek. For the remainder of the cruise, I had to live vicariously through stories of my shipmates' exploits in Naples, Italy; Malta; Palma Mallorca; and Rota, Spain. While the ship was in Naples, I attempted to go ashore by shinnying down the number-one mooring line, which led from the fo'c'sle to the pier. I had just maneuvered around the sheet metal cone-shaped rat guard attached to the line near the bollard, and stepped onto the pier, when I turned around, and almost had a heart attack. Standing there, with his enormous arms folded, was the Bos'n.

After regaining my wits, I managed, "Hey, Bos'n, thought I would just check the mooring lines since I was restricted anyway." When I didn't get a response, I climbed back up the mooring line, and clambered over the rail back onto the fo'c'sle. He never mentioned the incident and neither did I. (This method of getting off a ship, when unable to depart via the quarterdeck, was referred to as "mooring line liberty." Of course, you had to be both stealthy and fit to employ it successfully, lest you end up in the water.)

CONVERSION TO SIGNALMAN

Shortly after going to Mast, I submitted a Special Request Chit to strike for Signalman. My chain of command was not especially happy with my antics and my request was disapproved until it got to the captain who approved it. It helped that the Signal Gang was short two personnel. Unfortunately, Deck Department was also shorthanded so my transfer to Operations didn't take place until after we returned to Little Creek. We reached home port on a Saturday and I couldn't check out of Deck until Monday, so I spent the weekend relaxing and contemplating my future. I was up bright and early on Monday morning, sweeping and swabbing the fo'c'sle and shining brightwork. After breakfast I began the checking in/checking out process and by noon had joined the Operations Department.

Photo 2-9

Signalman aboard USS *Yorktown* (CV-10) uses a blinker lamp to send a message to the carrier's escorting destroyer, at night, circa late 1943. National Archives photograph #80-G-419960

In August 1962, I took the Navy-wide competitive examination for SM3. In those days, the exams consisted of 150 multiple choice questions based on all aspects of the particular rating a sailor was in. You had three hours to complete the test. The results would be promulgated in October and the first wave of advancements would be authorized in November. Subsequently, incremental advancements would be authorized each month until all who had passed their exams were advanced. Those sailors who passed, but not high enough to be advanced, were designated as strikers and authorized to wear a striker emblem (symbol of that rating) above their Seaman patch. While waiting for the exam results, *Lindenwald* got under way and proceeded to the Caribbean as part of the deployed Amphibious Ready Group.

CARIBBEAN DEPLOYMENT

In mid-October we pulled into Guantanamo Bay, Cuba, and anchored for a short break. I happened to be on watch when the alarm for General Quarters was sounded and the Boatswain's Mate of the Watch announced, "This is not a drill." Everyone went into a state of shock and some thought the boatswain's mate had messed up, but he was right. President Kennedy had established a military blockade around Cuba to prevent the Soviet Union from introducing ballistic missiles to Cuba and all the ships in the Caribbean would be part of that blockade.

Things were pretty tense for about two weeks and there were several vessel confrontations, but eventually the Russians backed down and things returned to normal. Shortly after, the results of the examination I'd taken in August came back and were posted outside the

Personnel Office. I was to be advanced to SM3 in the first increment in November.

Photo 2-10

Navy ships at anchor at Guantanamo Bay, Cuba; date unknown.
Naval History and Heritage Command photograph #NH 109393

DEPARTURE FROM *LINDENWALD*

We returned to Little Creek in November and, one afternoon, on a whim, I visited the Atlantic Fleet's Enlisted Personnel Distribution Office in Norfolk. In the 1960s, a sailor could walk into the EPDOLANT in Norfolk, or the one for the Pacific Fleet in San Diego, talk with a detailer and, in some cases, obtain a transfer to another ship. Detailers were shore based sailors, with whom one negotiated for orders. I talked to the guy that handled Signalmen and Radiomen and told him I was looking for something different. He asked if I had submitted a request for transfer through my chain of command and I told him I had, but that it had been "deep sixed" somewhere. He mentioned an opening for a Signalman Third aboard the attack transport USS *Mountrail* (APA-213).

I told him that sounded good to me and he said, "Ok, Flags, go on back to your ship and your orders will arrive tomorrow morning, detaching you within five days, authorizing five days leave en route and reporting to the *Mountrail* within two weeks." I thanked him and headed back to the *Lindenwald* and didn't breathe a word to a soul.

The next morning my orders hit the ship and my Division Officer asked what was going on. I played the dumb sailor and said I didn't know anything about it. The following Friday I checked out of the ship, slung my seabag over my shoulder, and walked down the *Lindenwald*'s accommodation ladder for the last time. It was with mixed feelings that I left, but I felt it was the right move at the right time for me. I have never forgotten my first ship and, over the years, have thought about her many times with fond memories of my time onboard.

3

Short Stint aboard *Mountrail*

Photo 3-1

Attack transport USS *Mountrail* berthed pierside.
USS *Mountrail* (LPA-213) Mediterranean 1968 cruise book

I reported to USS *Mountrail*, under the command of Capt. Emmett M. Compton, USN, in late 1962. Commissioned on 16 November 1944, the *Haskell*-class attack transport was a veteran of World War II and the Korean War. Of the 111 *Haskell*s built in time to see action in WWII, all had served in the Pacific Theater. Most participated in the Okinawa landings, and some had landed Marines and Army troops at Iwo Jima.

Ships of the class were among the first Allied ships to enter Tokyo Bay at the end of the war, landing the first occupation troops at Yokosuka. Most of the *Haskell*-class ships were mothballed (laid up in Reserve Fleets in 1946). A few of the ships were reactivated for Korean War service, with some remaining in service into the Vietnam War.

The service of *Mountrail* closely followed this pattern. She had been decommissioned on 12 July 1946, and laid up in the Pacific Reserve Fleet at Stockton, California. She was recommissioned on 9 September 1950 for Korean War service, and decommissioned a second time on 1 October 1955, farther down the California coast at Long Beach. She was later moved to Suisun Bay, Benicia, California, on 7 June 1960, joining the "ghost fleet" (National Defense Reserve Fleet) languishing there. She was withdrawn for reactivation a little over a year later, and recommissioned on 22 November 1961. *Mountrail* earned one battle star in World War II and three during the Korean War.

The *Haskell*-class attack transports were designed to transport 1,500 troops and their combat equipment, and land them on hostile shores with the ships' integral landing craft. In World War II, the ships had been used primarily in the final push across the Pacific. As part of the invasion fleets, they carried heavy vehicles and stores in their lower holds with 1,000-2,000 Army or Marine Corps troops quartered in the upper cargo spaces.

Mountrail was not sent to Vietnam. On 1 January 1969, she and the other APAs still in the Navy's inventory were redesignated amphibious transports (LPA). *Mountrail* was decommissioned for the final time on 13 August 1970, and laid up in the National Defense Reserve Fleet, James River Group, Lee Hall, Virginia. A little over six years later, she was struck from the Naval Register on 1 December 1976.

NORTH ATLANTIC NATO EXERCISES

I knew little about the *Mountrail* when I joined her, other than that she had been part of the Amphibious Ready Group with *Lindenwald* during the Cuban Missile Crisis. Shortly after I reported aboard, we sailed for southern Spain to take part in NATO exercises. We had a solid Signal Gang—a chief, an SM1, one SM2, three SM3s and three strikers—and I was welcomed and accepted. The signal bridge of the APA was huge compared to the one on the *Lindenwald*, and very well laid out to facilitate visual communications. During our deployment I was able to visit Madrid and Barcelona. I took in a bull fight in Barcelona and wished I hadn't—I never did so again. I guess I was naïve and really didn't think the bull would be repeatedly injured and then killed.

Photo 3-2

Signalman Third Lee Foley aboard the USS *Mountrail*, summer of 1963. Author's collection

We also visited Lisbon, Portugal, which was very enjoyable. I made the whole cruise without getting into any trouble and earned my keep as a signalman. When we returned to Norfolk, I found my enlistment nearly at an end. I had entered the Navy on a "Kiddie Cruise" which allowed you to sign up as soon as you turned 17 years old and serve a three-year enlistment instead of four, getting out of the service when you turned 21 years old. There was never a doubt in my mind that I would reenlist. I was just hopeful the Navy would let me stay. Although my tour on *Mountrail* was brief, I enjoyed it to the fullest.

Photo 3-3

Port of Barcelona, Spain.
USS *Mountrail* (LPA-213) Mediterranean 1968 cruise book

Photo 3-4

The semi-tropical city of Lisbon, Portugal, early 1900s.
Naval History and Heritage Command photograph #NH 122262

SHIPPING OVER

Despite life at sea often being hard and spare, some sailors choose to remain in the Navy at the end of their enlistment by reenlisting, which is known as "shipping over." The following poem (by an unknown author) aptly expresses the wishes of one individual to do so. The term "mast" refers to "Captain's Mast," a procedure whereby the commanding officer makes inquiry into the facts surrounding an offense allegedly committed by a member of the command; affords the accused a hearing as to such offense; and disposes of such cases by dismissing the charge, imposing punishment, or referring the case to higher authority for a court-martial. Standing at attention in front of one's commanding officer is not something that most sailors enjoy. "Request" refers to a "request chit." Sailors wishing to remain in the Navy must request this action, and their command must approve it in order for them to remain in the naval service.

Our Father who art in Washington
Please, dear Father, let me stay,
Do not drive me now away.
Wipe away my scalding tears
And let me stay my thirty years.
Please forgive me all my past
And things that happened at the mast,
Do not my request refuse,
And let me stay another cruise.

Post card of 1906, sent to a prospective re-enlistee
at the Brooklyn Navy Yard, advising him to "ship over."
Naval History and Heritage Command photograph #NH 82988

The Navy allowed me to reenlist, which I did, under the SCORE (Selective Conversion and Reenlistment) program. Based on my high aptitude scores, I was advised to convert from Signalman to Electronics Technician, and was guaranteed a series of schools culminating in Submarine School and SINS (Submarine Inertial Navigation System) School. Attendance at each one was predicated on passing the previous school.

I had taken general mathematics in high school, no algebra, and it wasn't sufficient. Even with voluntary extra study and hiring a tutor, I couldn't cut the academics. Nonetheless, I kept being moved forward despite my failing every 2-week long unit. I asked to drop; the school refused. I was adamant. A commander sent out from the Bureau of Personnel tried to convince me to stay. He told me the SCORE Program was in its infancy and if I was dropped, I would be the first, and it would embarrass the Navy.

I told him that if I got to the fleet as an ET and I didn't know anything it would embarrass the Navy a lot more. Eventually, they were forced to drop me. The SCORE Program was an excellent opportunity for qualified sailors, but wasn't for me. I had been advanced to SM2 while enrolled in the school, so I was happy.

4

Assignment to a "Bird Farm"

Photo 4-1

USS *Lexington* (CVS-16) under way on 15 July 1963, with T-28 training planes on deck. Naval Academy midshipmen were aboard to observe carrier qualifications. Naval History and Heritage Command photograph #USN 1086588

I had been in the Transient Personnel Unit at the Great Lakes Naval Training Command for almost two weeks after dropping out of ET "A" School when my orders came in. When told by the Personnel Man in charge of student orders that I was going to a "Bird Farm" (aircraft carrier) in Pensacola, Florida, I just looked at him in shock. Pensacola was okay, I guess, but not to an aircraft carrier. I didn't have to ask the name of the ship because there was only one carrier in Pensacola, the USS *Lexington* (CVS-16). Admittedly, she had a storied history in fighting the Japanese Navy during World War II, but to me the "real Navy" was a "Small Boy" (destroyer).

Having no choice regarding my assignment, I took a train from Great Lakes to Chicago and caught a plane to New York City. *Lexington* was in drydock in the Brooklyn Naval Shipyard undergoing an extensive overhaul. I had a bad feeling about this assignment, but couldn't really discern why I was so uneasy. After landing at the airport, in early evening on a Friday night, and claiming my seabag and suitcase, I caught a cab to the Brooklyn Navy Yard. Entering the gate to the yard on Flushing Avenue, I presented my ID Card and orders to the sentry, who provided me directions to the ship.

Photo 4-2

Navy Yard, Brooklyn, New York, looking northwest, 15 April 1945.
Naval History and Heritage Command photograph #NH 93237

I walked about two blocks into the yard and stood at the side of the drydock looking up at Lady LEX. She was huge and looked sort of forlorn sitting on blocks, high and dry. Taking one last look, I threw my seabag on my shoulder, grabbed my suitcase, and proceeded up the brow (gang plank) to check in. The lieutenant (junior grade) who had the watch endorsed my orders and told the messenger to take me to the Operations berthing compartment. After a long trek down ladders and through myriad passageways, we arrived at Ops Berthing. The messenger said, "Here you are, Flags," and returned to the quarterdeck.

Within the Navy, there has developed over its long history, nicknames or fleet "shorthand's" for different enlisted ratings. Some are shortened titles, such as "Boats" for Boatswain's Mate, and "Guns" for Gunner's Mate. Others resulted from the symbol of the rating. The Signalman rating badge had two crossed flags, thus I and others were addressed as "Flags." Quartermasters were called "Wheels" because their badges featured a ship's wheel. Some nicknames were based on humor, Cooks being "stew burners." Finally, there were collective terms: engineers, no matter what their ratings, were called "Snipes," while "Airedale" referred to all those involved with Naval aircraft.

The compartment was immaculate with metal lockers shining brightly and the deck buffed to a gloss in which you could almost see your face. Part of the compartment was darkened with only red night lights showing, in consideration of men sleeping, but there were bright lights at the other end of the compartment so I headed in that direction. I found a partitioned lounge and several sailors watching TV. I introduced myself, "Hey, guys, I'm SM2 Foley," after which the Operations Duty Petty Officer stood up, shook my hand and said "Welcome to the LEX, Foley, you'll be sorry." The latter comment was said with a grin. He assigned me a bunk and two lockers, and told me I would be put in a duty section on Monday. Therefore, I had weekend liberty in New York City. It only took a few minutes to stow my gear, shower, change into to a clean uniform and "hit the beach" (go ashore).

Exiting the Navy Yard, I walked up Flushing Avenue and took the subway to 42nd Street. Wandering around Times Square for a while, I took in the sights of the city that never sleeps. Tiring of walking past strip shows, porn shops, X-rated movie houses, panhandlers, hookers and the ubiquitous newsstands, I ate at a deli and then caught the subway back to Brooklyn. There were a lot of places to hang out in Brooklyn in those days, but I eventually narrowed it down to two bars, Dan's, and Carlucci's, on Flushing Avenue. Both were rough and catered to sailors and Merchant Marines, but I felt comfortable in them and they were close to the Navy Yard. This first night on the town I settled for Carlucci's, drinking beer and shooting pool until nearly 0200.

Lexington was the last carrier to undergo overhaul in the Brooklyn Navy Yard and the facility was closed soon after we departed. We were there for six months, most of that time in the winter, and that made for some real cold times. Those of us who had working spaces exposed to the weather would chip ice and shovel snow all morning, then preserve and paint in the afternoon if the temperature rose enough. At mid-morning and again in mid-afternoon, hot soup and hot chocolate in addition to 24/7 coffee was available on the mess decks. These welcome respites went a long way toward relieving the cold that seeped into every part of your body no matter how warmly you were dressed.

Seven sailors were killed in New York in various ways during the time that the ship was in the yard, and many muggings and robberies also took place. I must have had the luck of the Irish, because I never had a problem knocking around Brooklyn and Manhattan at night. Finally, the overhaul was completed, sea trials were conducted successfully, and *Lexington* stood out of New York Harbor, bound for Pensacola and home.

Photo 4-3

Fleet at anchor in New York Harbor, circa 1939.
Naval History and Heritage Command photograph #NH 923

Arriving in Pensacola (westernmost city on the Florida Panhandle, bounded by the Gulf of Mexico), we sat berthed pierside at the Naval Air Station for about a month. This time was spent correcting discrepancies in yard work that we found during our transit home. We then turned to the ship's mission, training students to be Navy pilots. A standard cycle for the ship involved one-week pierside in Pensacola, two weeks at sea in the Gulf of Mexico for touch-and-goes (carrier landings by student pilots), and one week serving as the training platform for advanced pilot training off Corpus Christi, Texas.

Photo 4-4

Aerial view of U.S. Naval Air Station, Pensacola, 1937.
Naval History and Heritage Command photograph #NH 113411

I never sailed with a more enigmatic bunch of guys than those that made up the Signal Gang, led by a nervous chief who was about five feet, two inches tall. When he was talking to you, he had a habit of taking off his chief's hat, pointing the anchor at you and saying, "See, this says I'm a chief petty officer." The leading SM liked to tell everyone that he was a former SEAL, and when ashore on liberty, he would give replica gold jump wings to girls. The middle First Class was a Kentuckian who was sharp, but kind of quiet. The junior First Class was the sharpest, but was not afforded much opportunity to lead. At some point in his career he had been badly burned over most of his body and his skin grafts were visible when wearing short sleeves. I had the utmost respect for him and did whatever he asked.

We also had four second class SMs including me, four thirds, and a couple of Seamen. SM2 Koskela had been an SMSN with me on the *Lindenwald* for a short time, and SM2 Vince Spears reported aboard after we arrived in Pensacola. I mostly hung with Koskela and Spears. With no other ships around in the Gulf or at Pensacola, our skills stagnated because the senior SMs didn't care to practice light or semaphore; and Koskela, Spears, and I found ourselves losing our expertise. Frustrated and unhappy, I started doing Officer Correspondence Courses.

Photo 4-5

Signalman Second Lee Foley writing down a visual message, while the big light is being used aboard the aircraft carrier USS *Lexington* (CVS-16), operating in the Gulf of Mexico. Author's collection

EFFORTS TO TRANSFER OFF THE SHIP

After a year on board, I started submitting monthly requests for transfer to a fleet ship that operated and deployed on a regular basis. Just as faithfully, the Leading SM approved them, but when they got to the division officer and department head, the requests mysteriously disappeared. Finally, in desperation I wrote a letter enclosing copies of my request chits to then Senator James William Fullbright, the senior

Senator from the State of Arkansas. Bill Fullbright was a household name in Arkansas.

I had met him lots of times, ran errands for him as a kid during his campaigns for reelection, and thought nothing about dashing off a letter asking him to intercede on my behalf and get me back to the real Navy on a deploying ship. What I didn't know, and therefore wasn't prepared for, was that when the Senator responded to my letter, a copy of my letter with enclosures, and his response went to my commanding officer.

Lexington was unique in that there were five captains assigned to the ship. The commanding officer of course, the executive officer, the operations officer, the air officer, and the navigator were all "Four Stripers." All incoming correspondence unless it is marked "Personal For" (for the eyes of the commanding officer) goes to the administrative officer and then to the executive officer (XO). When the XO received the copies of my journalistic endeavors, he became very irate.

He immediately called the operations officer (a captain), the assistant operations officer (a full commander), and the OS Division Officer (a full lieutenant), to notify my leading petty officer and myself that we were to assemble outside his stateroom at 2000 in full dress uniform to address my transgression.

At the appointed hour we were all standing tall outside the XO's cabin, me with a copy of Navy Regulations under my arm. The Marine Guard bade us enter and we all filed inside and stood at attention in front of his desk. It was my first time to see a four striper (the Ops Boss) standing at attention. The XO was livid and his face was mottled and red, as he started shouting and screaming like someone possessed.

After his initial tirade, he started chewing everyone out from the most senior, the operations officer, to the most junior, me. Eventually he asked what I had to say for myself. Thinking the worse was over, I said, "Sir, I brought a copy of Navy Regs with me in order to prove that I could write my Congressman or Senator if I wanted to." If I thought he was mad before, I was deeply mistaken. He ripped the copy of Navy Regs out of my hands and sent it flying across his cabin. En route to the impact site on the bulkhead, the heavy manual wiped out an expensive lamp, a crystal vase, and a plaque commemorating the Battle of the Coral Sea.

Having fully vented his anger, the XO reviewed the copies of my transfer requests and stated that he would deal with the Ops Department later for throwing my requests in the trash. I had actively sought a swap with any SM2 on any ship in Norfolk that might be interested in changing duty stations. An SM2 named Wilcox aboard the USS *Taconic* (AGC-17), had agreed to swap duty stations with me and his request had already been approved aboard the amphibious command ship.

Concluding the interview, the XO stated, "Foley's request to swap with SM2 Wilcox is approved forthwith and I want that son-of-a-bitch (pointing at me) off my ship before 2400 tonight. I want a 2.0 enlisted evaluation placed in his Personnel Record before he goes. Does everyone fucking understand me?" When affirmative responses had been received from all, we were dismissed. As we cleared the XO's stateroom, I was told to stay in my dress blues, pack all my fucking gear, take it to the quarterdeck, and then return to Personnel to pick up my orders.

And so, I found myself walking down the LEX's brow for the last time at 2345 on 3 January 1966. When I stepped on the pier, I laughed heartily. Once more I was running free before the wind, and with a little luck I'd catch the 0100 Grey Dog (Greyhound bus) out of Pensacola and head to Norfolk. In May, I received a letter from Vince Spears, wishing me well and hoping things were going better for me on *Taconic*. He said he was changing his rating to Data Systems and would be taking the test for First Class in August and felt good about his new career choice. I wrote him back, expressing my happiness for him and wished him luck on the rating examination. That was our last contact until many years later.

5

Flagship Duty

Photo 5-1

USS *Taconic* (AGC-17/LCC-17) signal bridge June/July 1969.
Naval History and Heritage Command photograph #UA 571.60.01

Taconic was the answer to my prayers. My tour aboard her, and my periodic temporary attachment to the staffs of commander, Amphibious Group Four, and commander, Amphibious Group Two, whenever they were embarked, formed the core of my drive to become a naval officer. But I'm getting ahead of my story. My department head, Lieutenant (later Captain) Bill Horne, reviewed my record with me on my first full day aboard. It was not a cursory review. We spent three hours going over things in detail. He read all of my evaluations including the detaching one from the *Lexington*, quizzed me at length about my decision to drop from ET "A" School, and wanted to know why the *Lexington* in their detaching evaluation had not recommended me for advancement or reenlistment. I told him the truth, and let him draw his own conclusions.

He had the evaluation from *Lexington* removed from my record and a new one submitted by *Taconic* with 3.8 grades across the board (in all categories) and a strong recommendation for advancement and retention. I was deeply shocked by all this, but Horne merely said, "I believe you have a lot of potential and did not get a fair shake on the *Lexington*. I'm giving you a clean slate and a once-in-a-lifetime opportunity. Don't make me regret what I'm doing."

Photo 5-2

Amphibious flagship USS *Taconic* (AGC-17) at sea in July 1968.
She was redesignated LCC-17 at the beginning of 1969.
Naval History and Heritage photograph #NH 107690

An SM2 with eight years of Naval service was the Leading Signalman aboard *Taconic*, and we got along well. We split the work and trained our junior signalmen and things were fun again. With lots of ships based at Naval Operating Base, Norfolk, there was no lack of SMs willing to practice flashing light and semaphore and my proficiency in both quickly returned, then exceeded what it had been before I reported to *Lexington*.

WORKING ON ADVANCEMENT

Once I was settled in, I started studying hard for the First Class Examination. Beyond the rank of Seaman, sailors compete with their entire peer group, Navy wide. Test scores are combined with performance marks (evaluations), and those individuals with high enough multiples are advanced in rank, based on the number of spots available. If you pass the test, but your combined score is not high enough to get one of the coveted spots, you were said to have Passed, but not Advanced.

Photo 5-3

From square riggers to nuclear surface ships, such as the carrier USS *Enterprise* (CVN-65), semaphore remains an important method of communication.
Naval History and Heritage Command photograph #L09-01.01.01

In those days, it was not uncommon to serve alongside sailors with only an 8th Grade education. Their reading comprehension might be relatively low, making it difficult for them to understand, and correctly answer questions on a test. This is most likely why there'd been two very old Boatswain's Mate Seconds aboard the *Lindenwald*. Of course, some believed in the old saw, "The best rank in the Navy is second class." For those who adhered to this philosophy, and didn't seek advancement beyond E-5, it was because they believed they could avoid the worse jobs given junior sailors to do, and not have to shoulder the leadership responsibilities and accountability of a first class or chief petty officer. I did not subscribe to this belief, and wanted to advance as fast as possible.

Everywhere I went, I had a study guide rolled up and stuck in my back pocket. I never saw the senior SM open any kind of study guide. I reviewed flash card information, listened to audio tapes, read constantly, and concentrated on making First Class by trying to get the best possible evaluation marks. In addition to my duties on the Signal Bridge, when in port, I was "Duty Operations," meaning that after the officers in the department went home for the day, I was the representative of the Operations Department. These duties extended well beyond those of a signalman.

NEARLY IN TROUBLE AGAIN

One of my running mates (buddies) aboard ship was a Hospital Corpsman Second and we stood duty in port on the same days. I was making my rounds one evening, checking on the security and quietness of the department spaces and stopped by Sick Bay to see my buddy. I noticed the door to the ward was ajar and I heard voices. Not thinking anything was out of the ordinary, I passed through Sick Bay and entered the ward. The sight that greeted me was startling, to say the least. My friend and a voluptuous female companion were both unclothed, doing what might be expected of two adults in that state of undress.

Sighting me, there began a frantic effort to disengage and simultaneously came the sounds of a baby crying. Needless to say, I was absolutely speechless. My friend however, was equal to the occasion. Without so much as a blush, he picked up half a bottle of Jack Daniels, held it out to me and said, "Have a drink, Lee, you look like you need one." While my mind was trying to assimilate this turn of events, avert my eyes and not ogle the girl, she stood there unembarrassed with a smile on her face. "What's the matter, Lee?" she asked. "Haven't you ever seen a girl get laid before?"

She then walked over to one of the unoccupied bunks, picked up the baby I had heard crying, and started nursing him like it was an everyday occurrence. Well, I grabbed the bottle and was well into a long pull, when in walked the command duty officer (CDO). As he looked around the room, everything seemed to be frozen in time. I stood there with the bottle of whiskey halfway between my mouth and my side, my friend was still unclothed, and the baby continued to nurse happily. The girl (also still undressed) then looked up, smiled and said, "Hi, Lieutenant, want to join us?"

This wisecrack galvanized my friend and I into action and we both started talking at once. However, the CDO's voice cut through our explanations and we froze once more. "Listen, up. If I'm not offered a drink from that bottle in ten seconds, everyone here is on report." I immediately placed it in his hand. As he sampled the Tennessee whiskey, the girl mused out loud from the corner, "If you put me on report, Lieutenant, should I wear a tight sweater and skirt for the skipper?" and then burst into laughter.

With the barest hint of a smile, the CDO looked at all of us, then turned to me and said, "Foley, make sure the Ops spaces and the rest of the ship is secure for the night and all visitors are off the ship by 2200. Also, I found this bottle of whiskey while making my rounds so I'm going to confiscate it and pour the contents down a commode. If you find any more, do the same." With that he turned on his heel and left Sick Bay leaving two very shocked but grateful sailors, one bemused girl, and a happy baby.

We had broken the rules and were in the wrong and the lieutenant was in the wrong also. However, that one incident, and how he handled it, did much to influence how I conducted business after becoming an officer. His actions made a lasting impression on me (teaching me that occasionally not going "strictly by the book" would more likely produce a desired outcome). They also helped to keep me squared away. In essence, I didn't want to throw away the chance he gave me.

ESCAPADE ASHORE

One day, I looked at the ship across the pier and thought I saw a familiar face. Grabbing a set of binoculars on the signal bridge, I took a closer look and couldn't believe my eyes. There was Chief Boatswain's Mate Alfred Holt, who had recruited me back in Mountain Home, Arkansas. I quickly went down to the quarterdeck, crossed to the other ship, and requested permission to come aboard to see Chief Holt.

When the chief finally ambled up and saw me standing there, he exclaimed, "Goddam, if it ain't Lee Foley from Arkansas. How you doing, boy?" My hand disappeared into a gigantic paw as he grabbed ahold of my hand and shook it. "Good to see you, son. Looks like you're doing okay for yourself since you are a second class. What rating did you end up in?" I proudly answered, "I became a signalman, Chief, and

I really love it." He smiled and said, "Let's go down to the Chiefs Mess and get some coffee."

We went through several cups of coffee as I brought Chief Holt up to date on my adventures and misadventures including the Masts for disciplinary infractions. I even included the latest escapade in the *Taconic*'s Sick Bay. When I was done, he said, "You're a real sailor now, and I'm proud that I recruited you. You got duty tonight?" I told him I didn't and was off for the next two nights. "Great," he said. "Meet me on the pier at 1800 tonight; we're going to hit the beach." With that he brought me back to the quarterdeck. He shook my hand again, said how good it was to see one of the guys he had recruited, and that he'd see me later tonight on the pier.

That evening, 1800 found me standing on the pier in dress canvas (dress blues) with my white hat perfectly squared and my neckerchief positioned just so. Chief Holt came down the brow of his ship in his dress blues with rows of ribbons and we set a course for East Main Street in downtown Norfolk. God, what a wild night. We must have hit every bar on both sides of the street, some of them twice. By midnight, neither of us was feeling any pain, whatsoever. As we stood somewhat shakily on the sidewalk outside the Texas Bar, deciding where to go next, we were accosted by the Shore Patrol.

Photo 5-4

Sailors on liberty ashore, during the early 1920s.
Naval History and Heritage Command photograph #NH 77308

The senior member of the two-man patrol, a First Class Gunner's Mate, sidled up to me and said, "Boy, you're out of uniform." I looked at him and then at myself, but I saw nothing wrong with my uniform. I sure hadn't disgraced it in any way. When I looked back at him it must have been the wrong way because he grabbed my arm and said, "I'm taking you to Shore Patrol Headquarters. Your hat is on the back of your head and you have a comb sticking out of your jumper pocket, your neckerchief is not centered on the vee of your jumper, and your sleeves are turned back with unauthorized designs on them (gold dragons). I just stood there looking at the GMG1 like he was an idiot.

The unauthorized designs he referred to were called "liberty cuffs," silk panels stitched inside the cuffs of my dress uniform. Although such adornment was popular among sailors, it was not authorized by the Navy. Thus, sailors usually turned their cuffs outward to display the silk art only in bars where there were no officers present. Meanwhile, Chief Holt said, "He's with me, Gunner. Why don't you let me handle it?"

That might have worked if the gunner's mate hadn't been a complete asshole. His response was, "I'd like to make that happen, Chief, but orders are orders." With that he handcuffed me, and put me in the Shore Patrol truck. As the truck was getting ready to shove off, Chief Holt told me to stay calm, do whatever they told me, and that he would get me bailed out. All the way to Shore Patrol Headquarters the gunner's mate continued to push his weight, bad mouthing me and then continually shoving me as we entered the Shore Patrol building.

The chief of the watch was a boatswain's mate and he could see I was steaming I was so mad. My face was almost blood red and I was really ready to wipe the deck with this clown. However, before I could do anything rash, the chief told the gunner to take off the cuffs and go write his report in the back room. The gunner protested this, saying, "Com'on, Chief, I've got four or five charges on this kid. We need to lock him up and place him on report." With a resigned look on his face, the chief said to the gunner's mate, "Just do what I fucking tell you to do, Gunner. Take the cuffs off and go write your fucking report."

As I stood in front of the chief's desk and slowly rubbed my wrists to get the circulation flowing again, I gradually started to cool off. He came around the desk and handed me a cup of coffee. "Son," he said, "Al Holt and I are old shipmates and he called about you before you were brought in. Just have a seat on the bench there and drink your coffee. By the time you're done, Al will be here to pick you up. Don't worry about the gunner's mate, I'll take care of him and his report."

By the time I finished my coffee, Chief Holt had shown up. Thanking his friend, he grabbed my arm and said, "We've had enough fun for one night." A short while later we were on the pier. Shaking hands and saying goodnight, we each went up our respective brows.

PHILADELPHIA NAVAL SHIPYARD

Photo 5-5

Philadelphia Naval Shipyard, Pennsylvania, 19 May 1955.
National Archives photograph #80-G-668656

Not long after, *Taconic* entered the Philadelphia Naval Shipyard for overhaul. We spent twelve months in the yard, but I only went ashore a handful of times. All of my spare time was spent studying for the First Class Examination. All the second class petty officers eligible to take it mustered on the mess decks in August to try our luck. Each examination had 150 multiple-choice questions, and those taking it were monitored by a commissioned officer. Finishing quickly, I started reviewing all my answers. I did that three times, and then turned in my exam and materials. I was relieved to have the test behind me and could forget about studying for a while. To occupy my free time, I continued the practice I started on *Lexington*, of doing Officer Correspondence Courses.

6

Return to the Caribbean and the Mediterranean

The days in the yard passed quickly and before long the advancement list came out and was posted outside the Personnel Office. The usual crowd gathered and there were happy yells, and curses and grunts of disappointment. When I could finally get through the crowd and looked at the list, I saw quite a few guys had made third class and second class. Of the thirty-two second class who had taken the First Class Examination, I was the only one to be advanced. My elation more than justified all the study I had invested in preparation. Our SM1, a great guy named Perry, made chief and we had one new SM2 and three new SM3s, so it was a pretty happy Signal Gang, for the most part.

In mid-1967, we left the Philadelphia Naval Shipyard and headed home to Norfolk. Arriving at Naval Operating Base, Norfolk, we worked at correcting discrepancies left over from the yards and began "workups" (training at sea) for a brief Caribbean deployment.

Photo 6-1

Aerial view of Naval Operating Base, Norfolk, 25 May 1979.
National Archives & Records Administration #DN-SN-88-06418

AMPHIBIOUS GROUP TWO

Photo 6-2

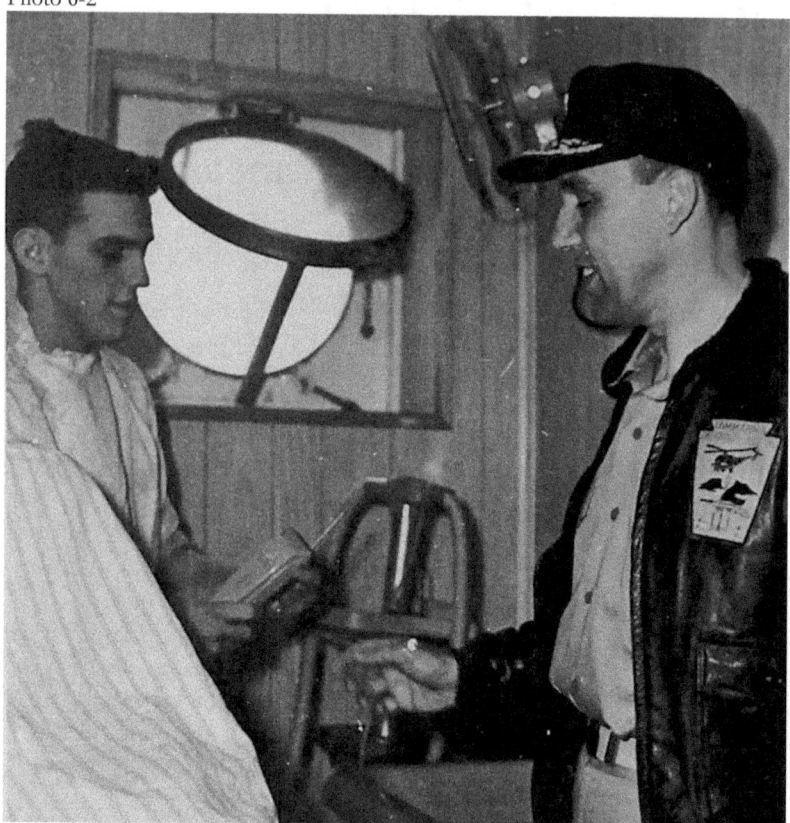

Commander, Amphibious Group Two, Rear Adm. Raymond E. Peet, USN, visiting the barbershop aboard the dock landing ship USS *Shadwell*, 1967.
USS *Shadwell* (LSD-15) Mediterranean 1967 cruise book

Late that year, 1967, we set sail for the Caribbean with commander, Amphibious Group Two (ComPhibGru 2) embarked. I had been reading a book, *United States Destroyer Operations in World War II*, and learned that Rear Adm. Raymond E. Peet had served aboard the destroyer USS *Converse* (DD-509) during battles in the Solomon Islands and the Central Pacific. As officer of the deck during General Quarters (battle stations), he'd had a bird's eye view of the combat action. His ship was a unit of Destroyer Squadron 23, the famed "Little Beavers." DesRon 23 was led by Commodore Arleigh A. Burke (commodore being the title of a Navy captain in command of a squadron of ships).

As a four-star admiral, Burke served an unprecedented three terms as Chief of Naval Operations (17 August 1955–1 August 1961).

When ComPhibGru Two and his staff embarked, *Taconic*'s signalmen and radiomen were temporarily assigned to the staff—comprised of officers and senior enlisted members. A master chief signalman and an SM1 took control of our Signal Gang and directed our efforts in support of the Amphibious Ready Group, of which *Taconic* was a part. *Taconic*'s job as an amphibious command ship was to provide command and control capabilities for amphibious invasions. Stretching 459 feet in length, she'd been laid down as a Maritime Commission ship (type (C2-S-AJ1 hull), before being acquired by the Navy. Following conversion at Atlantic Basin Iron Works, Brooklyn, New York, she had been commissioned on 16 January 1945.

Photo 6-3

"Flag plot" aboard an amphibious force command ship. The sailor (whose arm is shown in the foreground) is writing backwards with a grease pencil on a Plexiglas status board to plot information for users in the command center.
National Archives photograph #USN 1113998-B

The deployment came off without a hitch and we returned to Norfolk for the Christmas holiday and leave period.

DEPLOYMENT TO THE MEDITERRANEAN

Photo 6-4

Rear Adm. William P. Mack, USN, 2 October 1963.
National Archives photograph USN 1075283

In January 1968 we began preparations to deploy to the Mediterranean. There, we would be part of a Naval Task Force supporting Operation DAWN PATROL, an exercise involving ships from NATO countries including England, Italy, and Greece. This time, our embarked commander was Rear Adm. William P. Mack, commander Amphibious Group Four.

I spoke to the senior watch officer aboard *Taconic* before we left Norfolk, and requested permission to stand junior officer of the deck (JOOD) watches, under instruction, under way. He asked me if it would interfere with my signal bridge duties and I told him that it wouldn't. Visual communications wouldn't suffer and while I was learning to be a JOOD, I would be checking on things on the signal bridge. With that, he acceded to my request, but told me, "I won't put you in a normal rotation so you can balance your duties. However, I'll expect you to stand at least one watch per night as JOOD/UI."

"DRIVING THE SHIP"

> *One of the most important principles of ship handling is that there be no ambiguity as to who is controlling the movements of the ship. One person gives orders to the ship's engine, rudder, lines, and ground tackle. This person is said to have the "conn."*
>
> —James Alden Barber in *The Naval Shiphandler's Guide*

In addition to at least one watch at night, and I rotated them, I tried to stand at least one day watch on the bridge, as well. Within a short period of time, the officer of the deck allowed me to "have the conn" under extremely close supervision. On several occasions the ship had a chance to practice "bumper drills." These involved throwing a large object over the side, usually an empty box or sometimes "Oscar" (an orange canvas dummy used for Man Overboard Drills).

After the object had cleared the ship, and was astern off the port or starboard quarter, the conning officer would make a sharp turn, and attempt to bring the ship alongside the object. The trick was to do so without running over, or past it. This may sound easy, but in addition to wind and wave acting on the ship and target, there were the effects of advance and transfer to consider. Ships do not turn immediately when the wheel (ship's helm) is put over. "Advance" refers to how far a vessel will continue along its track before it starts to turn, and "transfer," how long until it steadies up on the new course. This point is made to highlight the fact that there are delays between when speed and rudder orders are given to the helmsman and lee helmsman, and when the results of these orders take effect. When coming alongside a pier, or in this case a box, the conning officer must visually gauge how the ship is doing, and rapidly order any necessary changes.

I took my turn conning the ship with junior officers, and my experience as a deck seaman driving small boats and landing craft helped immeasurably. I was able to lay the ship alongside the box or Oscar without embarrassing myself. I was unaware at the time, that during the first such training period the admiral and his chief of staff had observed my efforts from the flag bridge and were pleased. You see, enlisted men conning naval ships just didn't happen in the 1960s. I was an oddity, an experiment, if you will, to be monitored carefully. I was acquitting myself well, and so would get further opportunities.

That night, our commanding officer, Capt. John V. Peters, and the executive officer dined with the admiral and chief of staff. One of the Filipino stewards who was a friend of mine told me later that I was the object of much favorable discussion during dinner. This was certainly a change, because I normally only came to the attention of senior officers if I did something wrong. Not surprisingly, I was happy with this turn of events and hoped it would continue.

LOSS OF THE SUBMARINE *SCORPION*

At the conclusion of DAWN PATROL, *Taconic* headed for Rota, Spain. We arrived early on a Tuesday morning and would sail for the States the following day. I had duty for our one night in Rota, but didn't mind. I was exhausted from my efforts at sea and needed rest.

Photo 6-5

Entry gate to Naval Base, Rota, Spain, on the road to Puerto de Santa Maria, circa the mid-1960s. Donkey traffic is visible on the overpass in the background.
Naval History and Heritage Command photograph #NH 92353

We were scheduled to conduct and monitor exercises with the USS *Scorpion* (SSN-589) during the homeward crossing of the Atlantic. She was a *Skipjack*-class nuclear submarine and the sixth vessel of the U.S. Navy to carry that name.

Photo 6-6

Fast attack submarine USS *Scorpion* (SSN-589) comes alongside USS *Tallahatchie County* (AVB-2) outside Claywall Harbor, Naples, Italy, 10 April 1968. *Scorpion* was lost with all hands in May 1968, while returning to the U.S. from this Mediterranean deployment. Naval History and Heritage Command photograph NH 70304

The next morning, we sailed and had two good days of exercises as we headed in a general direction toward the eastern seaboard of the United States. On the third morning neither *Taconic*, nor any of the other ships involved in the exercises were able to communicate with *Scorpion*. As the day wore on, tension increased dramatically and the highest priority radio messages flew between Rear Admiral Mack and commander, Submarine Force, Atlantic Fleet. I'm sure messages flew to Washington, D.C., and back as well.

That night, *Scorpion* was declared missing and Mack was designated on-scene commander to direct search and rescue operations. As part of this effort, each of the ships in company was assigned to a 10-mile square search grid. I had the midwatch as JOOD (under instruction). The actual JOOD, an ensign, was a quiet, introverted officer who appeared reluctant to aggressively discharge his duties. The OOD was Lt. Claude Farmer. He was a very good officer of the deck, and I loved standing watches with him because he was very patient with his bridge team and spent time training all of us. (After leaving *Taconic*, I would have the pleasure of running into him again, several years later, off the coast of Vietnam.)

I requested permission from the OOD to take the conn, and, when granted, relieved the JOOD of his conning duties. Around 0245, as we were steaming in our assigned grid, our port side was lit up by the high intensity signal lights of a Russian destroyer. Our radar had been down since 0130 and the ET's were working frantically on it. We had added two additional lookouts while the radar was down. Unfortunately, we didn't see the Russian until his searchlights stabbed out of the darkness. Lt. Farmer took the conn, and told me to notify the captain and chief of staff and to check on the ETs. The destroyer was close aboard, about 500 yards off our port quarter, requesting via flashing light that we identify ourselves immediately. Silhouetted by its own light sources, we could see the destroyer's guns trained on us, and her crew at battle stations.

Captain Peters and the admiral's chief of staff arrived on the bridge, and Lt. Farmer gave the CO a status report including that the radar was still down and that I was supervising the ETs as they worked and was assisting them in any way I could. He also told Peters that we were under the guns of the Russian ship, and being interrogated by flashing light. The captain walked out on port bridge wing with the admiral, who'd arrived on the bridge, and chief of staff. He told one of the signalmen to tell the Russian who we were, and ordered those not actually on watch to get inside the skin of the ship.

After our identity was conveyed, the destroyer slowly closed us with her lights still illuminating our port side and her guns still trained. She asked if she could be of assistance in helping us find our lost submarine, which begged the question, How the hell did the ship's commander know that, and who gave him the information? This solicitous offer ran counter to his menacing behavior. With the admiral's concurrence, the CO thanked the Russian for his offer of assistance, but assured him that we had everything well in hand. After acknowledging receipt and understanding of that message, a long fifteen minutes went by before the destroyer trained her guns centerline, turned off her lights, moved away from our port side, and slowly increasing speed as the distance between the two ships widened.

Photo 6-7

Soviet *Krupny*-class guided missile destroyer conducting surveillance during the NATO exercise, Operation DAWN PATROL in the Mediterranean, April 1968. National Archives photograph #K-50255

Very slowly, normalcy returned to the bridge and we continued to steam in our assigned grid. The admiral and chief of staff went back into flag plot and the captain came back into the pilot house and climbed up into his chair on the starboard side of the bridge. I told the boatswain's mate of the watch to get the CO a cup of coffee and then announced to the bridge that "the radar is now up and working." Lt. Farmer responded with the time-honored acknowledgement, "Very Well," and the ship settled down to routine. The captain remained on the bridge until the watch had been relieved, then went to his at-sea cabin. As he passed me, he patted me on the shoulder and said, "Good Job, Flags, you're steady when it counts."

We remained in the general area for a lengthy period, but never regained contact with *Scorpion*. The hunt was finally terminated and the ships in our group were released to steam independently back to Norfolk. We were happy to finally be going home, but saddened at the loss of our submarine and ninety-nine undersea shipmates. When we tied up at NOB, there was a group of flag officers waiting on the pier. As soon as the brow was in place, they stormed aboard and went up to "Admiral's Country." I don't know what transpired there, but liberty wasn't granted for about three hours, until after they had all departed.

Later in the year, *Scorpion* was found crushed on the bottom of the sea at a depth of ten thousand feet, about four hundred miles southwest of the Azores. The naval research ship USNS *Mizar* (T-AGOR-11) photographed a piece of wreckage on the seabed on 27 June 1968; the wreck proper was found nearby on 29 October. There were rumors in the fleet that she had been sunk by the Soviets. Fifteen years after her loss, it was disclosed that *Scorpion* had been sent to surveille a Soviet naval exercise southwest of the Canary Islands, that included a least one Soviet nuclear submarine. There had been much speculation about the cause of her demise since then, within both the Navy and the press, but the loss of *Scorpion*, at least in "open sources" remains a mystery.

TRANSFER TO USS *RALEIGH*

Following three wonderful years aboard *Taconic*, it was time for a change. I visited EPDOLANT in Norfolk, and was able to get a set of orders to another amphibious ship. My new home would be the USS *Raleigh* (LPD-1). Fairly new, she had been commissioned on 8 September 1962, lead ship of the *Raleigh*-class amphibious transport docks.

7

Short Stint aboard *Raleigh*

Photo 7-1

USS *Raleigh* (LPD-1) off Guantanamo Bay, Cuba, on 1 February 1963. The amphibious transport dock has two H-34 helicopters parked on her afterdeck.
Naval History and Heritage Command photograph #NH 107694

I have always been the type of sailor that was ready to move on to a new ship or duty station after a couple of years. If you do this in civilian life, you end up in each new place not knowing anyone or what to expect. Additionally, your résumé will be suspect if you move around like a gypsy. Not so in the Navy. You can go from an aircraft carrier to a minesweeper, from an amphib to a supply ship, and everything in between. The people may be new, but there is continuity because you'll still be doing the same kind of work called for in your particular rating. Thus, going to a new ship is not something to be faced with trepidation.

For me it was always exciting to learn the mission of a new ship and take on challenges beyond the special expertise required of a Signalman.

My time aboard the *Raleigh* would be brief, encompassing a cruise to the Caribbean, and some experiences new to me. One such experience, meant to help me advance in my career, inadvertently caused friction between *Raleigh*'s commanding officer, her executive officer, and myself.

PASSED UP OPPORTUNITY

The executive officer sought to nominate me for the Navy's Enlisted Scientific Education Program (NESEP). This was a super program by which selected enlisted personnel were able to attend a college or university free, all the time drawing their normal pay and being allowed to compete for advancement in their rating. Upon graduation, students were commissioned as ensigns in the regular Navy.

NESEP enabled bright young sailors to realize the two-fold dream of a college education and becoming a naval officer. Of course, upon graduation you had to agree to remain on active duty for a specified number of years. Since most applicants, when accepted, already had one or more enlistments behind them, the Navy was fairly certain of retaining NESEP graduates for a full twenty-year career, and maybe longer. It was a great honor to even be considered for this program and I was flattered.

When I respectfully declined to accept the nomination, the CO and XO were floored. I was summoned to the CO's stateroom where he and the XO asked if I was in my right mind. I could understand their point of view. I did harbor a desire to be an officer, which is why I had started doing officer correspondence courses. Nonetheless, I wanted to make chief petty officer first. This goal, while important to me, didn't make sense to the CO and XO. They just couldn't understand why someone would turn down such an opportunity to gain a commission, in order be a chief. They said the word like it was insignificant, while being called Chief seemed to me the epitome of being a sailor.

Chief Petty Officers are the backbone of the Navy, the glue that holds everything together and makes it work efficiency. They teach young sailors about the Navy and guide young officers to become effective leaders. Our meeting came to an abrupt end, and I was summarily dismissed. I guess I must have really disappointed them, and perhaps even caused them to question their judgement in nominating me in the first place, because the CO and XO never spoke to me again unless it was in the line of duty.

PORTS OF CALL

As a part of our Caribbean deployment, *Raleigh* visited Cartagena, Columbia, in South America. I did some sightseeing and quaffed some beers with shipmates, but steered clear of the women. I was glad that I did. Every single sailor that indulged in sex developed a weird strain of VD that resisted normal treatment with penicillin, but which the doctors eventually found a way to cure. There was also a tense feeling in the air, like everyone was waiting for something to happen. Drugs were prevalent even then, and maybe this was the cause of fear among the people. In any case, I felt a lot better when I was back aboard ship.

Photo 7-2

U.S. Navy sailors walking down a city street in Colon, Panama, date unknown. Naval History and Heritage Command photograph UA 18.01.01

The second port we visited was Colon, Panama, on the Atlantic side of the Canal Zone. Like Cartagena, it was a wide-open town with all the usual vices available to sailors for very little money. Although shabbier than Cartagena, it was more inviting. The destroyer escort USS *O'Callahan* (DE-1051) was also in port with us. She had just been commissioned and was on her way to San Diego, California, her new home port, via the Panama Canal. Upon her arrival there, she would become the newest member of the Pacific Fleet Destroyer Force.

Photo 7-3

Destroyer escort USS *O'Callahan* (DE-1051) at sea in the Pacific, 7 April 1975. National Archives photograph #KN-23382

The problem, as explained to us, was that she was rushed to completion and had not yet received her full manning. Thus, she was desperately looking for volunteers to augment her crew for the transit through the Canal and then up the coast to San Diego. The volunteers would disembark in San Diego and be flown back to their parent ships courtesy of the Navy. Having never been through the Canal, I quickly volunteered and was accepted.

TRANSIT THROUGH THE PANAMA CANAL

The Panama Canal is a series of locks, which raise a vessel from, and lower it to, sea level, during passage across the Isthmus of Panama. This narrow strip of land between the Caribbean and the Pacific, links North and South America and contains Panama and the Panama Canal. Entering Gatun Locks (the only lock on the Atlantic side), vessels are raised a total of 26 meters in three distinct chambers. Vessels then proceed across Gatun lake (formed by damning the Chagres River) and into the Gaillard Cut (carved through the Continental Divide). Exiting the cut, there remain a lock, a lake, and another lock on the Pacific side. Vessels descended 9 meters in one step in the Pedro Miguel Locks, pass through Miraflores Lake (a small artificial body of fresh water), then descend 18 meters in two distinct steps in Miraflores Locks, before exiting the Canal.

Photo 7-4

Heavy cruiser USS *Houston* (CA-30), with President Franklin D. Roosevelt and his party on board, as she passes through the Gatun locks, Panama Canal, on 11 July 1934. Members of the presidential party are visible near turret #2.
National Archives photograph #80-G-455963

As the *O'Callahan* moved through the locks, she was guided by "mules" on each side. These "mules" were actually small diesel engine tugs on rails that are attached to a ship using its own mooring lines. By this means, the ship is moved forward through the locks using the power of the "mules" instead of ship propulsion. At the entrance to each lake, the "mules" are disconnected and the ship proceeds under its own power. Upon reaching the departing locks, the sequence is repeated until the ship is clear of the last set of locks. Exiting the Canal on the Pacific Ocean side, a ship can berth at Panama City or proceed out into the Pacific. Our transit was a wonderful experience. We even received certificates that attested to our transit. Many versions of "Order of the Ditch" certificates exist; two examples follow:

Photo 7-5

Certificates offering proof of having made ship passage through the Panama Canal.

O'Callahan remained overnight in Panama City, the capital city of the Republic of Panama. Another great night of liberty was had, although tamer than Colon. We stood out of port the following morning, and sailed up the Pacific Coast, stopping overnight in Mazatlan, Mexico. Beautiful, sun-drenched beaches, ice-cold beer, great-looking women, and friendly local people (if you had money). What more could an American "bluejacket" (enlisted sailor) ask for? There were also terrific souvenirs that were inexpensive by U.S. standards.

Photo 7-6

Panama City, Panama, street scene, date unknown.
Naval History and Heritage Command photograph #NH 122227

We finally arrived in San Diego and tied up at the Naval Station at 32nd Street. Those of us who had ridden the ship as volunteers were given plane tickets back to our parent commands and paid up to date.

We only had to go to the airport and check in for our flights. I decided to catch a cab downtown and see the sights before heading for the airport. We had about eight hours before our various planes were due to depart, so that left plenty of time for other things. I spent the afternoon and early evening in a bar called the China Doll. While enjoying the oriental atmosphere, I shot pool, drank a lot of beer, flirted with the waitresses, ate some chow, and watched the dancers on stage. I made it back to Lindberg Field in time to catch my plane and, feeling no pain, settled in for a flight to Norfolk, to rejoin the *Raleigh*.

DESIRE FOR DUTY ABOARD A DESTROYER

Back aboard ship, I was bored and restless. I had never lost my appetite for assignment to a destroyer, and I wanted desperately to go to the Orient—a desire rekindled by the afternoon spent in the China Doll. So, I visited EPDOLANT in Norfolk. I was told I didn't have a year on board *Raleigh*, and so couldn't be transferred. Not one to be put off so easily, I continued talking to the detailer. In the course of our conversation, it somehow came up that I had a case of Johnny Walker Black Label Scotch. During the back and forth, I sensed that he was considering the scotch, so I just kept dangling it out there.

Eventually, he looked at me and allowed that something might be done and, while he couldn't accept a bribe, if he happened to find a case of scotch whiskey, then it could be liberated. I agreed, and added that I wanted an assignment to a destroyer so bad I could taste it. My second wish was to go to the Orient, but I knew that would be hard to do when based on the East Coast. "You know, Flags, I just might have something that you'd like. I can transfer you to the USS *Noa* (DD-841), home ported in Mayport, Florida."

Learning that she had just sailed from Mayport with Destroyer Squadron 14, bound for the western Pacific and Vietnam, I told him I'd love to have orders to her if that could be arranged. Preparing to leave his office, I told him to follow me outside for a few minutes and we'd both be satisfied. Getting up, I left the building and went out to my car. I opened the trunk and took out a box and set it on the sidewalk near him. "You know," I said, "you never can tell what you might find on the streets these days." We both grinned, shook hands, and took our leave of one other. My orders to *Noa* arrived in the mail the next day.

After getting numerous shots in Sick Bay mandated for overseas duty, I was detached from *Raleigh* and given travel pay and a plane ticket to San Francisco, California. From San Francisco International Airport I would go by bus to Travis Air Force Base in nearby Fairfield, where I would catch a government-chartered Northwest Orient airliner that would take me to Clark Air Force Base in the Philippines. I was then to take a bus from Clark to the Subic Bay Naval Station where I would presumably catch up with the *Noa*.

The first challenge in this itinerary came at the MAC (Military Airlift Command) Terminal at Travis. After checking in at the MAC desk, I was informed by an airman that my luggage was overweight, and that I had been bumped off the initial flight and would have a two-day delay in departing Travis. Neither of these setbacks dampened my enthusiasm, but they did put me to thinking. I couldn't do too much about the delay, but I was damned if I was going to leave any of my gear behind. Like servicemen the world over, I ate in the terminal cafeteria, and slept on hard metal chairs in the passenger waiting section. I also purchased several paperback books, magazines and newspapers to pass the time.

In between eating, sleeping, and reading, I racked my brain in an attempt to figure out how to beat the weight limitations. The MAC desk was manned by shifts, however each successive person on duty told me the same story after weighing my gear. On my second and last night in the terminal, a young female airman was manning the desk. Using what little charm, I possessed, I was able to learn her name was Jan, and talk her into letting me buy her dinner in the cafeteria. Dinner and a couple of drinks enabled me to prevail upon her to weight my baggage yet again. This time around, the baggage was just under the limitation.

Overjoyed with this development, I took the young lady to the Airman's Club for a few more drinks, then we repaired to the apartment she shared with an Air Force girlfriend, and spent the night together. When her alarm went off at 0500, I was a little hung over and disoriented, and it took me a few minutes for reason to return. A quick shared shower woke us both up. We followed that with a glass of juice and a cup of coffee, hurriedly dressed and went back to the MAC Terminal. Jan had the first shift and I had a plane to catch. When we got inside, Jan went to man the desk and I to get us some more coffee. When I got back to the desk my baggage had been checked as being of legal weight. The girl was a saint. We enjoyed our last cup of coffee together before they called my flight. A quick hug and kiss and I went to board my plane – finally!

8

"Destroyer man" at last

Photo 8-1

Destroyer USS *Noa* (DD-841) in heavy seas, date and location unknown.
National Archives photograph #USN 1046594

Noa would prove to be everything I had dreamed of and wanted, many times over. My time aboard her would be the highlight of my enlisted service at sea, and I have harkened back on those experiences many times in later years. She was a 390-foot *Gearing*-class destroyer, built at Bath Iron Works, Bath, Maine, and commissioned on 2 November 1945. Fast and nimble, she had a top speed of 36.8 knots. Originally armed with three twin 5"/38 gun mounts, twelve 40mm anti-aircraft mounts, eleven 20mm AA mounts, and ten 21-inch torpedo tubes, she had been modernized several years before I joined her.

By the late 1950s, the U.S. Navy's destroyer force was outdated in its ability to defend against modern aircraft and submarines. A FRAM (fleet rehabilitation and modernization) program was begun to upgrade and rebuild existing ships. FRAM I was intended to extend the useful life of ships by eight years. Restricted to *Gearing*-class ships, it included the removal of one 5-inch/38 mount and the addition of anti-submarine warfare weapons, sensors, and delivery systems:
- DASH (drone anti-submarine helicopter)
- ASROC (anti-submarine rocket)
- SQS-23 Sonar
- VDS (variable-depth sonar)
- Mark 32 torpedo tubes

Noa had entered the Philadelphia Naval Shipyard on 25 May 1960 for her FRAM I overhaul. Leaving the yard on 2 May 1961 with the latest in ASW weapons, she rejoined the Atlantic Fleet.

Photo 8-2

USS *Noa* (DD-841) after her FRAM 1 conversion, date and location unknown. Naval History and Heritage Command #NH 81823

ADVENTURE-FILLED TRAVEL TO THE SHIP

Everyone on my flight was either in the service or dependents of service members. However, it was a civilian plane chartered by the Air Force, so we had Northwest Orient flight attendants working our plane. From the West Coast of the U.S. to the Philippines was about a 14-16-hour flight, if non-stop. We would be stopping at Midway Island for approximately two hours, so adding that to the flight time made it about

18 hours from Travis AFB in California to Clark Air Force Base in the Philippines.

Since it was a service-chartered aircraft, there was no distinction between First Class and Coach. That was great, because the female attendants treated all of us first class. About three hours into the flight, three other sailors, myself, and Brenda, one of the attendants, were in a semi-closed alcove playing poker. After a few rounds of drinks, traditional poker gave way to strip poker. It was a long and languorous flight and we sailors were fairly accomplished poker players. By the time we were an hour out of Midway, Brenda had been divested of every bit of her clothing, and was even more stunning than with her clothes on. We finally had to break up the game and prepare for our dissent into Midway Island, but we parted friends and all of us agreed that we had never before spent our time on an airplane so enjoyably.

Photo 8-3

Two of the many Gooney birds on Midway Island.
USS *Lloyd Thomas* (DD-764) Western Pacific 1972 cruise book

Midway didn't offer much but a change of flight crews and the opportunity to watch Gooney Birds use the runway for touch-and-goes (landings and immediate takeoffs). We lifted off the runway two hours later, landing at Clark the next morning. After the air conditioned-comfort of the airplane, the tarmac at Clark was like a blast furnace. The oppressive heat would definitely take some getting used to. Customs was only a perfunctory check, and then we were through the line and into the terminal.

Approximately thirty of us needed to get to the Naval Base at Subic Bay and, wonder of wonders, there was one of those long gray Navy buses at the terminal for that very purpose. We loaded our gear and settled in for the trip to Subic. Passing through the main gate at Clark, our bus headed through Angeles City. In 1969, Angeles City was a pretty wild place. Not quite as wild as Olongapo, but close. Wall to wall bars, Sari-Sari stores, old men and women selling barbeque meat on a stick, little kids begging for pesos and, everywhere, the girls.

Photo 8-4

Subic Bay, gateway to the Philippine Islands.
USS *Du Pont* (DD-941) cruise book

On the outskirts of Angeles City, the bus stopped and we all chipped in and bought a big wash tub full of yellow (Tagalog for ice) and San Miguel beer. This tub was quickly consumed and we stopped for another, something we would do three more times along the road. By the time we got to the last hill that overlooks Subic, we were all inebriated including our Filipino driver. As we came down off the hill drinking, singing, and carrying on, we missed the sentry and wide-open gate by a good ten feet and crashed through a chain link fence that bordered the base, finally coming to a halt against a very large tree. We were all unhurt, but the bus wasn't going to move anywhere under its own power. Base Security arrived, took in the scene, and sent for another bus to take us to the Transient Barracks.

Arriving at the barracks, the Master at Arms (MAA) issued us linen and assigned us to two-man rooms. I ended up with a room to myself, perhaps because I was the only first class petty officer. All the rest of the guys were thirds, seconds, and non-rated. I intended to just take a shower and hit my rack. However, the shower revived me and left me ready to go exploring. Slipping into a light-weight short sleeve shirt and some chinos, I put on my mirrored sunglasses and felt ready to tackle the world, or at least Olongapo. First, I went to the Staff NCO club and had a great steak dinner and salad, washing it down with San Miguel beer. I then left the base, and walked across the bridge between the naval station and adjacent city of Olongapo, to experience my first taste of the Orient.

Photo 8-5

Olongapo City, Philippine Islands.
USS *Canberra* CAG-2 1966-1967 cruise book

Entering Olongapo, I walked up and down Magsaysay Drive for an hour or so, just soaking up the sounds, sights, and odors. The streets were filled with laughing sailors and Marines, most of them walking hand in hand with girls. I have never seen so many girls concentrated in one place in my entire life. It seemed as though there were five girls for every guy, no matter where you went. The cacophony of sounds was deafening. No matter what you liked, you could find a bar with music that appealed to you: hard rock, mellow rock, country and western, soul, and everything in between. Most of the bars had live bands and they were, by and large, pretty talented. Some of the singers were quite adept at imitating singers of international stature. In fact, had you not been watching the performance, you might have thought that the actual star was entertaining, rather than an imitator.

A few of the bars featured Go-Go dancers in skimpy costumes, which left little to the imagination. Interspersed with the many bars were hotels, restaurants, silk-screening shops, and souvenir stores, and myriad street vendors selling everything imaginable. The entrances to the bars were guarded by armed Filipinos and Philippine Constabulary Police, who made their presence felt on the streets along with Navy and Marine Corps Shore Patrolmen. Hustlers of all types plied their trades, vying for a share of the "American green."

Photo 8-6

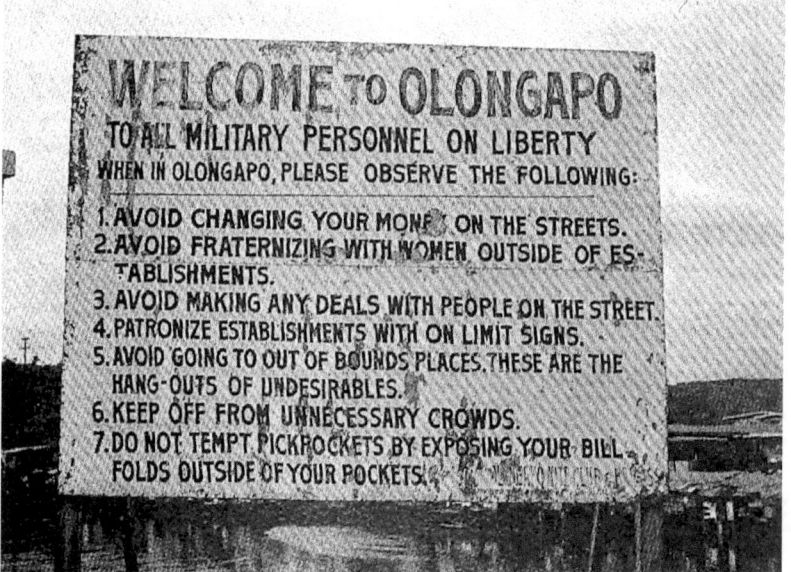

Guidance for sailors and Marines embarking on liberty in Olongapo.
USS *Du Pont* (DD-941) cruise book

Among the many bars in Olongapo were JoLo's, which was famous throughout the western Pacific, the Alamo Club, the Cherry Club, and the Old West #1 & #2. The two main streets were Magsaysay Drive and Rizal Boulevard. Ramon Magsaysay was a former president of the Philippines and Jose Rizal a national hero. Back then, neither of these streets were paved as they are now. Rather, they were just dirt and gravel roads with ruts caused by the ubiquitous jeepneys. These colorful rides are known for their crowded seating and wild decorations, and have become a symbol of Philippine culture and art.

Photo 8-7

The Jeepney was the popular form of public transportation in the Philippines.
USS *Canberra* CAG-2 1966-1967 cruise book

Inside the darkened establishments, bar girls sat at tables waiting for customers to entertain. When a sailor or Marine came in to the bar and sat down at one of the tables, a girl would immediately approach and ask if she could sit down. If the answer was yes, she would sit and make conversation for a few minutes, then ask if the serviceman would buy her a drink. She also ensured that the guy never lacked for whatever it was he was drinking. At closing time, the girls were free to make their own arrangement for the night. However, if you found a girl you liked and the feeling was mutual, and you wanted to take her out of the club before closing time, you had to "buy" her out (complete a contract with the mama-san in charge of the girls). In this way, the club was reimbursed for the girl's services, even though she had left for the night.

If you entered into this type of "buyout," you both could then go bar hopping, go to a restaurant, a movie, or better yet, go to the base. There, the two of you could go to one of the clubs, eat, bowl, see a movie, go horseback riding, or ride a go-kart. If you lived in the BOQ (Bachelor Officer's Quarters) or BEQ (Bachelor Enlisted Quarters) you were allowed to bring a girl to your room. However, most sailors opted to use the plentiful hotels out in town. I have been all over the world. From Sydney to Bangkok, Hong Kong to Tahiti, Hawaii to Brazil, Columbia to Cuba, Spain to Portugal and all the Med, and from Saigon to Bombay (now called Mumbai). Yet, I have never found a place to rival Olongapo for shear sailor delight. Olongapo was an absolute paradise where your only limitation was the extent of your pesos.

When I staggered back through the base gate early the next morning, I was absolutely exhausted, but grinning from ear to ear. A hot shower and some steaming hot coffee at the BEQ got my blood circulating and I felt ready to meet the morning halfway. I reported to the Transient Personnel Office and asked about *Noa*. Unfortunately, she had sailed the day before I arrived at Clark and no one knew when she might return. Therefore, I would be put on one of the ships passing through Subic on the way to Vietnam. Since every ship in WestPac (the western Pacific) was involved in supporting operations for the Vietnam War, it seemed logical that the ship to which you were sent TAD (Temporary Additional Duty) would eventually come across the ship to which you were permanently assigned.

Photo 8-8

Battleship USS *New Jersey* (BB-62) bombarding enemy targets near Tuyho, on South Vietnam's central coast, in March 1969.
Naval History and Heritage Command photograph

It actually worked out that way about 95 percent of the time, so it was as good a method as any. The battleship *New Jersey* (BB-62) had been re-commissioned for Vietnam service, and she had arrived in Subic for the first time on the same day I arrived at Clark. I immediately started lobbying to be assigned TAD to her. Alas, all my efforts came to naught. Every other transient sailor had the same desire and there were a lot of us who were en route to our ships. Waiting on assignment to a ship, I had "open gangway" (no duty), and opportunity to learn the meaning of the old saw, "too much of a good thing." After four days and four nights of liberty in Olongapo, I was ready to go to sea.

When I checked at Transient Personnel on the 5th morning, I was told that I was being assigned to the fleet oiler USS *Mattaponi* (AO-41), and that she would eventually rendezvous with *Noa* somewhere off Vietnam. I packed my gear and made my way aboard her. About midafternoon, she quietly slipped her lines, moved out into the harbor and headed fair around Grande Island, bound for the open sea and Vietnam.

Photo 8-9

Signal station in old abandoned lighthouse tower on highest point of Grande Island, looking up Subic Bay, circa 1903.
National Archives photograph #USN 903055

In the ten days I rode *Mattaponi*, we replenished approximately thirty-eight ships. This was my first introduction to the "Underway Replenishment (UnRep) Navy" and I loved the pace as well as the evolutions. One morning we were scheduled to refuel the *New Jersey* at about 0500. At 0400 we set the UnRep Detail and quietly stood on station drinking hot coffee and eating fresh rolls. My station, of course, was on the signal bridge helping ship's company SMs handle visual communications. The *Mattaponi*'s Signal Gang was solid and they treated me like one of their own.

Photo 8-10

Empty five-inch shell casings being brought aboard the USS *Mattaponi* (AO-41) in the South China Sea, for storage and return to the manufacturer, January 1969.
National Archives photograph #USN 1137267

It was a real pleasure to work with them. As *Mattaponi* moved through the offshore Vietnam fog at a leisurely 15 knots, we gradually heard the sounds of a band playing. As the musical strains increased in volume, we searched in puzzlement for their source. Then, like a grey ghost, the *New Jersey* materialized out of the fog and slid alongside to port at a distance of about 100 feet. The source of the music was then clear, as we could see her Marine Corps Band in dress uniforms playing Anchors Aweigh. It was an awe-inspiring sight to say the least.

The battleship remained alongside for two hours taking on fuel and stores. With the UnRep complete, we recovered our rigs, and she moved off, disappearing into the fog as quickly and as quietly as she had come alongside. Later that morning, we were on station awaiting the arrival of the hospital ship USS *Sanctuary* (AH-17). The fog had lifted and we could see the lush coastline of Vietnam as we steamed steadily north at 15 knots. Directly, we sighted the *Sanctuary* approaching on our port quarter. However, her angle of approach was almost 45 degrees in relation to our port quarter rather than coming up astern, parallel to our course, as she should have. As the distance continued to close and the relative angle of approach remained constant, we began to wonder just what the hell was going on.

Photo 8-11

Hospital ship USS *Sanctuary* (AH-17) at Wakayama Harbor, 13 September 1945. National Archives photograph #80-G-351801

Our commanding officer—an old aviator wearing a light-weight green aviator jacket and a ball cap—watched the *Sanctuary*'s approach. Finally, we could make out the captain of the hospital ship on his bridge wearing an Australian bush hat and waving. The only problem was our CO wasn't waving back. In fact, he was flapping his arms violently in what I guess was an attempt to tell the *Sanctuary* shear off. Repeated attempts to communicate with her by radio, flashing light and semaphore had all been to no avail. When all seemed lost, *Mattaponi* turned hard to port in order to minimize any damage from collision.

Sanctuary obligingly turned with us and plowed right into our port quarter doing some fairly heavy damage including crunching the captain's gig (boat). Fortunately, no one was physically hurt. For our part, the rigs were still intact and we were able to maintain our UnRep schedule. We managed to get the hospital ship alongside, but her station-keeping was atrocious and we broke (recovered) the rigs after transferring only a token amount of fuel. When they requested to come back alongside, our captain shouted across to her captain, "The only fucking way you'll ever come back alongside *Mattaponi* is if my XO comes over and drives your ship for you." With that, we increased speed and left *Sanctuary* wallowing in our wake.

The morning after the *Sanctuary* fiasco, we rendezvoused with *Noa*. As UnRep Detail was being set, I said goodbye to my shipmates. Then I ducked into the pilot house and thanked the skipper for *Mattaponi*'s hospitality and the privilege of serving aboard, even if only in a TAD status. I had packed my gear the night before so I went down to the berthing compartment, grabbed my stuff and went up to the personnel transfer station as *Noa* was sliding into station to starboard.

Once in position and hooked up, *Mattaponi* sent the Bos'n's Chair (transfer-at-sea chair – an aluminum rig with a high back and a seat belt) across to the *Noa* so they could transfer one of their officers to the *Mattaponi*. In this way, the officer could ride the oiler back to Subic for further transfer to the United States. After unrepping with the *Mattaponi*, *Noa* would return to the gunline off Vietnam.

Personnel transfer at sea is a dangerous evolution at best, but sailors are wont to find a way to enjoy themselves even in sobering situations. And so, it came to pass that as the officer was being transferred from *Noa* to *Mattaponi*, the line handlers aboard *Noa* slacked off just enough on their lines to give the officer a quick salt-water bath between the ships. When he finally set foot on the deck aboard *Mattaponi*, he was soaking wet and mad as hell. The sailors on the *Noa* hee-hawed him some, but he just ignored their antics and stalked off the transfer station.

Photo 8-12

Vice Adm. Marc A. Mitscher, USN, commander, Task Force 58, is highlined from a destroyer to aircraft carrier USS *Randolph* (CV-15) via boatswain's chair, 15 May 1945. This was the third time he had transferred his flag in four days, as his two previous flagships, USS *Bunker Hill* (CV-17) and USS *Enterprise* (CV-6) had both been badly damaged by Kamikaze hits off Okinawa.
National Archives photograph #80-G-320987

Then it was my turn. After donning a kapok lifejacket and being strapped into the chair, *Mattaponi* transferred me to the *Noa* and I was home. I arrived on the ASROC Deck Personnel Transfer Station of *Noa* dry as a bone and sailors shook my hand and welcomed me aboard. I was shocked and tremendously impressed that her CO, Commander Horace D. Mann Jr., was also on the ASROC deck, shook my hand and personally welcomed me aboard. The fact that the commanding officer of a warship would come down on deck from the bridge to greet an arriving first class petty officer in the middle of an alongside evolution spoke volumes for the trust he had in his crew. It also evidenced the genuine care he had for enlisted men. That welcoming foreshadowed an outstanding tour aboard the destroyer.

Photo 8-13

CDR Horace D. Mann Jr., USN, commanding officer, USS *Noa* (DD-841). USS *Noa* 1968-1969 "Welcome Aboard" brochure

Captain Mann asked, did not direct or order, one of the sailors on deck to take my gear to the Operations berthing compartment, while he took me up to the bridge to observe the final portion of the UnRep. He introduced me to embarked commander, Destroyer Squadron 14, Capt. (later Rear Adm.) John S. Kern, and to the executive officer, an enormous Viking of a man named Olsen, if memory serves. When the UnRep was complete and *Noa* had disengaged and was pulling away smartly, the CO turned me over to BM1 Wesley Golon.

Wes would prove to be a tremendous guy. He had a chest full of ribbons including the Bronze Star for in-country service in Vietnam and was a top boatswain's mate. I couldn't have asked for a better partner or running mate had I chosen him myself. Grabbing my hand, Wes welcomed me aboard, saying, "Welcome to *Noa*, Lee, you'll love it here. The skipper knows everyone in the crew by their first name, knows the name of their wives or girlfriends, and knows who has problems. Best of all, he really and truly cares for each one of us as individuals."

9

First Combat Tour aboard *Noa*

Photo 9-1

The attack aircraft carrier USS *Bon Homme Richard* (CVA-31) with the destroyer USS *Noa* (DD-841) in the background. National Archives photograph #USN 1142865

After praising the *Noa*'s commanding officer, Wes gave me a run down on the other officers on board, as well as the chief petty officers, and fellow first class petty officers:

> We got a solid Chiefs Quarters and good junior petty officers and non-rated guys. By far the best deal on board though, is that the First Class run the ship and the Old Man supports that 110 percent. Com'on, I'll take you up to our First Class Lounge. We still have our DASH helicopter hangar on board, but no more DASH helo, so the CO let us First Class turn the hangar into a lounge.

Photo 9-2

A drone anti-submarine helicopter (DASH) operating off the flight deck of the destroyer USS *Nicholas* (DD-449), off Hawaii, on 10 February 1965. National Archives photograph #USN 1111342

For readers not familiar with Navy shipboard accommodations, the commanding officer has a cabin and eats with the officers in the wardroom. On larger ships, the commanding officer usually has both an in port and a sea cabin, and eats in a private mess. The other ship's officers have staterooms located in an area of the ship termed "Officers Country" and use the wardroom as a lounge and dining area. Chief petty officers have their own "Chiefs Quarters" encompassing their berthing and a lounge/dining area.

Photo 9-3

Chiefs Quarters aboard the USS *Brooklyn* (CL-40), 18 January 1938. Naval History and Heritage Command photograph #NH 56633

The remainder of the crew, from seaman recruit through first class petty officer (E1-E6), reside in cramped berthing compartments, with their racks (beds) stacked three high. Many first class petty officers are older, mature individuals, long-past the rowdy activity engaged in by younger sailors, particularly after a night drinking ashore. As such, this collective group aboard any given ship often lobby for their own mess and berthing, similar to Chiefs Quarters. Space limitations normally prevent this action. The First Class aboard *Noa* obtained a private lounge as a result of the failure of DASH technology.

This small helicopter was developed to find Soviet submarines, acquired on sonar, and attack them with torpedoes before the subs could close the ship employing it to within range of their anti-ship weapons. A number of destroyers were modified to carry two small radio-controlled, unmanned drone anti-submarine helicopters with the addition of a hangar and flight deck. Despite extensive trials, the DASH system did not prove reliable. There were a number of reasons for this; one was that the helicopter, once airborne, was susceptible to jamming of its radio control system. In short, after being launched, the radio-controlled "birds" often crashed into the sea, instead of returning to the ship. Aboard another *Gearing*-class destroyer, the *George L. MacKenzie*'s (DD-836) hangar and landing deck were neither sizable enough, nor strongly built enough, to service manned aircraft after this occurred, so she suddenly had a fine movie theater.

As Wes led the way up to the DASH hanger, I reveled in the feel of the ship rolling gently under my feet as we proceeded up the Vietnam coast at 20 knots. When we entered the hangar, I was quite surprised to see large lockers lining two of the four bulkheads. We walked down the row on the port side, and I was pleased to see that one already had my name and rate on it. That indicated to me that this ship was organized and knew how to take care of its people. There were several couches and some lounge chairs, a refrigerator, stove, and sink, plus a rather large mess table. For entertainment, there was a movie screen and projector, a color TV, and an impressive stereo system—all the comforts at home.

I was introduced to some of the other First Class and would get to meet the rest of them as time went by. They gave the promise of being good shipmates and I hoped this proved to be true. I would wait and see, and I'm sure they were probably thinking about me in the same way. I was to learn, over the next few days, that I was the senior first class petty officer, based on years in grade. After having a cup of coffee and shooting the breeze for a short time, I went below to stow my gear.

Photo 9-4

View looking forward, over USS *Perkins'* (DD-877) after 5"/38 gun mount, of her hangar and flight deck for DASH drone anti-submarine helicopters. Naval History and Heritage Command photograph #NH 99527

I then went to the signal bridge to see what we had. The leading signalman before I arrived was an SM2 named Lee Ferrier. Lee was superb at his job and we formed a good team, along with the rest of the Signal Gang. Lee was a great shipmate, who introduced me to Louis L'Amour Western novels. I have enjoyed these books ever since.

The Signal Gang was in a three 2-man under way watch rotation, which seemed like an equitable setup to me. It would leave me free to oversee all the sections at given times and pitch in wherever and whenever I was needed. Satisfied for the time being that all was in order, I went to the mess decks for the evening meal. First class petty officers had head of the line privileges, in addition to all the other perks. I certainly didn't see how anyone could ask for more. After chow, I went about exploring my new ship. I was assigned to a destroyer, we were in the Orient, and to top it off, we would actually be firing shots in anger and engaging the enemy, albeit infrequently. The feeling was terrific.

Photo 9-5

USS *Oriskany* (CVA-34) catapulting an A-4 Skyhawk attack aircraft during operations off Vietnam, 30 August 1966.
Naval History and Heritage Command photograph #USN 1117395

For two weeks after I reported aboard, *Noa* carried out gunfire support missions and served as plane guard destroyer for the aircraft carriers *Oriskany* and *Bon Homme Richard* ("Bonnie Dick"). I have great respect for carrier pilots. In takes great skill and courage to land aboard a fast moving "flattop" not to mention being catapulted off it. A catapult failure can result in a plane plunging into the sea just forward of a carrier's bow. Few pilots survive such accidents. A few years later, Australian Naval aviator Sub Lieutenant Barry Evans was lucky to escape unhurt when a catapult failure saw his aircraft virtually fall into the sea on 8 November 1973. Evans remained in the Skyhawk A4G attack aircraft as the screws of the aircraft carrier HMAS *Melbourne* churned overhead and freed himself underwater.

Plane guard duty involved a destroyer being in position astern of a carrier conducting flight operations, to rescue any pilots that went into the sea during the launch or recovery of aircraft. Some planes also had aircrews, and COD flights (Grumman C-2 cargo planes used for ferrying personnel, mail, supplies) might be carrying passengers as well.

Photo 9-6

Grumman C-2A cargo plane.
Naval History and Heritage Command photograph

Whenever we were near the Vietnam coast, and particularly during gunfire support operations, first class petty officers manned .50-caliber machine guns mounted just below each bridge wing. Additionally, I was assigned to Mount 52 (*Noa*'s second forward 5"/38 gun mount), initially as a loader, later as a spotter, and finally as mount captain. Everything was new and exciting, and the icing on the cake was that we were in a war zone. Therefore, mail could be sent to the U.S. free, our pay was tax free, and we also drew combat pay. For the first time, I had more money than time or a place to spend it.

LIBERTY IN SUBIC

Photo 9-7

USS *Samuel Gompers* (AD-37) providing tender services to four destroyers, May 1969, probably in Subic Bay, Philippines. Ships alongside are (left to right): USS *Higbee* (DD-806); USS *Douglas H. Fox* (DD-779); USS *Robison* (DDG-12); and USS *Leary* (DD-879). Naval History and Heritage Command photograph #USN 1139041

Our time at sea passed rather quickly and soon we were relieved on the gunline and set a course for Subic Bay and some R&R (rest and relaxation). With my wallet fairly bulging, I could hardly wait. Arriving in Subic, we moored outboard the destroyer tender *Samuel Gompers* (AD-37) at anchorage. (Years later, I would become her first lieutenant in my first at sea assignment as a Limited Duty Officer.) Wes Golan and I crossed her deck that evening, went down her accommodation ladder to the waiting liberty launch, and proceeded to the Fleet Landing and, from there, to the NCO Club. We ordered the biggest steak dinner on the menu, washed it down with several San Miguels, and then headed out to tackle Olongapo.

Photo 9-8

A sight typifying the life in Subic Bay was a view of children in small boats begging for coins beneath the Olongapo Bridge. The presence of children at this location, day and night, made sailors realize how lucky they were to live in America.
USS *Canberra* (CAG-2) 1966-1967 cruise book

Of the five days in port, I had liberty on three of them, and Wes two, so we went ashore together twice, and I by myself once. It seemed as though each night's liberty was better than the one before. On our last night, liberty expired at midnight, for first class and below, so it was with some disappointment that we reluctantly caught the launch back to the *Noa*.

10

Second Combat Tour aboard *Noa*

Map 10-1

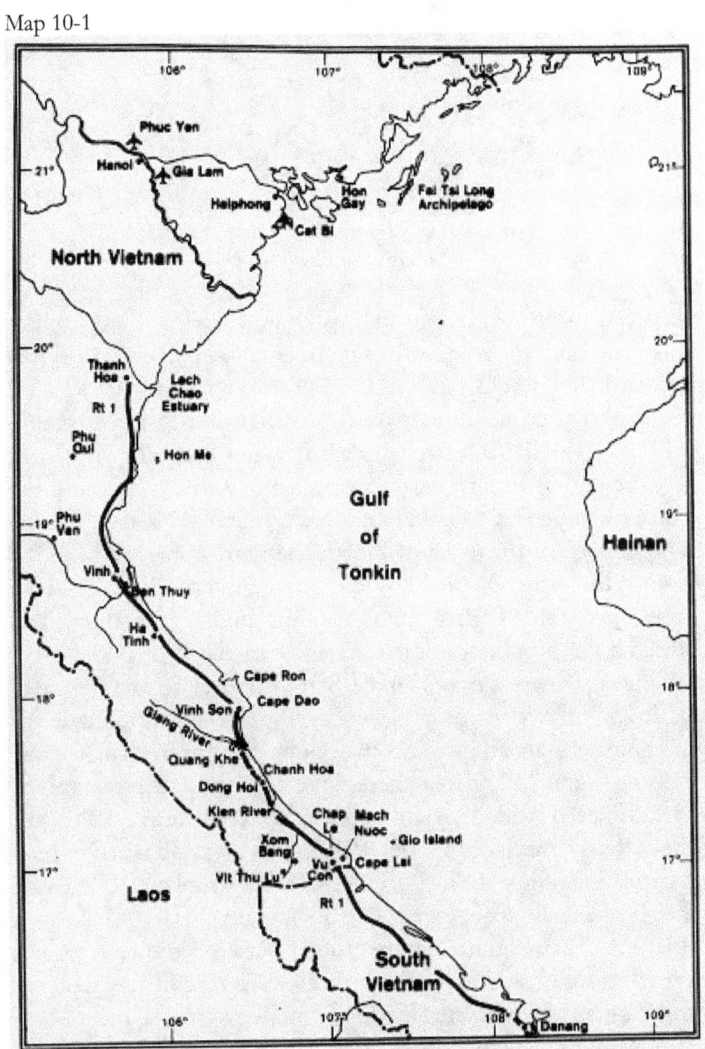

Area of U.S. Naval Operations in North Vietnam, 1964-65.
Naval History and Heritage Command photograph #NH 96352

BACK ON THE GUNLINE

Photo 10-1

Guided missile destroyer USS *King* (DLG-10) under way on 26 February 1965.
Naval History and Heritage Command photograph #NH 106808

We were to remain at sea, a month this time, carrying out gun fire support missions and plane guard assignments as before. For this particular period, we would have one additional assignment, PIRAZ Operations. With the commencement, in February 1965, of Operation ROLLING THUNDER (the large-scale sustained bombing of North Vietnam), participating aircraft carriers operated from a location in the Gulf of Tonkin designated 'Yankee Station.' Initially, Yankee Station was about 400 miles off the coast of North Vietnam, in part to keep the carriers beyond the range of North Vietnamese aircraft. This distance required long over-water flights (many needing mid-air refueling), and greatly restricted the number of sorties flown per day.

The solution was to move Yankee Station closer to the intended targets, about 150 miles offshore. However, the new location made the carriers vulnerable to air attack, and it became very important for the task force commander to know if there were any hostile aircraft mixed in with friendly air traffic. An air defense concept, termed Positive Identification Radar Advisory Zone (PIRAZ), was established, which called for stationing ships about 30 miles off the mainland to provide radar coverage of the air space over North Vietnam.

The PIRAZ ships were to be positioned between the land targets and carriers to monitor and keep track of all air traffic in the area. In addition to being armed with surface-to-air missile systems, these ships would be under the protective umbrella of the carrier's fighter aircraft, and could call in an interceptor at any time. Additionally, because of the possibility of North Vietnamese torpedo boats so close to the mainland, each PIRAZ ship was to have an accompanying destroyer, termed a 'shotgun,' as added protection against these threats.

Our job off North Vietnam was to act as protector, blocker, and shotgun for the guided missile destroyer USS *King* (DLG-10). *King* was tasked with monitoring U.S. planes flying combat missions against North Vietnam. Extreme vigilance was the word, especially when carrier aircraft reported "feet dry" which meant they had crossed the coastline and were bound in-country on their bombing missions. *Noa*'s job was to prevent any aircraft, or surface craft, from getting close to *King*.

We twice sighted North Vietnamese patrol boats, but none came closer than approximately 6,000 yards from us. This was prudent on their part, because our two ships packed a pretty potent punch. When we completed our support of *King*, we headed back down south and stood by for gun fire support missions as an on-call destroyer. One night, we were lying to, real close inshore, in hope that we would receive a call for gunfire support. We were standing easy at our General Quarters stations and all was quiet. We could clearly see a UH-1 Huey gunship (helicopter), about a mile inland, slowly circling an area, but nothing seemed to be happening.

Photo 10-2

Overhead view of a Bell UH-1 helicopter gunship firing a 2.75-inch rocket in support of two river patrol boats (PBR) in the Mekong Delta, South Vietnam, October 1969. Naval History and Heritage Command photograph #USN 1131566

All of a sudden, tracers started coming up out of the jungle at the Huey and, just as fast, tracers marked the answering rounds on their way down. Although we were in contact with forces ashore, we were strictly forbidden to interfere in the firefight. In helpless and angry frustration, we watched the Huey get shot out of the sky by the Viet Cong. I don't ever remember a time in my life when I felt as helpless and impotent as I did right then, and I knew for certain that the rest of the crew felt the same. We never did learn why we were kept out of the fray, or if the aircrew died or were taken prisoner.

Worse, we were directed to remain in our present position in anticipation of a mission in the waning hours of the evening. Thus, we couldn't escape the scene of the firefight and the fiery crash. I'm sure others relived that scene in memory, as I did, seeing life wasted, as we stood easy on station. As the sun slowly pushed over the horizon to start another day, we were released and told to resume plane guard operations.

FRIENDLY FIRE INCIDENT

About a week later, we were lying to again, this time off the mouth of a river. We were to rendezvous with a boat-load of ROKS (Republic of South Korea Marines), replenish their supplies, and give them big gun support while they conducted an infiltration operation against the Viet Cong. *Noa* and the ROKS had been given a series of light signals which were to be used to positively identify one other. If the wrong recognition signals were used, our orders were to open fire and destroy the small craft.

Because this was such a delicate operation and so much of it depended on reading the light signals correctly, I was on the signal bridge with binoculars and I asked SM2 Ferrier to be there also. With the two of us, plus the regular 2-man watch, I was pretty sure we would convey accurate information to the bridge. Around 2130, we saw, in the distance, a small boat approaching from up river in the shadows. There were small light signals emanating from the boat, but they were incorrect. When we challenged them by light, our signals must have been incorrect also, because we started taking small arms fire from the boat.

We quickly took the boat under fire and sank it, killing everyone aboard except for one man. The captain had deck department lower our small boat with an armed crew, who went to ascertain the results of our short-lived action. What we found were indeed ROK Marines. The boat brought the survivor back to the ship where our chief corpsman patched him up, as best he could. The ROK was alive, but in bad shape, so we moved to seaward and set flight quarters. Presently, a helicopter from the *Bon Homme Richard* was hovering overhead and lowering a basket so the Marine could be hoisted aboard. As the aircraft returned to "Bonnie Dick," the *Noa* headed back toward the coastline.

The next day, we learned that the injured ROK Marine had made it through surgery and was eventually going to be able to rejoin his unit. We also learned that due to a bureaucratic glitch at MACV headquarters (Military Assistance Command, Vietnam) in Saigon, both *Noa* and the ROKS had been given the wrong recognition signals. In hindsight, the damn mission was doomed before it even started.

The rest of the month went by smoothly for us. We carried out our gun fire support missions without a hitch, and operated as plane guard for the fast carriers when directed. Every third or fourth day, we rendezvoused with an oiler for UnRep (underway replenishment). I loved being part of a real warship's crew and reveled in our different assignments. However, I couldn't help but admire the crews of the oilers and ammunition ships that replenished us. For a boatswain's mate running the rigs, it must have been a thrill.

LIBERTY IN KAOHSIUNG, TYPHOON AVOIDANCE, AND RETURN TO SUBIC BAY

Photo 10-3

Indigenous craft at Kaohsiung, Taiwan.
USS *Fechteler* Southeast Asian 1967 cruise book

When we left Vietnam after our month was done, we sailed to Kaohsiung, Taiwan. We were to be in Kaohsiung for three days of liberty, after which we would return to Subic for some much-needed engineering maintenance with the help of the ship repair facility. I was chosen to be the ship's representative assigned to the Armed Forces police during our stay. Reporting to the chief petty officer in charge at the police headquarters in downtown Kaohsiung, I learned that they had a room booked for me at the Empress Hotel, and that I would be working the 1800-0200 shift.

My duties involved patrolling the main street, where the bars were concentrated, with one of the permanently assigned Armed Forces policemen. The ship had provided me plenty of money for the hotel and food, and it seemed that life couldn't possibly get any better, but then it did. I had met and was spending my free time with a young lady. After the second night, a typhoon came up, forcing *Noa* to sortie (depart Kaohsiung and stand out to sea) for storm avoidance, leaving about fifteen sailors and myself stranded on the beach.

During *Noa*'s ten-day absence, life ashore became ever more wonderful. Mei and I became inseparable and enjoyed every possible moment together. *Noa* pulled in only long enough to recover my shipmates and me, and with heavy heart, I hugged and kissed Mei while standing on the quay wall. With a last touching of hands and fleeting smiles, I boarded the ship as Mei departed in a taxi.

Arriving at Subic, we were able to berth at Riviera Pier, rather than outboard a tender at anchor. Our schedule called for five days in port, but this was soon shortened to three days, owing to an urgent requirement for several destroyers to return to the gunline, as soon as possible. Nevertheless, Wes, Lee Ferrier, and I packed many days' worth of liberty into our limited time ashore.

11

Final Combat Duty aboard *Noa*

Photo 11-1

Vietnamese junk used to intercept Viet Cong craft in search of contraband, May 1965. National Archives photograph #USN 1111098

Arriving off Qui Nhon, South Vietnam, to begin our third combat tour of the deployment, we rendezvoused with a South Vietnamese junk. We lowered a Jacob's ladder to port for a Special Forces major and a Vietnamese woman to quickly make their way on board. The executive officer met them, and immediately escorted then to the commodore's cabin where, I assume, they discussed our forth-coming mission. The woman, Co Binh, was drop-dead beautiful. A Mestiza blending of the best of French and Vietnamese parentage, she was tall, slender, and elegant, with a voluptuous figure not often seen in the Orient. She was to serve as our guide and as director of our mission, while Major Farris, the Green Beret, acted as her interpreter, since she spoke only French and Vietnamese.

They remained aboard for about a week, while we conducted classified operations along the Vietnamese coast. While they were aboard, the commanding officer gave Co Binh his in port cabin and he stayed in his sea cabin. On the third day, as we proceeded up the coast while at General Quarters, international relations almost suffered an irretrievable setback. Co Binh, Major Farris, the commodore, and the captain were in discussion in front of Mount 51. Wes was mount captain, and I was next to him on the mount. After admiring Co Binh's looks for a while, Wes, who spoke good Vietnamese, looked over at me and remarked in Vietnamese, "Co Binh has Saigon tits" indicating she might have had surgery to enlarge her breasts.

Co Binh heard the remark and she started yelling and screaming at Major Farris, while the commodore and captain stood there wondering what was going on. Eventually Major Farris was able to calm her down while explaining to the others what one of the *Noa* sailors had said in Vietnamese. Wes and I had both ducked down so she really didn't know who made the crude statement. However, only three people on the ship were fluent in Vietnamese, so the commanding officer had a pretty good idea who was responsible. Later that afternoon, the CO told Wes in passing that sometimes language fluency could cause major problems for large numbers of people. He never accused Wes, it was said as a matter of fact, but Wes got the hint, and no more comments were made during our visitor's stay.

REUNION OF OLD ACQUAINTANCES

Ten days later, we were again off Qui Nhon when we were hailed by a Swift boat requesting permission to come alongside. We stopped and lay to, as the Swift came alongside to starboard. Looking down in the boat, I was surprised to see Lieutenant Farmer, whom I had served with aboard the *Taconic*. While his crew held the boat alongside, Farmer came aboard to pay his respects to our commanding officer. It seems that Captain Mann had been his NROTC (Naval Reserve Officer Training Corps) commanding officer when he was in college, so he wished to say hello and perhaps acquire some ice cream and goodies for his crew. We broke out a couple of cases of soda, a box of ice cream, some luncheon meat, cheese, and some other goodies, and lowered them over the side to the waiting boat. I spoke with the lieutenant for a few minutes, saying it was good to see him and to stay safe in-country. He said that it was nice to see me also, and I was in good hands with Captain Mann.

Photo 11-2

Drawing of a Fast Patrol Craft ("Swift boat") by Ensign John Roach.
National Archives photograph #USN 1163487

Following this brief interlude, we took up our trade on the gunline. The time passed slowly but happily. One day, I was in Radio Central talking to the RM1 on duty, when the teletype started clattering. We both leaned over it to see what was coming in and, as we read the incoming message, looked at each other in horror. USS *King*, the DLG we had run shotgun for during PIRAZ Ops, had suffered a boiler explosion which killed eight sailors. When word of the incident was finally relayed to our crew by the skipper, we all felt a sense of loss and knew that "there but for the grace of God, goes *Noa*." We never learned the cause of the accident, but the captain ordered our chief engineer to review boiler operations with an eye to cinching up our procedures.

FRANK E. EVANS CUT IN HALF BY *MELBOURNE*

A couple of weeks later, we steamed back to Subic for two weeks of well-deserved R&R, which allowed the engineers to do some much-needed maintenance. It was the first time in the cruise that I ran short on money, but that was because I was ashore every chance I got. All too soon we left port, but this time, instead of going back to Vietnam, we were scheduled to participate in the SEATO exercise Sea Spirit.

(The Southeast Asia Treaty Organization is an international organization for collective defense in Southeast Asia, established on 19 February 1955.)

This joint exercise with Navy ships from Allied countries around the Pacific Basin promised to be an exciting alternative to what we had been doing. I was pleased to learn, when I read the operation order, that it mandated, to the greatest extent possible, communication was to be by visual means. However, shortly after departing Subic, we got a message cancelling our participation. Since we were freshly topped off with ammunition, it was decided to send us back to the gunline and to send the destroyer *Frank E. Evans* (DD-754) in our place.

Photo 11-3

Destroyer USS *Frank E. Evans* (DD-754) under way in January 1969.
Naval History and Heritage Command photograph #NH 107148

Anyone who was in the Navy at this time will never forget the tragedy that befell the *Evans* in early morning darkness on 3 June 1969. Operating as a screening destroyer, she was running with the Australian aircraft carrier HMAS *Melbourne*. Operating with a carrier is tricky at best. Their myriad lights confuse you and they sometimes signal they are going to do something and then do just the opposite. You have to be especially vigilant and alert whenever you operate with a carrier; one moving at flank speed through the water is an awesome beast almost impossible to stop. For whatever reason, *Evans* crossed the bow of *Melbourne* and the carrier sliced through the combat information center of the destroyer, cleaving her cleanly in two.

The first that the commanding officer of *Evans* knew anything was amiss was when he found himself in the water. Only the grace of God prevented more fatalities than there were. It was a tragedy of epic proportions that never should have happened and could have been prevented. I obtained pictures of the *Frank E. Evans* when she was a whole ship and of her aft section being towed back to Subic. (The bow sank, taking 6 officers and 68 men to the bottom with it.) Those pictures have been sobering reminders, ever since, of the responsibility entrusted to the officer of the deck on a ship at sea.

Photo 11-4

Frank E. Evans' after section, made up alongside USS *Everett F. Larson* (DD-830), after she was cut in two in a collision with the Australian aircraft carrier *Melbourne*. Naval History and Heritage Command photograph #NH 98651

Noa had fired a lot of shells in anger since arriving off Vietnam so it was only natural that during our last tour of duty on the gunline, we found a way to commemorate our combat duty over the course of the deployment. The brass casing from the first shell fired in the war, was cut in half lengthwise, with one half-relief section mounted on the wardroom door and the other on the door to the CPO Mess. Associated brass plates proclaimed, "This is the casing from the first shell fired in anger by USS *NOA* DD-841 off Dong-Hoi, Vietnam," with the date of this occurrence.

Noa had left Mayport, Florida in February 1969 and now it was September 1969, and we were completing our last gun fire support mission for this deployment. The captain had several buddies who were pilots operating from the carrier USS *Hancock* (CV-19). Somehow, he must have contacted them because, on the day we finished our final mission, three F-4 Phantom fighter aircraft buzzed us as we were turning back out to sea. They made several high-speed, low-level passes over the ship, then waggled their wings and departed for the carrier, which was stationed well out to sea.

COLLISON WITH THE OILER *PONCHATOULA*

Photo 11-5

The fleet oiler USS *Ponchatoula* (AO-148) prepares to refuel the guided missile destroyer USS *Coontz* (DLG-9) in the South China Sea, July 1969. Another destroyer is breaking away, following completion of fueling.
Naval History and Heritage Command photograph #USN 1139571

Leaving the gunline, we rendezvoused with the fleet oiler *Ponchatoula* (AO-148) to top off our fuel before heading to Kaohsiung, and then on to Hong Kong for Christmas. It was a beautiful, sun-filled day and the South China Sea was like glass. We were on the *Poncho*'s starboard side while on her port side another oiler was consolidating. This practice of a nearly empty oiler transferring her remaining fuel to another oiler, allowed one to return to port and replenish, while the other remained on station supporting the fleet.

As we steamed along at 15 knots it appeared to me that the *Ponchatoula*, required to maintain the designated replenishment course and speed, was closing the distance between her and us. A minute later, she sounded the danger signal, six short blasts on her whistle, and began coming right rapidly. As she did so, the oiler to port turned to starboard, as did we, in an attempt to avoid or to minimize the damage from an apparent, forthcoming collision. At the same time, each ship was frantically trying to disengage the tensioned span wires supporting the fuel rigs in order to get clear of the others.

The three ships came together with a tremendous crash and only the cool steadiness of our commanding officer, kept a potentially fatal situation from happening. As we continued to try and disengage, fuel hoses started parting and spewing NSFO (Navy Standard Fuel Oil) all over the ships. We finally cut the span wires to clear the two oilers, which continued to turn lazy circles while trying to break free of each other.

Once clear, *Noa* lay to, while a survey of the damage was done. Some handrails had been carried away, our TACAN (tactical air navigation system) antenna torn off, and the gig smashed, not to mention the ship and crewmembers being drenched in fuel oil. However, no one had been hurt by parting lines and wires on the rigs, and no one had been thrown over the side during the violent maneuvers. It could have been a whole lot worse. It took us two days of scrubbing to get *Noa* shining again, but no one had to go to the hospital. Due to the damage, the planned visit to Kaohsiung was cancelled and we proceeded, instead, to Subic for repairs.

LIBERTY IN SUBIC

During this time in Subic, I took the chief petty officer's advancement exam for the first time. I hadn't cracked a book—nobody stays aboard ship and studies in the "P.I." (Philippine Islands)—because Wes and I were running the streets almost every night, and when I wasn't with him, Lee Ferrier and I hit it hard. Such was the case, the night before the examination. Early in the morning I stumbled to the mess decks and started drinking coffee. At 0800 when we assembled for the exam, I still was really hung over. I don't remember much about the test. Six of us First Class took the CPO test, but only a cook and myself passed it. The cook got advanced but I PNA'd (Passed, Not Advanced) which meant I would be taking it again in another six months. Wes made BMC the next time around.

HONG KONG

The ship repair facility at Subic finished our repairs in record time and we were able to sail, as planned, in time to arrive in Hong Kong for Christmas. Nestled in a valley, it is one of the most cosmopolitan cities in the world. Ruled at that time by the British, the place was clean and crime was very low. High-rise buildings dotted the waterfront, floating restaurants lined the wharf in Aberdeen, ferries plied the waters of the harbor, and everywhere was the scent of money. Hong Kong was a fabulous place to visit in the 1960s, and really not all that expensive when everything was considered.

Photo 11-6

Lockhart Road, Wan Chai, Hong Kong.
USS *Floyd B. Parks* (DD-884) Western Pacific 1972-1973 cruise book

Christmas Eve found Wes and me in a bar about half tight. The place was crowed, and I guess we were taking up a lot of room as we played with a couple of toys we had purchased to take back home. Trouble began when a first class radioman off one of the other Navy ships in port told Wes, "Get the fuck out of our way, you fucking drunk." He then went into a karate stance and stated, "My hands are registered. If you don't get out of the fucking way, I'll hurt you. This is your first and only warning." During this invective, Wes was looking at me, and not the antagonist, because I was laughing so hard.

This RM1 had about as much chance of whipping Wes's ass as I had of getting a date with Elizabeth Taylor. It just wasn't going to happen. By this time a circle had formed around Wes, me, and the RM1. I just told everyone to stay out of it and give them some room. Well, as this dumb radioman weaved and bobbed in front of Wes in a drunken, poor imitation of Bruce Lee, Wes shook his head and said, "You may know karate, asshole, but I know Kabreaka."

With that he grabbed the guy by the crotch with one large hand while the other hand sort of cupped the RM's head. He then bodily picked him up and slammed him down onto the floor, and then stood back to see what was going to happen. Several things became obvious rather quickly. The RM1 was not very good at Karate, Wes was by far quicker and stronger and not near as drunk as he looked, and the radioman was not about to get up under his own power. A chief petty officer broke into the circle, but when Wes pivoted to face him the chief hastened to explain, "He's off my ship, Boats, I'm just going to help him out of here. I don't want, or need, the kind of trouble he asked for."

The crowd broke up after that, and everyone went back to what they had been doing before Wes cleaned the guy's clock.

DESTROYER SQUADRON 14 HOMEWARD BOUND

On December 27th, we sortied out of Hong Kong Harbor and lay a track to return to Subic for our final visit. We arrived two days later, and party time took up where it had left off when we were last there. Celebrating New Year's was definitely a wild time. By the time we sailed for Pearl Harbor on January 2nd, we were tired, but refreshed. The ships of Destroyer Squadron 14 spent two days at Pearl Harbor for upkeep and maintenance. Upon our departure, we formed up and proceeded northeastward, steaming in formation while conducting maneuvering and mutual ship exercises. At the end of the second day, the commodore detached each ship to proceed independently at best possible speed to San Diego, where the squadron would spend three days before beginning the final leg of our journey.

Our destroyers were all old but *Noa* managed to crank up 34 knots. At that speed, the whole ship shook as she plowed through the water and we had our doubts that she would hold together. The engineers declared that the Old Girl was singing. We arrived in San Diego one full day before our squadron mates, tied up at the naval station, and enjoyed a one-night head start on liberty. Leaving "America's finest city" (as San Diego now proclaims itself), we made our way down the coast and through the Panama Canal, before proceeding onward to Mayport, Florida. *Noa* had been gone from homeport for almost twelve months. I didn't realize it at the time, but I had made my last cruise, and served aboard my last ship, as an enlisted sailor.

A couple of weeks later, I went to see the captain and requested permission to reenlist. He looked at me with a big smile and said, "No time like the present, Lee. Let's do it now," and so we did. Two weeks after that I received orders to shore duty. I would be going to the Naval Reserve Training Center in San Mateo, California, as an instructor and station-keeper for three years. First though, I was to report to the Navy's Instructor School in Great Lakes, Illinois, for six weeks of training.

12

Naval Reserve Center Duty

Great Lakes Naval Training Center in the winter isn't no picnic, even for someone like me who likes snow and cold. Checking in for attendance at instructor school in early 1970, we were issued three blankets. When we got to the barracks, we found out why. Most of the windows were cracked or broken and the heating system didn't work. I guess the Navy could have put us up in motels or something similar, but that would have been quite expensive. Had we been civilians, we definitely would have been given adequate lodging. However, we were sailors, so into the barracks we went. I spent all six weeks of the school in long underwear, blues (my uniform), and three blankets whenever I went to bed at night.

The school itself was great. We were taught how to speak in front of an audience, the proper gestures to use, as well as those not to use, because gestures can add to or detract from your presentation. We were taught how to prepare a lesson including visual aids to enhance the effect, the proper way to ask questions, and how to get the audience working with you. At the end of the six-week course, I stood first in a class of twenty-two chiefs and first class petty officers, and was asked to remain at the school as an instructor. I was flattered at the offer. The lure of California being stronger, I forsook the opportunity and headed west for the famed San Francisco Bay Area.

I arrived at the San Mateo Naval Reserve Center with an ambivalent attitude toward the Reserves and their programs. I left, seventeen months later, with the highest degree of respect for the same Reserves and programs. The commanding officer of the Center was a TAR lieutenant named Phil Mansell. (TAR was an acronym for Training and Administration of Reserves). Officer and enlisted TARs were full-time career active-duty personnel, whose job was to provide administrative support for reservists drilling one weekend a month ("weekend warriors").

Mansell was very sharp, and it was a pleasure to work for him. He was the only officer assigned to the Center. The remaining fourteen of us were regular Navy chiefs and first class, with one TAR storekeeper second. Normal work hours were 0700 to 1500, Monday through Friday. If you had the duty, you remained until "colors" (lowering of the American flag at sunset), after which you could lock up and secure for the evening. We had a duty bunkroom, if you chose to spend the night, and a really nice lounge complete with refrigerator, pool table, color TV, and stereo.

Fridays were devoted to sports, either among ourselves or with members from other Reserve Centers in the Bay Area. The third weekend of every month was "drill weekend," when reservists showed up for formal classroom training; shipboard orientation tours; damage control training; and practical, hands-on training in rating specialties. Since we worked Saturday and Sunday on drill weekends, the Monday following was considered a holiday.

During my tour, I submitted numerous requests for transfer back to the Fleet. My persistence in this endeavor was likely a source of irritation to the CO, but he never said so, and I never got transferred.

Most all of the enlisted men work part-time jobs to offset the prohibitively high cost of living in the Bay Area. I moonlighted running a telex/teletype communication relay network for a company called RMK-BRJ. This company was a subsidiary of Morrison-Knudsen Construction of Boise, Idaho, the main building contractor in Vietnam. Our relay network included most of the countries on the Pacific Rim, as well as several key U.S. locations. My duties consisted of sending and receiving messages as directed, Xeroxing copies of incoming messages and routing them to the appropriate departments, and night-time security of the installation. I went to work at 2000, Monday through Saturday, and got off at 0630 the following morning. Though the hours appear long, we could, and did, sleep between midnight and 0500 if nothing was going on. This part-time job doubled my Navy pay.

I had previously taken the Navy-wide exam for advancement to chief signalman on three separate occasions. I PNA'd all three times. The first time I took the test at the Center, my fourth time overall, I received superior scores in all eight categories. Still, I again PNA'd. I called my detailer in Washington and asked him what was going on. He was sympathetic, but told me, "You are just too young and too junior in time in the Navy, Flags. Hang in there, you'll make it." I didn't even study for my fifth try at making chief and, sure enough, I passed and was selected for advancement.

As soon as I found out I made chief, I called the detailer and asked if I could go back to sea duty. I can still remember him laughing as he said, "Your initial tour was for three years, Foley, but now that you've made chief, we're extending your tour by one year. You'll spend four years at that Reserve Center instead of three." He was still laughing as I hung up. I then concocted a plan which, if successful, would ensure my return to sea duty. I would apply for the Warrant Officer Program. If selected, I knew that Washington would order me back to sea.

APPLICATION FOR WARRANT OFFICER

When I approached Mansell with my request, he was enthusiastic and supportive. I really didn't want to be a Warrant Officer. I wanted to be a Limited Duty Officer, but the only path to LDO was through the warrant grades, and you could only apply for warrant as a first class or chief. (LDOs are former senior enlisted personnel or CWOs, who are very highly skilled in their Navy job, and are selected to become a commissioned officer.) I put in my request. The skipper approved it on the spot and forwarded it.

Candidates had to take an 8-hour written examination comprised of naval history, simple mathematics, algebra, geometry, American history, chemistry, English composition, logic, and American government. The exam was required to be completed in a single sitting and had to be proctored by a commissioned officer. You were allowed breaks, but if you left the room you had to be escorted by a commissioned officer. Lieutenant Mansell had me take the exam at a table in his office so he could monitor me.

I had little knowledge of the higher math disciplines and some of the chemistry questions, so I just randomly picked multiple choice answers by looking at the clock and selecting whatever quadrant the second hand was in. Mansell must have been watching me breeze through the math because he said to me, "Foley, I had no idea you were so good in math. You don't even have any scratch paper filled out." I replied, "I don't even know what they're talking about so I'm just dive-bombing the answers." He looked at me like he thought I had lost my senses, then just shook his head and went back to his work.

When the result of the examination came back, I had scored exceptionally high in naval history, American history, English composition, and American government. I was above average in simple mathematics and logic, and average in algebra, geometry, and chemistry. The next requirement was an oral interview by a board of at least five commissioned officers. When I showed up at Naval Base, Treasure Island, on the appointed day, I found that I was one of fourteen candidates from throughout the Bay Area being interviewed. We all looked our best in dress uniform as we waited in the anteroom outside where the interviews were being conducted. There was a window in the door so it was possible to view the proceedings, but no conversation could be heard. The interviewing officers were smoking and drinking coffee as they asked their questions, while the candidates sat at attention and conducted themselves stiffly.

Being the tenth interviewee, it occurred to me that the officers were probably looking forward to finishing up the process and departing for the day. When my name was called, I walked into the room and instead of immediately taking a seat, I went directly to the coffeepot, filled a Styrofoam cup with black coffee, and then sat down. Crossing one leg over the other, I lit a cigarette and declared, "Gentlemen, I'm your number one candidate for the Warrant Officer Program and I'm ready to answer your questions." I watched looks of astonishment cross the faces of some of the officers, and a smile crinkle the grizzled face of the senior lieutenant commander who was a Limited Duty Officer.

You could have heard a pin drop in that room at the conclusion of my opening statement. Then surprisingly, they started asking questions in a decidedly friendly fashion and I knew that my approach was going to work. There was one exception, a lieutenant commander who was openly hostile. Near the end of the interview, he asked sarcastically, "Foley, what makes you think that you could fulfill the duties of an officer in the Fleet? Your record is spotty to say the least, and you certainly have no higher education as an officer should."

I looked at him for several seconds, then answered, "Sir, although my record is spotty as you call it, my evaluations have consistently been 4.0 in performance. I've completed 38 officer correspondence courses, all with top-notch grades." I continued, "While it's true I don't have any higher education, I do have an abundance of common sense and that is what is really needed to be a successful officer." When I was finished, he was flushed with anger. The rest of the board could barely conceal their smiles so I felt I had at least survived. Dismissed, I went over to the club on Treasure Island and indulged in a few too many drinks, relieved to be through with the interview process.

The next day I received a phone call from the LDO lieutenant commander. "Foley, you received one adverse recommendation from our interview yesterday, and you know who that was from. However, I exercised my right as the senior board member and negated his write-up. I was able to get a buddy of mine, another LDO, to write a positive recommendation based on what he gleaned from mine and those of the other board members, so I think you're pretty much set. I like your approach and attitude. We need more of that in the Fleet. Good luck, son." I replied, "Thank you, sir. Thanks for everything."

ADVANCEMENT TO CHIEF SIGNALMAN

I was promoted to chief signalman on 1 July 1971. We had six CPO's (chief petty officers) assigned to the Reserve Center and I was the only one advancing to join their ranks, so my initiation was held there. I was put through my paces as it were, but it wasn't nearly as rough as some I have subsequently witnessed. I was finally allowed to clean up and don a brand-new chief petty officer khaki uniform. Our senior CPO read the Chief Petty Officer Creed, and then he and the next senior chief pinned gold fouled anchor devices on my collars. I was officially a chief, my proudest moment to date.

SELECTION FOR WARRANT OFFICER

A few days later, Mansell called me into his office and handed me a message. It was official notification that I'd been selected for the Warrant Officer Program as a (WO-1) Boatswain, one of only twelve individuals. I was to be promoted to WO-1 on 1 August 1971 and could expect to receive orders to sea duty in the near future. (All of this wonderful news was contingent on my passing a complete physical examination.) Finally, the message directed that I contact the warrant boatswain detailer concerning my initial assignment.

Navy Warrant Officer Shoulder Boards and Collar Devices

	Warrant Officer 1 (WO)	W-1
	Chief Warrant Officer 2 (CWO2)	W-2
	Chief Warrant Officer 3 (CWO3)	W-3
	Chief Warrant Officer 4 (CWO4)	W-4

I passed the physical with flying colors, and went about trying to assemble the uniforms representing my new status. The hardest items to locate were Boatswain shoulder boards and collar devices. None of these items were available locally, so I called a friend of mine in San Diego. He found what I needed in the uniform shop and overnighted a package to me.

Tradition dictates that a newly commissioned naval officer give the first sailor to salute him a silver dollar. My crafty shipmates at the Center had positioned themselves in a group inside the front door, in order that they salute me all at once as I entered the building, and receive silver dollars, one and all. Anticipating this possibility, I had a friend of mine let me in the back door on 1 August. He saluted me, earned a silver dollar and, by this means, I turned the tables on my shipmates. It didn't matter. We had a celebration and it was such a joyous time for me. To make Chief was the pinnacle; to make Warrant was the icing on the cake.

Soon after, I had orders in hand. The warrant boatswain detailer, Commander Les Kelsey, had assigned me to a fleet tug in San Diego. I was to detach from the Reserve Center on 17 August 1971, and report to USS *Apache* (ATF-67). By noon the following day, I was packed and on the road to San Diego.

Reporting aboard *Apache*

Photo 13-1

Fleet ocean tug USS *Apache* (ATF-67), circa 1972.
National Archives photograph #USN 1153269

During the ten-hour drive down the California coast, I let my mind wander. I was excited about returning to sea, of course, but somewhat apprehensive about going aboard ship as an officer for the first time. I had asked for orders to a fleet tug because a small ship was generally more informal and laid back. Also, I would be a department head (the 1st Lieutenant/Gunnery Officer) rather than just a junior officer on a larger ship lost in the shuffle. Any concerns that I may have had soon gave way to eager anticipation and I sped up as I neared San Diego.

I arrived there about 2130 and went straight to the Navy Lodge. Tomorrow could not get here soon enough to suit me. At 0530, I was up and dressed. It being kind of early to report aboard, I drove down to the mole pier (a massive structure of concrete, used as a pier) and just looked at the *Apache* from a short distance away. After twenty minutes or so, I reluctantly broke away and went to a diner for breakfast. Finally, at 0830, I just couldn't wait any more. I quickly finished my coffee and headed for my new ship.

Photo 13-2

Newly commissioned Warrant Officer Lee Foley, USN. Author's collection

INITIAL MEETING WITH COMMANDING OFFICER

I parked on the pier and, as I was walking toward *Apache*, I noticed a short, heavyset red-haired lieutenant standing near the brow. Knowing that the executive officer was a full lieutenant, I automatically assumed that this was the XO. Arriving at the top of the ship's brow, I saluted the Ensign (American flag on the fantail), then the officer of the deck (a second class petty officer), and stepped aboard. Turning to the lieutenant, I saluted and said, "Bos'n Foley reporting for duty. You must be the XO." "Nah, I'm just the fucking captain," was his reply. As we shook hands, I spied a command at sea pin—the most coveted uniform adornment in the fleet—above his right shirt pocket.

Needless to say, I was embarrassed and knew I had started off on the wrong foot. I later learned that Luther "Red" Blevins had expected a salty Bos'n, who'd been a boatswain's mate. What he got was a former chief signalman who had a lot to learn. He, like myself, was a Mustang, a former BM1, and the best ship handler I had ever seen. The XO was called to the fantail and I was turned over to him. Lt. Norris Ewalt appeared to be a solid leader, and I liked him immediately.

The Bos'n that I was supposed to relieve had been transferred to Balboa Naval Hospital two weeks earlier. A bad nervous disorder had resulted in his being medevac'd off the ship during a salvage operation. This left the chief boatswain's mate running the show. Almost from day one we were locked in a struggle regarding who was running the Deck Department. BM2 Ree Dossey was the leading petty officer and a sharp boatswain's mate. BM3 Chuck Richardson was his assistant. Richardson was without peer as a salvage and towing boatswain's mate, and he taught me salvage operations from A to Z.

In addition to being the 1st lieutenant and gunnery officer, I was also the collateral duty supply officer. The Navy does not assign Supply Corps officers to small ships. Instead, a junior officer onboard is given some rudimentary training and fulfills the duties. This system works when the right officer is assigned.

APACHE'S UNIQUE ASSIGNMENT

Photo 13-3

The auxiliary repair dry dock *White Sands* (ARD-20) stands by as the bathyscaph *Trieste* operates independently. The *Trieste* is being prepared for a dive. These two units and the fleet ocean tug *Apache* (ATF-67), which tows the *White Sands* with the *Trieste* aboard, are called the Integral Operating Unit (IOU), circa 1972.
National Archives photograph #USN 1153268

Apache did not operate like most other fleet tugs. She was attached to Submarine Development Group One in San Diego to provide services for the bathyscaph *Trieste II*, a navigable submersible vessel used for deep-sea exploration. Together with the self-propelled floating dry dock *White Sands*, the three vessels formed the Integral Operating Unit. *Apache* later supported the Deep Submergence Rescue Vehicle (DSRV) program as well as attending to the needs of *Sea Cliff* and *Turtle*. The latter submersibles were smaller than *Trieste II* and were used for different purposes than the bathyscaph.

Trieste II was the first deep submergence vehicle (DSV) built by the U.S. Navy and the successor to the original *Trieste* bathyscaph. *Trieste I* set a deep diving record on 23 January 1960, which stands to this day, when she made a 35,800-foot descent into the deepest part of the world's oceans, the Challenger Deep. In 1963, *Trieste I* took part in the search for USS *Thresher* (SSN-593), a nuclear-powered submarine lost off Cape Cod, Massachusetts, on 10 April while conducting drills. During a series of dives, *Trieste I* found a large debris field in over 8,000 feet of water, identified as remains of the submarine.

Photo 13-4

A portion of a sonar dome identified as that of the *Thresher*, photographed by the bathyscaph *Trieste I* on 24 August 1963.
Naval History and Heritage Command photograph #NH 97563

Trieste II, with whom we worked, had examined the remains of the nuclear submarine *Scorpion* (SSN-589) in 1969. (Her suspected demise at the hands of Soviet naval forces is described earlier in this book.)

Photo 13-5

Bathyscaph *Trieste II* at sea.
National Archives photograph #USN 1140948

LOCAL TRAINING AND OPERATIONS

The day after I came aboard, *Apache* got under way from the naval station for local training. Proceeding outbound, we first conducted "bumper drills" at the La Playa Fueling Pier at Ballast Point. Smaller ships use the fuel pier (located near the submarine base, just inside the harbor entrance) to practice shiphandling skills by coming alongside and getting under way from it. Unlike large ships which use tugs and pilots to assist them in and out of port, fleet tugs, minesweepers, gunboats, and other smaller ships enter and leave port without assistance.

Thus, junior officers assigned to smaller ships generally get more hands-on training in "ship driving" and maneuvers than do their counterparts on larger ships. However, regular practice is needed to maintain and improve seamanship skills. It was particularly tricky to moor and unmoor alongside the fueling pier because of the natural elements. The wind, sometimes quite strong, invariably set (pushed) ships down onto the pier while the current set them off it. However, wind strength varied as did the currents, depending on whether the tide was flooding, ebbing, or at slack water. Captain Blevins made ship landings there look like child's play and probably could have done it with his eyes closed; he was that good.

Despite my experience driving small boats and some shiphandling drills while aboard *Taconic*, I made a fool of myself when given the opportunity to moor at La Playa. Nervousness, combined with scant knowledge of the ship's characteristics, and innate stubbornness, became my undoing. It was as if the ship had a mind of her own; no matter what I did, she would not put herself alongside the pier. After an hour of ineptitude on my part, the skipper took over, gave four orders to the helm and lee helm and *Apache* was solidly alongside the pier. He then looked at me, shook his head and left the bridge. The executive officer, operations officer, and chief engineer tried their hand next. Two had no real difficulties, the other managed to get alongside after a fashion.

Apache then headed out of the harbor, rounded Coronado, and anchored off the Silver Strand to practice laying beach gear. This type of equipment was used to refloat ships gone aground. *Apache* carried a plethora of wire, stoppers, extra anchors, and sundry other items, which enabled her to put herself in an exceptionally stable moor. Once set up, the tug's towing cable would be sent to a stranded ship and shackled to its anchor chain. At high tide (when the ship was most likely to float free), *Apache* would heave around on her anchor chains (bring them in) while simultaneously cinching up on the beach gear and heaving around on the towing cable. This pulling power was generally sufficient to free a beach-gripped vessel. If not, additional tugs could provide assistance.

Photo 13-6

Naval Amphibious Base, Coronado, with San Diego Harbor in the background. The Silver Strand connects the city of Coronado (to the left in the photo) with the southern end of the harbor near Chula Vista and Imperial Beach.
Naval History and Heritage Command accession #UA 486

Wire dragging on the main deck played havoc with the deck plates and the paint. Thinking that coating the main deck with non-skid would cut down on the excessive maintenance then required to deal with the recurring abrasion, I asked the chief to get it organized and started. He responded, "Yes sir," but, as I was to learn, he immediately went to the captain and told him it was a lousy idea. The captain sent for me and told me the same thing. Stunned, I said, "Am I the 1st lieutenant or not, sir? Surely you're not going to tell me how to run the Deck Department." He angrily retorted, "Go ahead with your non-skid plan, Bos'n, but it isn't going to work. You'll just make more work for your men in the long run."

I left the CO's cabin and went to find the chief. After telling him to get the job started, he said, "Goddammit, Bos'n, the Old Man said no." As soon as he had spoken, he realized he had given himself away. "Chief, if you ever go to the captain behind my back again, I'll physically kick your ass. Do you fucking understand me?" He replied, "Yes, sir," with a scared look on his face. I backed off then, believing that I had brought him into line, but I was wrong. He would continue to be a liability, and thorn in my side, until the ship was finally rid of him.

ORDERED TO HAWAII FOR CLASSIFIED OPS

One Monday, I came to work and had a weird feeling, that something was either different or was going to happen. At around 0830, the word was passed to set the Sea and Anchor Detail. No advance word or reason why, just do it. We proceeded to Ballast Point where the *White Sands*, with *Trieste II* (hereafter shorted to *Trieste*) inside her dock, was already laying fair in the channel, waiting for us to take her in tow.

As the CO maneuvered to make up to the *White Sands*, rumors ran rampant throughout the ship. Still, no one really seemed to know what exactly was going on. Once the tow was connected and the towing watch set, we proceeded slowly out the channel and headed seaward. After clearing 1SD (the first buoy encountered by ships inbound to San Diego, and the last one leaving it), the captain told the executive officer, who was also the ship's navigator, to lay out a track for Hawaii. That simple statement really got the ship buzzing, but still no word on what was happening. Finally, about two hours after clearing the channel and heading west, the captain got on "the horn" (1MC, ship's announcing system) and told us we were en route to Hawaii in order for *Trieste* to conduct a classified operation in the vicinity of the island of Kauai.

As we plowed along during the transit, the *Trieste* would periodically be let out of her pen and put in tandem tow. *White Sands* would then station a tow watch (sailor) on her stern, to monitor the bathyscaph, while the tow watch aboard *Apache* continued to monitor the towline to *White Sands*. When in this configuration, *White Sands* was responsible for reporting the status of *Trieste* once an hour to us.

NEAR COLLISON/LOSS OF THE BATHYSCAPH

One night, I was the officer of the deck on the midwatch (0000-0400) when *Trieste* was in tandem tow. Reports from *White Sands* had been timely and nothing seemed amiss as we steamed along peacefully. Late into my watch, I was already contemplating being relieved and going below to hit my rack, when suddenly it became deathly quiet. For some reason we had lost all power and were now drifting. Worse, with the wind from astern, the rectangular drydock, boasting large sides ("sail area") was being blown down on us. In rapid succession, I sent the boatswain's mate of the watch to the engine room to find out what had happened, ordered the helmsman to put his rudder hard right, asked *White Sands* if *Trieste* was riding okay, and tried to contact the captain to let him know what was going on.

The phone was on the forward bulkhead of the pilot house facing the fo'c'sle, so I had my back to the inside bridge door as I attempted unsuccessfully to reach him. Exasperated, I exclaimed, "You can never reach the old SOB when you need him." Just then this voice behind me said, "The old SOB is right behind you, Bos'n, what the fuck is going on?" I was never so glad to see someone as I was to see him right then. As quickly as possible, I explained that we had suddenly lost power and what steps I had subsequently taken before he arrived on the bridge. Grunting, he climbed up in his chair and quietly observed the situation as it continued to unfold.

My hard-right rudder order to the helmsman had succeeded in getting us turned at right angles to the *White Sands*, which missed us close aboard as the wind pushed her by. The BMOW (boatswain's mate of the watch) returned from the engine room with information that a fire in No. 2 propulsion engine had automatically "tripped it off the line." When that happened, a new watchstander shut down the General Motors 12-cylinder diesel-electric engines online, without realizing the consequences of taking that action. Eventually we regained propulsion, maneuvered back in front of *White Sands*, and resumed our slow trek westward.

A week later, I was again on the bridge as OOD (officer of the deck), this time standing the 0800-1200 in the morning. As required, I called up *White Sands* on the radio to ascertain how well *Trieste* was riding in tandem tow. When no response was forthcoming, I walked out on the bridge wing and looked aft. I could plainly see *White Sands* riding smoothly astern. However, because of her bulk I could not see *Trieste*. I tried several more times to raise *White Sands*. When I still didn't get a reply, I called the captain and told him the situation.

Arriving on the bridge, the CO walked out on the bridge wing and looked aft. Coming back into the pilot house he commented that, "It looks like *White Sands* is riding okay back there. I wonder what their problem is?" He then picked up the radio handset and called *White Sands* himself. When there was no answer he tried again. Getting pissed, he yelled into the handset, "*White Sands*, this is *Apache*'s CO. Get your CO on the horn now!" Amazingly, that irate blast received a muffled reply, but a full fifteen minutes went by before the CO of *White Sands* came up on the radio, very shaken.

"Red, the *Trieste* is gone." The captain looked at the radio and then around at the bridge team like he couldn't believe his ears. "Gone? What the fuck do you mean it's gone?" he fairly screamed into the handset. "The fucking pig isn't back there, Red. That's what I mean. The son-of-a-bitch is not in tow behind us. I'm questioning everyone that stood watches back aft last night in an attempt to figure out just when it disappeared. All I can say right now is it isn't there, and I don't know where the hell it is." Our skipper responded. "All right, I'm going to break the tow so that we can go back along our track and find the sucker. Stand by to break the tow." With that we set the Towing Detail and prepared to break our connection with *White Sands*.

With the tow broken and our gear recovered, we turned to port to a reciprocal course to the one that we'd been on throughout the night. We steamed east all the rest of the day and night without success. Finally, around 0530 the next morning, one of the lookouts spotted the *Trieste* about three miles ahead, bobbing fiercely in an ever-worsening sea. While the captain maneuvered *Apache* in as close to the bathyscaph as he could without endangering it, BM2 Dossey and BM3 Richardson fashioned lariats. They were able to snag *Trieste*'s conning tower, and it was then short work to get her alongside.

Placing *Trieste* at short stay, about 100 feet astern, we turned to a westerly heading and made best possible speed to return to *White Sands*. En route, the captain called the drydock, told them we had the pig in tow, and were proceeding to join them. He also told them it would take an awful lot of beer for him to hush up the story. Needless to say, a promise of such was forthcoming. The 2000-2400 tow watch aboard *White Sands* had fallen asleep, and no reliefs were awakened for either the midwatch or the 0400-0800. Sometime during that 12-hour period, the *Trieste* came loose, and drifted away. Because of the lax attitude that prevailed on the *White Sands*, we had lost a priceless submersible. Had it sunk or been recovered by a foreign navy, many would likely have faced court-martial.

Arriving in Pearl Harbor, we remained in port for about ten days while *White Sands* performed repairs on the *Trieste*. We used the time for voyage repairs and needed maintenance aboard *Apache*. Just prior to our arrival, the skipper had found out that he'd been selected for lieutenant commander, so celebrations were the order of the day. Although we had our personal differences, I had the highest respect for him. His tour was ending and his relief had been identified. It was decided that *Apache* would return to San Diego for the change of command, spend a week there, then return to Hawaii with the new captain. *White Sands* and *Trieste* would remain in Pearl Harbor.

14

New Command Atmosphere

The transit to San Diego was quiet and uneventful. Without *White Sands* and *Trieste* dragging behind us, we made good time, arriving at the naval station, ten days after leaving Hawaii. Once moored at the mole pier, a flurry of activity began in preparation for *Apache*'s change of command. After things settled down a bit, we all had a chance to meet with the prospective commanding officer. Lieutenant Mike "Mad Dog" Barker was a 6'8" tall "Okie," whose previous duty had been chief engineer aboard the USS *Rogers* (DD-876), a *Gearing*-class destroyer like the *Noa*.

He spent a little time with each department head and with the XO and CO in order to get a handle on the crew before he relieved. We had a long discussion and I told him there was a good possibility I was going to revert back to chief petty officer. He became quite concerned with this pronouncement, but I refused to elaborate. I told him that if he was interested, I would explain the entire situation after the change of command. I had become very frustrated, owing to friction with my chief boatswain's mate, which I alluded to earlier, and with *Apache*'s chief engineer, a fellow warrant officer. More about him shortly.

However, fortune smiled on me and my situation began to change even before the change of command, when my useless chief boatswain's mate departed and I got a winner in return. BMC "Pappy" Poulson reporting to *Apache* was like a breath of fresh air. Tall and skinny almost to the point of emaciation, he smoked a large-bowled pipe like those favored by the literary figure Sherlock Holmes. The crew took to Pappy and he, in turn, embraced us all like a wise and benevolent grandfather.

With a real BMC and a fresh start with a new CO, things began looking brighter as I moved forward. BM2 Dossey had elected to get out of the Navy at the end of his enlistment and left before we sailed back to Hawaii. Chuck Richardson had made BM2 and he took over as the leading petty officer. He and Pappy made an unbeatable team.

In the coming months, I grew by leaps and bounds, as a boatswain and as a naval officer, as a result of the new captain becoming my "Sea Daddy." This term refers to a skilled seaman who is assigned to instruct a young or green hand. I was older than Mike and had more time in the

Navy, but he really took me under his wing and mentored me. He also quickly corrected some longstanding problems aboard ship.

The first week he was in command, the chief engineer and his merry men overflowed their fuel tanks onto my main deck, a common occurrence many times in the past. As he and I stood yelling at each other, the captain walked up, looked at the mess and said, "CHENG, get your men up here on deck and have them clean up this mess." The CHENG (chief engineer) immediately started to protest, but the captain cut him short, saying, "I'm not asking you to clean it up CHENG, I'm telling you! When I was an engineer, I didn't dump on the first lieutenant and as long as I'm CO of *Apache*, you aren't going to. If you did it before, this is a different ball game. Get it cleaned up now!" As the skipper walked away, he winked at me and went on about his business. I just smiled at the chief engineer and thought to myself, what goes around comes around, sucker.

RETURN TO HAWAII

En route to Hawaii, it became readily apparent that the captain enjoyed teaching, by showing us how to do things correctly. He never lost his temper or berated us. Instead, he would just have us try again, whatever it was we were having difficulty with. The feeling of teamwork and cohesiveness that began to permeate the ship was amazing and most welcome.

Mike and I did have our differences and there were arguments of a sort. However, any harsh words were spoken privately, never in public, and remained between him and me. Invariably, and this is hard to admit for a hardheaded former LDO, Mike was right in his judgments and assessments. Eventually, I consciously started to pattern myself after him—not his personality, but how he conducted business. He was a professional and that is what I aspired to be.

We made quick passage to Pearl Harbor, rounded Hospital Point and proceeded to the submarine base to tie up. The first night in port, Deck Force decided to throw a party at the Beeman Center Recreation Hall on the Sub Base, and of course they invited me. By the time I left the ship, all of the other officers had departed for the evening as Pappy was the Command Duty Officer. The first mistake I made was even going to Beeman Center, the second was in wearing my khaki uniform.

The party was in full swing when I entered the center. An all-girl Filipina band was playing on stage and things were getting pretty wild. I went through one pitcher of beer rather quickly and was starting on a second while watching the show, when one of my sailors jumped on stage, dropped his pants and started shaking a part of his anatomy at everyone. Out of my peripheral vision I saw someone heading to the stage highly irate. I couldn't let him hurt one of my men, could I? Of course not. Therefore, as he drew abreast of me in full stride, I clouted him alongside the gourd with a half empty pitcher of beer. He dropped like he had hit a brick wall and the situation quickly turned worse. Everyone seemed to be fighting, but the brawl soon ended when the HASP (Hawaiian Area Shore Patrol) descended on the scene like a "dose of salts" (very quickly and thoroughly) and restored order.

The HASP are the roughest, toughest Armed Forces police, bar none, in my experience. Many sailors were apprehended; Richardson and I were handcuffed and taken back to the *Apache*. Pappy, on the quarterdeck, looked pretty grim. The commanding officer had returned to the ship for something, and was aboard when a call came in about the fight. He came up to the quarterdeck just as the HASP arrived with us. To say that he was angry would be a gross understatement. Nevertheless, he had Pappy sign the custody papers, releasing us, and he dismissed the police.

The skipper told us both that we were to remain aboard for the rest of the evening, and he went ashore. As soon as he departed, Richardson and I turned in for the night. About 2300, Pappy came and woke me. "What's up, Chief?" I replied sort of groggily as I swung my feet to the deck. "Bos'n we got big trouble. The commanding officer of the submarine base called a little while ago and decreed that the captain present himself at 0800 tomorrow morning in dress whites, to explain the fiasco at Beeman Center." I was resigned to the consequences, and answered, "Okay, Pappy. All you can do is just tell the captain when he comes back to the ship. He'll probably put me in hack (confinement to quarters) for the rest of my time on board."

Breakfast in the wardroom a few hours later was a surprisingly civil affair. The skipper was in his whites but did not seem upset. He merely told me not to leave the ship until he returned from seeing the CO of the submarine base. He obviously was on the receiving end of whatever discussion took place because, when he got back to the ship around 1000, he immediately sent for me. I knocked on his cabin door, stuck my head in, and inquired, "You wanted to see me, Captain?" "Get your butt in here, asshole, and sit down," he said, in a normal tone of voice. "Yes, sir," I replied, as I gingerly took a seat.

"Lee, your little stunt last night caused me to get my ass chewed out by that stupid submariner who runs this base." He explained that he had been directed to move *Apache* forthwith, and moor at the naval station; submit a formal apology, in writing, for the actions of his first lieutenant and deck force; and that the ship had been 86ed (barred) from the Beeman Center forever. Mike then addressed how he intended to deal with me. "I hope you're happy with yourself. From now on, you will not go ashore with your men unless I personally authorize it. Instead, you'll go ashore with me so that I can show you how to act like a naval officer instead of a hooligan. Any questions?"

I felt really bad and wished that he had yelled and screamed at me. Instead, all of his statements were said calmly, in a matter of fact way, which only made me feel like more of an asshole than I already did. "No sir, Captain, I'm really sorry that I embarrassed you and the ship. I guarantee you it will never, ever, happen again." He ended the meeting with, "Okay, Lee, I accept that and I'll hold you to your word. Go tell them to set Sea Detail, and we'll move to the naval station." As I was leaving to do as he asked, he gripped my shoulder and said, "Don't sweat it. Just put it behind you."

I stayed aboard for the next several days, full of good resolve. By the third day I was going crazy. Fortunately, Mike called me up to his cabin to tell me, "Lee, I'm taking you ashore with me tonight so you can see how officers act on the beach, as compared to the troops." With relief, I answered, "Great, Captain, just let me know whenever you're ready."

Mike and I went to the "O" Club (officers' club) that night for dinner. Afterward, we joined Charlie Hoepper, our operations officer, and one of his friends from another ship, and went into the bar.

We danced with some cute Army nurses and the evening was holding forth promise. However, three Army officers took offense at our socializing female members of their service. They made their way to our table and told us to leave the nurses alone; that they were for Army officers and not Navy pukes. We allowed as how perhaps the ladies should make up their own minds, and they should just run along.

The situation deteriorated quickly. What was shaping up to be just verbal jousting went awry when one of the Army officers shoved the captain's shoulder while he was sitting down. As the skipper unfolded himself from his chair to his full height, it was obvious the Army officer was having second thoughts, but this insight came too late. Mike grabbed the Army asshole by his shirt and tie, and tagged him with one hell of a punch. I was proud of that blow. No enlisted sailor could have thrown one any better.

As soon as Mike hit the guy, I kicked the feet out from under one of the others. Before too much more could transpire, the club manager asked us all to leave for the evening, and we did. No report ever came of this incident. As we stood in front of the building contemplating our next move, I asked Mike, "Captain, what's the difference between what just went down here tonight, and what happened at Beeman Center?" "Well, for one thing, Lee, you're not in handcuffs. For another, there will be no report made to anyone, and lastly, it was among officers so it will be kept quiet." We hailed two of the nurses, who were giggling as they came out of the club. They happily joined us, and we grabbed a cab to hit other nightspots in Waikiki.

CLASSIFIED MISSION A SUCCESS

Our days in Hawaii were devoted to taking care of business, and our classified mission finally came to fruition. On 26 April 1972, *Trieste II* emerged from the water about 350 miles north of the Hawaiian Islands with the remains of a Hexagon film capsule. A classified U.S. photo reconnaissance satellite, code-named Hexagon, had ejected a capsule containing extremely valuable images over the Pacific a little over ten months earlier. The cannister's parachute had failed and the data package had settled to the ocean bottom at a depth of about 16,400 feet.

Two previous attempts by *Trieste II* to retrieve the capsule on 3 November and 31 November 1971, had been unsuccessful. Details about this CIA program and capsule recovery remained classified for forty years. (Additional information may be found in the article, "CIA declassifies spy satellite saga with a deep-sea twist" by Denise Chow.)

As *Trieste II* broke the surface on 26 April, divers jumped into the water and quickly retrieved the capsule for which we had searched so long. It was covered and quickly hoisted aboard *White Sands*. *Trieste* was moved into her pen, and *Apache* hooked up in tow. We then set a return course for Pearl Harbor. The Integral Operating Unit (IOU)—*Apache*, *White Sands*, and *Trieste*—was later awarded the Armed Forces Expeditionary Medal for its successful efforts. With our mission finally over, we departed Pearl, on a beautiful Friday morning, for San Diego. We arrived in home port with brooms flying from our yardarms to indicate a clean sweep of our lengthy mission.

ANNUAL CERTIFICATION REQUIREMENTS

Despite being attached to Submarine Development Group One and a dedicated member of the IOU, *Apache* still had to successfully complete annual salvage training requirements. During the one week each year dedicated to this, a derelict ship hulk, maintained for salvage practice, was towed out to the Silver Strand, and beached. *Apache* would then come out, set up off the strand with her beach gear legs, and attempt to extract the hulk from the beach. If this evolution was successful, the hulk was then cast loose after being set on fire. We were then required to maneuver alongside and make up (moor) to it, in order that our fire parties could board the hulk and fight the blaze. If these exercises were evaluated as successful, we then took the hulk in tow and returned to port.

Any type of salvage evolution required absolute concentration, split-second timing, and teamwork. Visualize a fleet tug maneuvering into position with her stern to the hulk and the shoreline. Hanging off each of her quarters are 6,000lb Eels Anchors resting on 2 x 4s and secured with line. Along each side of the ship are coils of wire also secured with line. On the fantail, the tow line (fabricated of 6x38 plow steel wire) is fed through the roller chocks on the front of the Johnson towing machine, out through H-Bitts, and through the roller chock on the centerline of the stern.

Photo 14-1

Fleet tug USS *Salinan* (ATF-161) under way, circa 1968, displaying the array of heavy towing and lifting gear used to salvage and tow ships of the fleet.
Naval History and Heritage Command photograph #NH 98805

Sometimes, for various reasons, wire could not be used. When that happened, 7-inch line was substituted as a towing hawser (a thick cable or rope used in mooring or towing a ship). During our commitments in Hawaii with the IOU, we had not had much time to practice our salvage skills. On the day we got under way with an observer to grade us, we had not laid beach gear for quite some time. We had tested our salvage pumps weekly, and knew they all worked, and had also continually inspected and properly maintained the equipment. What we hadn't done was actually lay out the gear and use it.

I provided the captain this pre-salvage operation assessment, and expressed some anxiety regarding our prospects. He just said, "Lee, you and your boys go out and do your best. I can't ask for more than that." I shouldn't have worried though, Pappy and Boatswain's Mate Second Richardson never, ever, let me down. We rigged our gear the night before getting under way. I was a nervous wreck, checking, double-checking, and even triple-checking everything. I must have driven the chief and Richardson crazy. To their credit, they maintained their composure. I twice got up in the wee hours to re-inspect the rigs. Unbeknown to me until after the exercise, they too had rechecked their work.

When we got under way at 0800, I was exhausted and we hadn't really even started yet. Once positioned off the Silver Strand, we moved into our moor like we had been doing it every day for a month. The full commander, who was grading us, was quite impressed with our initial efforts and told the Old Man, "Captain, if you do as well tomorrow as you did today, your final score will be the best so far of the six fleet tugs I have graded." Barker merely smiled and replied, "Thanks, John. We just try to do our best. I've got the best tug crew on the West Coast and I'll pass on your kind words to them."

With that, Mike got on the 1MC and praised everyone's efforts so far. He let us know what the observer had thought of our first day and exhorted us to do even better tomorrow. As we settled in for the night, each of us was highly motivated by the captain's words and were determined to do even better on the morrow.

When operating with the hulk, we always kept it manned by at least one sailor with a hand-held radio. This precaution enabled us to determine how hard aground it was, if there was significant movement resulting from wave action, and how difficult or easy she might be to refloat. As Dave Bond and I sat on the fantail drinking coffee late that evening, we deduced the hulk was experiencing a good deal of movement in the surf. Warrant Officer Bond (WO-1) was the relief for my nemesis, the chief engineer, who had finally transferred off *Apache*. Dave and I got along great, meshing well professionally. Nine years later I would report to a ship as first lieutenant, as he was being relieved as chief engineer. In the Navy, you constantly run into people you have served with before, or have met somewhere.

When I queried our guy on the hulk, he indicated he felt like he was almost afloat. Hearing this, I decided to ease the hulk off the beach and into the surf, well before commencement of the exercise. By this means, she could easily be salvaged. Before I went to catch a few winks, I asked Dave to give us power to the tow machine about 0500. When that time arrived, Pappy, Chuck, I, and other members of the Deck Department were at work on the fantail, trying our best to be quiet. By 0615, the hulk was riding free inside the surf line. However, looking aft from *Apache*, she still appeared to be high and dry on the beach.

We shut down everything as quietly as possible, grabbed some breakfast, and mustered on the fantail to commence the exercise. At 0800, the CO and the observer showed up on the fantail and asked if we were ready to go. My men and I were on station, so I gave the captain a double thumbs-up and said, "Let's do it, Skipper." He looked at the observer who nodded his head, and then said to me, "Heave around, Bos'n," upon which, I yelled, "Up Five." (Heave around means to pull at or haul a rope or cable.)

BM2 Richardson energized the Almon-Johnson towing machine, at top speed in the Retrieve Mode. The hulk slid into deeper water as nice as pie, while we kept heaving around so as to keep a steady strain on the tow line. As soon as the hulk had cleared the surf line, I told Chuck to stop heaving around. Turning to the captain, I asked, "What next, sir? She's riding clear. Should we bring her all the way in and get ready for firefighting?"

This evolution had been expected to last up to four hours, and we had completed it in a little over thirty minutes. Both the captain and the observer had incredulous looks on their faces, but all the Old Man said was, "Yeah, Bos'n, get set up for the firefighting part of the exercise." As he and the observer stood back and watched the hulk being retrieved, the observer commented, "Your crew is really something else, Captain. What the hell do they do for an encore?" The skipper said, "Well, John, I guess we go out and finish up the last evolution and get back in port around 1300, instead of late this evening."

The firefighting portion of the exercise came off flawlessly. We returned to the naval station, dropped off the hulk and secured it, then proceeded to the mole pier and moored. The CO walked the observer back to the fantail. As he got ready to depart, he turned to the captain and said, "You lied to me, Captain. You said we would be moored by 1300 and here it is 1315." Grinning, he added, "You truly have a superb team, you better buy them all a beer, because they sure earned it."

REMAINING TIME ABOARD *APACHE*

Mike Barker taught me how to be a naval officer by his personal example, and I was promoted to CWO-2 during my tour aboard the fleet tug. I now felt that I could hold my own as a salvage and towing boatswain, and wanted to return to the "Amphib Navy" as an officer. With his wholehearted support and encouragement, I applied for a split tour to a "gator" (amphibious ship). While I was waiting to learn whether or not my request would be approved, Mike received orders to the Naval Postgraduate School in Monterey, California. His relief, Lt. Jim Howick, was a former enlisted man (Electronics Technician First) commissioned via NESEP (the Navy Enlisted Scientific Education Program).

Howick was a complete gentleman and professional naval officer from the same mold as Mike Barker. I missed the closeness and mentor-to-student relationship I had shared with Mike, but I thoroughly enjoyed working for Jim Howick.

I eventually received orders to another San Diego-based ship, the dock landing ship USS *Mount Vernon* (LSD-39). In the interim, I had the good fortune to be involved with the DSRV (Deep Submergence Rescue Vehicle) Program.

Photo 14-2

The Navy's deep submergence rescue vehicle (DSRV) being loaded onto a flatbed trailer in Sunnyvale, California, prior to being airlifted to San Diego for launching on 24 January 1970. The submergible is capable of "mating" with the escape hatch of a submarine, while operating at depths to 5,000 feet.
National Archives photograph #USN 1142506

The Navy had developed the DSRV to rescue trapped crewmen on stricken submarines. Our tasking was to determine if it was feasible for a DSRV to be towed while completely submerged and, if so, whether the handling characteristics of the DSRV would be adversely affected. *Apache* conducted these trials off the southern California coast. We were able to prove that the concept of towing a submerged DSRV was sound, practical, and safe, while establishing handling data for *Apache*, as well.

Eventually we were able to tow the DSRV at a surface speed of 10 knots, while her crew drove the craft like a glider plane deep below us. The whole idea worked great, but I left the ship too soon to learn if the Navy ever adopted the process. I do remember standing on the fantail of *Apache* and staring at my tow line as it led down into the deep. If an observer hadn't known the DSRV was down there, they would likely have been mystified.

My Hail and Farewell Party, on the eve of my departure from *Apache*, was terrific. This tradition bids good bye to an officer being transferred, and welcomes their relief aboard. My successor, CWO-3 James Ryan, was an old-school boatswain, similar to Bos'n Yarborough on my first ship. Jim Ryan fit right in with the crew of *Apache*. He and Pappy Poulson perfectly complemented each other, while Chuck Richardson continued his stellar work as a fleet tug boatswain's mate. They would all go on to distinguish themselves in the Navy.

15

Duty Aboard *Mount Vernon*

To the many, many memories of this, our first WESTPAC from the raw majesty of typhoon seas to the placid serenity of a tiny harbor ... from the jammed and bustling waterways of Hong Kong to the desolate waves surrounding Triton Island ... to whatever this ship touched ... to whatever was left behind.

—USS *Mount Vernon* (LSD-39) WestPac 73-74 cruise book

Photo 15-1

USS *Mount Vernon* (LSD-39) off the Massachusetts coast, circa April 1972. Naval History and Heritage Command photograph #NH 79119

Mount Vernon was my eighth ship since joining the Navy, and by far the newest one. The *Anchorage*-class dock landing ship had only recently arrived in San Diego from the Boston Naval Yard, where she'd been commissioned following construction, down the coast, in Quincy. Her shakedown cruise had been the voyage from Boston to San Diego, around Cape Horn. Since arriving in San Diego, she had undergone Refresher Training (required periodically of all Navy ships) and more specific Amphibious Refresher Training along with amphibious operations off Camp Pendleton and the Silver Strand. (Marine Corps Base Camp Pendleton, the major West Coast base of the U.S. Marine Corps, is just up the coast from San Diego.)

Photo 15-2

Attack transport USS *Pickaway* (APA-222) and her embarked Marines prepare for an amphibious assault on Camp Pendleton's White Beach in connection with exercise PINE TREE, 26 May 1964.
Naval History and Heritage Command photograph #L45-228.05.01

Mount Vernon was "shipshape and Bristol fashion," an old phrase meaning in good and seamanlike order with reference to the condition of a ship. (The expression had its origin when Bristol was the major west coast port of Britain at a time when all its shipping was maintained in good order.) She had a sharp crew and I was pleased to have been assigned as her boatswain.

Every morning without fail, Monday-Friday, when the ship was in port, Capt. William F. Keller Jr., *Mount Vernon*'s commanding officer, held a staff meeting from 0900 until 1030 or so. The executive officer and all department heads were required to be present at these meetings. Other attendees included: any division officer where something in their division was a topic of discussion; a warrant officer when any technical opinion on some subject was required; the administrative officer or the ship's secretary to take notes; and sometimes the chief master at arms. Division officers and Warrants were dismissed as soon as they had contributed what was required. The more senior officers were there for the duration.

Photo 15-3

Capt. William F. Keller Jr., USN.
USS *Mount Vernon* (LSD-39) Western Pacific 1973-1974 cruise book

Mount Vernon was Captain Keller's fourth command. He had previously commanded the fleet tug *Sioux* (ATF-75), destroyer escort *Voge* (DE-1047), and Destroyer Division 72. He had begun his Navy career as an enlisted man aboard the destroyer *Sigourney* (DD-643), and was later commissioned as part of the Harvard NROTC V-12 program. He ran a taut ship, and his meetings were only to be interrupted for such things as *Mount Vernon* sinking at the pier involuntarily, or being engulfed in flames, or a crewmember being killed.

This edict resulted in important items of business requiring key decisions to languish until the meeting was adjourned. Nothing of consequence was done during them, unless you had the aplomb to make a command decision on your own. One morning, I did just that. The captain's gig (boat) had been out of commission while the engine was being worked on. In order for the engineers to test the engine, the boat had to be launched. With the CO's meeting in progress, no one, and I mean no one, was going to presume to put the gig in the water.

"What the hell, I'm the damn ship's boatswain and responsible for all the boats." Acting on this thought, I had the boatswain's mates put the gig in the water and told the "snipes" to check it. Directly, the engineman in charge of small boats got hold of me and said the gig was working fine and was once more operational. I then had the boatswain's mate lift the gig up in its davit. As I stood watching the sailors gripe the boat in place, I heard, "Bos'n Foley, your presence is requested in the commanding officer's cabin" passed over the ship's announcing system. (Gripes are metal fastenings for securing a boat in its cradle.)

Arriving outside the CO's cabin, I knocked on the door and was told to enter. As I stepped inside, the Old Man was chewing the first lieutenant's ass about putting a boat in the water without first obtaining his permission. Interrupting, I said, "Excuse me, Captain. I put the gig in the water. The first lieutenant was in the morning meeting and didn't know a thing about it. The engineers told me they had the engine repaired and wanted to test it, so I gave them permission. The test was satisfactory and the gig is operational again." The captain looked at me, and then said in a quiet and matter of fact way, "Thanks for getting the gig back on the line, Bos'n. However, in the future I would prefer you get my permission, okay?" I quickly responded, "Yes, sir, no problem. It won't happen again." With that I beat a hasty retreat.

PREDEPLOYMENT LANDING EXERCISE

Photo 15-4

Amphibious Squadron Five plaque, proudly displaying a V (squadron number), a gator signifying amphibious forces, and the motto: "No beach beyond reach." Naval History and Heritage Command photograph #NH 76292-KN

Photo 15-5

View from inside USS *Mount Vernon*'s wet well deck during PAGASA II, a joint U.S.-Philippines exercise in late September 1973.
USS *Mount Vernon* (LSD-39) Western Pacific 1973-1974 cruise book

Prior to sailing from San Diego on our first "WestPac" (Western Pacific) deployment, *Mount Vernon* and the other ships of Amphibious Squadron Five conducted a full-scale amphibious landing off Camp Pendleton. This dress rehearsal put the finishing touches on our landing techniques and prepared us for amphibious operations while deployed. Working the wet well of a dock landing ship is an art. Color-coded sets of mooring bitts line each wingwall: red, yellow, blue, white, and green. As a boat enters the well, lines are passed from the wingwalls to sailors in the boats. These lines are attached to cleats on either side of the boat while the bitter ends are handled by the sailors on wingwalls. As the small craft move farther and farther into the well, lines are shifted on the walls from one set of bitts to another.

The person running the well deck orchestrates the action thusly: "One to Red, Three to White, Two to Blue, etc." As the line number and the color are yelled out, sailors shift the properly numbered line to the bitts corresponding to the color designated. The noise level is deafening with small boat engines revving and other sounds related to an amphibious landing, requiring these instructions to be yelled at the top of your voice while using a bull horn. As soon as a boat clears the dock sill and moves forward into the well, another takes its place.

This sequence continues until all small craft are loaded. When the boats are secured, the ship "ballasts up," using compressed air to expel water from the ballast tanks. This action lifts the ship, allowing water in the well to run out. With the small craft now resting on the dry bottom of the well deck, the stern gate is closed and dogged (latched shut) and the well deck is secured. All that remains then is to gripe down the boats so they are secured for heavy weather. Captain Keller came back to observe wet-well operations as we were recovering our small craft. He watched the evolution closely, from several vantage points, and then left. He never said a word to me, but his expression indicated he was pleased with the work of my men, and the boat crews in the dock.

EARLY PART OF THE DEPLOYMENT

After departing San Diego on WestPac, I requested to stand bridge watches as OOD (under instruction) and was assigned to Dusty Rhodes' section. Lt George "Dusty" Rhodes was our chief engineer. He taught me how to be an OOD under way on a ship much larger than a tug, and with more diverse duties including aviation operations. (Upon leaving *Mount Vernon*, Dusty would take command of a patrol gunboat. Years later, I ran into him in Newport, Rhode Island, where he was preparing for command of a new *Whidbey Island*-class dock landing ship, USS *Fort*

McHenry LSD-43, and I the ocean minesweeper USS *Excel* MSO-439.) I learned one hell of a lot from him and became a very competent OOD. Nevertheless, Captain Keller kept me under instruction and I was anxious to be in charge on the bridge, instead of an understudy.

One day while steaming along in formation, someone aboard yelled, "Man Overboard, Port Wingwall Aft." Nothing is scarier than losing a sailor overboard. The captain was in his chair and Dusty was studying a chart at the navigation table. I had the "conn." (The conning officer aboard a Navy ship is the only person allowed to issue orders to the helm or lee helm, until relieved of these duties.) Without thinking, I told the boatswain's mate of the watch to pass the word, "Man Overboard, Port Wingwall Aft; sounded six short blasts on the ship's whistle; and grabbed the bridge-to-bridge radio to tell the other ships that I was coming to starboard to clear the formation. While this was going on, I had the messenger go aft to the port wingwall and told him to report the situation once he got there.

The sailor reported overboard was actually dangling by a line he had wrapped around his arm, and two other sailors were trying to knock him loose with fire hose applicators (functioning as batons). Upon clearing the formation, I stopped the ship and ordered the Master at Arms Force to the scene. The MAA's handcuffed the two sailors (who had been trying to kill their shipmate) and took them below, while other crewmen brought the rightly terrified sailor up on deck. I then got the ship under way and resumed our station in the formation.

Captain Keller listened to my various reports and responded, "Very Well," without leaving his chair. Dusty observed my actions closely, but had little to say. When the watch finally ended, I went below. I don't know what transpired on the bridge after I left, or if Dusty and the captain even spoke about the incident, but when I checked my in-box in the Deck Department office that evening, there, to my surprise, was a letter signed by Captain Keller designating me as a Fleet OOD. I went up to the wardroom and found Dusty talking with the XO and told him about the letter. He just smiled and said, "I think you earned it this afternoon, Lee, congratulations."

ENCOUNTER WITH *RANGER* BATTLE GROUP

While en route to Subic Bay, Philippine Islands, I was the OOD when we encountered the USS *Ranger* (CVA-61) and her escorts. Prudence and good seamanship dictate that Navy ships give way to aircraft carriers maneuvering and conducting flight operations. The relative positions of *Mount Vernon* and *Ranger* to one another made her the burdened vessel—requiring her, in accordance with the nautical rules of the road, to give way (maneuver around us). However, in such situations, the "stand on" vessel typically gave way, after coming to an agreement with the carrier to do so, so as not to interrupt flight operations.

Photo 15-6

Painting of USS *Ranger* (CVA-61) by R. G. Smith, 1969.
Naval History and Heritage Command accession #88-160-FF

The captain was in his chair and I told him I would like to come right, so as to avoid the carrier and her escorts. He looked at me with just the hint of a grin, and told me to maintain course and speed. I replied, "Aye, aye, sir," and did as I was told. *Ranger* soon contacted us by flashing light and requested that we give way. When the signalman brought the message to the skipper, he signed it and then looked at me and said, "Maintain your course and speed, Bos'n." I did so, and then the *Ranger*'s signal bridge erupted with flashing light messages conveying that *Mount Vernon* OOD's was a piss-poor ship handler, my seamanship was atrocious, and I did not understand rules of the road. All flashing light messages are originated/released for transmission by a ship's CO. This one ended with a demand to speak to our captain immediately.

By now I was pretty embarrassed, but I was following what the CO told me to do, so I continued to maintain course and speed. After a few minutes, Captain Keller had me call a signalman down to the pilot house and he wrote out a message to send to *Ranger*'s commanding officer. He handed it to me to give to the SM and as I was doing so, I saw what he had written. "Check your lineal number," was his message to the *Ranger*

CO. As this was transpiring, I had destroyers, previously stationed in a moving screen around the carrier, going every which way, maneuvering around *Mount Vernon*.

Several minutes went by and then a reply came back. "Having checked my lineal number and yours, I have regained my sense of humor and apologize for my formation interfering with your independent steaming. I withdraw my comments concerning your officer of the deck." (Keller outranked the commanding officer of the *Ranger*, who yielded.) As we proceeded on our track, *Ranger* and her escorts regrouped astern of us and continued their operations. The captain just sat in his chair for a while with a half-smile on his face and then went below. We proceeded to Subic without further incident, moored at the naval station, and made preparations for Captain William Holt to relieve the most senior captain in the U.S. Pacific Fleet, Captain William F. Keller Jr., USN.

Keller was relieved of command on 9 December 1973, and retired on 1 January 1974. He had entered the Navy in August 1941. During the change of command, his successor announced that all existing ship's instructions and policies were to remain in effect.

DARKEST AND BRIGHTEST MOMENTS

During the deployment, I experienced the darkest moments of my naval career, as well as the zenith of my personal life. As alluded to in the preface, *Mount Vernon* was caught up in Super Typhoon NORA, resulting in millions of dollars of damage to Marine Corps equipment aboard and as a result, disciplinary action for the first lieutenant and myself. The following elaboration may provide some lessons learned.

Mount Vernon carried all the rolling stock and equipment belonging to the Marines embarked aboard ships of the ARG (Amphibious Ready Group). Filling our well deck and mezzanine deck, it had to be secured properly in case the ship encountered heavy weather. The reference for doing so was a manual published by the Marines with detailed guidance for securing their gear at sea, in the air, and in containers. The manual included photographs and diagrams showing how to connect, position, and adjust the gripes to ensure that everything rode well, especially in heavy seas. Separately, I believed that everything should be well lighted, so anyone checking the cargo could easily discern if something were amiss.

The captain's policy was that no lights were to be turned on in the well deck or on the mezzanine deck, at night, when we were under way. The nautical rules of the road specify what lights ships are required to display between sunset and sunrise, and the commanding officer did not want to "show" other lights. It was also our ship's policy that no watch was stationed in the well deck. During a transit by *Mount Vernon* and the tank landing ship USS *Barbour County* (LST-1105) from Subic Bay to Hong Kong, the weather began to deteriorate rapidly with increasing winds and seas.

Photo 15-7

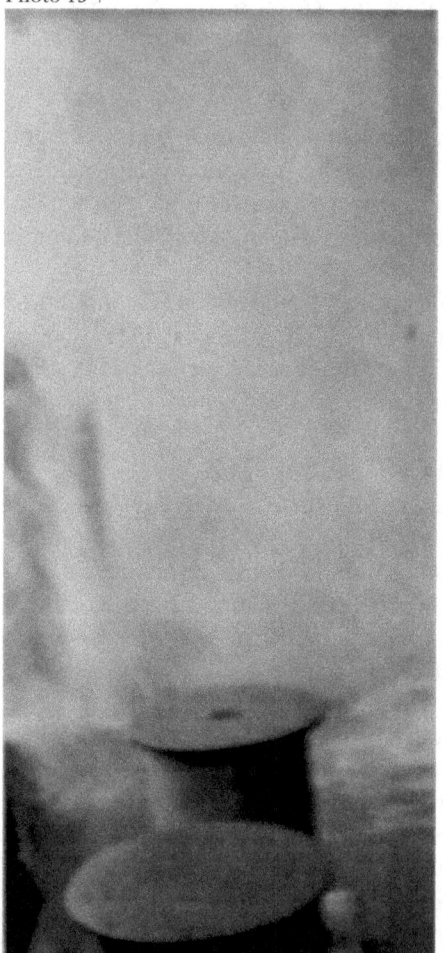

During her 1973-1974 Western Pacific Deployment, *Mount Vernon* encountered Typhoons PATSY, RUTH, OPAL, and NORA.
USS *Mount Vernon* (LSD-39) Western Pacific 1973-1974 cruise book

We checked the well deck and mezzanine deck frequently and everything was riding as securely as possible, even though equipment and rolling stock was working back and forth within their gripes. As the weather continued to build, I went to see the captain and requested that we light up the mezzanine deck and well deck and station a watch. With the weather picking up, I wanted to be able to see what I was checking. This request was denied. My chief boatswain's mate, leading petty officer, and I checked everything meticulously one last time around midnight and then turned in.

Around 0500 Chief Marteney woke me, Bos'n, you better come down to the well deck. We've got big problems." I stumbled around getting dressed as quickly as possible wondering what the fuck was up and, grabbing my flashlight, hastened to the well deck. Upon entering it, I almost went into cardiac arrest. I was now the exclusive owner of the world's biggest fucking junkyard—consisting entirely of twisted, mangled, and smashed Marine Corps equipment. Apparently, a D-8 Diesel Caterpillar had broken loose and careened around, breaking other equipment loose and smashing everything in sight.

I did a quick visual assessment, then called the first lieutenant and told him about the damage. While I was doing this, BM1 Martin and the chief had got Deck Force out of their racks and they were all trying to secure everything in place as the storm continued to rage. Some Marines, who weren't seasick, lent a hand. The first lieutenant met me at the CO's cabin and we gave him the bad news. Then the three of us went down and surveyed the damage. After several minutes, the captain left and went to notify the embarked Staff. Deck Force and Marines continued to secure everything where it was and with a little luck, we could prevent the equipment from breaking free again.

As we began to clear the storm, we rode somewhat better and securing the junkyard became easier. *Barbour County* had also suffered damage during the night. When her crew started checking their spaces, they discovered much to their horror that the bow doors had been ripped off by the fury of the storm. She reversed course and returned to Subic for major repairs while we continued on to Hong Kong. After mooring to a buoy on a cold blustery morning, and with the Sea and Anchor Detail secured, I quit the fo'c'sle and went below to get warm.

My time spent ashore in Hong Kong was wonderful, except for one night when I caught an assignment as the Senior Shore Patrol Officer on Fenwick Pier. The pier area was quiet, relatively speaking, in the early evening hours. Nearing midnight the action picked up. By 2300, my men and I had put scores of drunks into boats and sent them back to their ships, but not without some difficulties. Nonetheless, we were congratulating ourselves on maintaining control with only a few problems. Then ten minutes after midnight, all hell broke loose.

Down the pier came three Australian Marines, two American Marines and five sailors, and four British sailors arguing, pushing, and shoving. Our efforts were not sufficient to quell the resultant fight. During the nearly 20-minute melee, I lost one shoe, my ribbons were ripped from my uniform, my uniform blouse torn, and my hat crushed. Each of my men's uniforms suffered similar fates. The British and Australian Shore Patrol eventually showed up and took their mates away. We sent our sailors and Marines back to their respective ships. The remainder of the early morning was relatively calm. The biggest problem we had was a 6'6" 250lb drunk-on-his-ass sailor. It wasn't that he was causing a stir. He was just extremely big, and nearly comatose, requiring us to manhandle him into the boat. God, what a night.

On our next-to-last day in Hong Kong, I ran into the staff secretary of commander, Amphibious Squadron Five. He was an administrative type LDO. The sun being already over the yardarm (approaching sunset), we decided to "splice the main brace." As we sat in the bar at the Hong Kong Hilton, having a couple of drinks, he warned me, "Lee, you better watch your ass. There is talk of convening a formal Board of Inquiry and a court martial could devolve from that proceeding. The chief staff officer is adamantly opposed, but the Marines are insistent. For God's sake, don't tell anyone where you got this info, just be prepared." I took a swallow of my drink before answering. "Okay, Tom," I replied, "Thanks for the heads up." We took leave of each other, and I returned to the ship.

BOARD OF INQUIRY PROCEEDINGS

Sure enough, the day after we arrived back in the Philippines, the CSO came aboard. Setting up shop in a corner of the wardroom, he sent for me and the first lieutenant. After we both arrived, he told us he was sorry to be the bearer of bad news, but that he had been directed to advise us that formal charges were being drawn up as he spoke. He was here to inform us of our rights under the UCMJ (Uniformed Code of Military Justice) and offer what advice he could. The charges levied were dereliction in the performance of our duties, in that we had failed to ensure that the vehicles were secured correctly and failed to station watch personnel with sufficient lighting to ensure the safety of the rolling stock.

It was a subdued meeting and didn't last very long. When the chief staff officer departed the ship, I went to my stateroom to contemplate the situation. After about 30 minutes of reflection, I was angry through and through and left the ship to try and drown my anger in San Miguel beer. The drowning didn't work too well, but for a while the beer took my mind off the tremendous problem I now faced. As if the impending Board of Inquiry wasn't enough, I had some financial difficulties as well.

In the 1970s when our U.S. bases in the Philippines were at their height, several large American banks had branch offices in Makati, Manila's financial district. One such was Bank of America. I had set up a bill pay system with them before deploying. They were to take funds from my account, monthly, and apply it to bills I had designated. This was all in writing and signed by bank personnel in the U.S., and myself. However, when we arrived in Subic from Hong Kong, I had several dun (debt collection) letters awaiting me in the mail for non-payment of bills.

I was arranging for some leave to go to the Bank of America branch in Manila to get this problem squared away, but was forced to delay this action. The CSO returned aboard *Mount Vernon*, summoned the first lieutenant and me, and read the formal charges to us. He then informed us that the Board of Inquiry would convene the next morning, and that we were to appear at 0900 in dress white uniform.

The board was comprised of two Navy captains and a Marine Corps colonel. The decision, or verdict, that the Board of Inquiry would hand down was a foregone conclusion in my mind. A Marine major, who conducted the proceedings for the board, kept referring to a manual for securing equipment that was published after the accident, and was not the manual that was in use at the time. When the major had finished his presentation, the first lieutenant was asked if he would like to make a statement. He merely said he thought the equipment was secured correctly and he was sorry for its destruction.

When it came time for me to make my statement, I was mad clear through. "Gentlemen, with all due respect to your respective ranks and positions, it is my firm belief that the outcome of this proceeding has been predetermined and nothing I say will change that. I then, however, did my best to counter the assertions made. Only the most important points I made follow:

- You claim that I was derelict in my duties by not securing the vehicles properly and you cite the latest publication as your reference. However, your reference did not become available in the fleet until a month after this tragic incident had occurred.
- Further, this board has the only copy available in the Western Pacific, because it was flown out here by special plane just for this inquiry. The vehicles that were destroyed were secured in accordance with the guidelines set forth in the manual that pre-dates your reference.
- I have been told that I cannot use that as evidence. Likewise, I have been prevented from submitting Polaroid photos I took

of the vehicles showing how they were secured and how those pictures matched the pictures in the manual that was in force at the time of the incident.

I forcefully expressed my belief that I and the first lieutenant were being railroaded, then thanked the board members for their patience and professionalism and returned to my seat. The board determined that the first lieutenant and I had been derelict in our duties and that was that. The commanding officer received a non-punitive Letter of Caution, more of an embarrassment than anything since it could not be addressed in a fitness report (officer evaluation) and no one got a copy. We each received a punitive letter of admonition. These type letters can become public knowledge, were mandated to be addressed in our next fitness report, and a copy of the letter was inserted in our official records in Washington, D.C.

CHANCE MEETING WITH A BEAUTIFUL GIRL

With the Board of Inquiry completed, I travelled to Manila to try and square away my accounts with the Bank of America. I was foisted off on a bunch of underlings before I finally got to the branch manager and I blasted him verbally. I was angry and finally, he signaled for a young girl to come over. He introduced her as Zenaida Antonio and stated she could help get my accounts back in order.

I turned to confront her and choked up. She was gorgeous and my anger quickly faded. Her English was fluent and in a short period of time she had identified what had caused the glitch, paid the bills that were delinquent, wrote letters of explanation that would be sent to my creditors, and then asked if there was anything else, she could do to help. While we were doing this, I was making small talk, but I don't know what we talked about. I just kept staring at her like I had never seen a girl before. Finally, I said, "You could really help me a lot if you would go out with me."

She smiled and then said, "I live with my parents and I can't go out with someone without their permission. Even if I wanted to and they allowed it, we would have to be chaperoned because I'm under age." That kind of formality probably existed in the U.S. in the 1930s, but this was 1973 and I was shocked. I told her I had to return to my ship in Subic, but when able, I would like to meet her parents and get their permission for us to go to dinner and a movie. Her smile lit up the entire bank and she said that she would like that.

Photo 15-8

Nida and her mother, 8 July 1978.
Author's collection

I left the bank with my mind in a whirl and caught the Victory Liner back to Olongapo. Today there are many bus lines in PI (the Philippines) and the vehicles are air conditioned, curtained, have TV and Wi-Fi, and are very comfortable. The Victory Liner I caught that day had zero amenities. Its windows had to be kept open to get even a minimal breeze, and every time the bus slowed down, children would run up and have their hands in the windows begging.

When I got back to *Mount Vernon*, the first lieutenant told me that we were allowed to appeal our letters to the next senior in the chain of command within fifteen days, should we choose to do so. I considered this option, but did not pursue it for several reasons. First, you never win when you start trying to shovel shit uphill because even more runs back down on you. Second, my conduct during the inquiry, although respectful, was probably not conducive to an appeal being seriously considered. Third, I still believed in Navy justice. Underneath the bureaucracy and occasional bullshit lay a basically fair system. Lastly, pointing my finger at superiors would not endear me to anyone.

I chose, instead, to submit a letter of rebuttal, addressing each specific point of contention set forth in my letter of admonition. By this means, I could make my case without casting aspersions on the Marines or my seniors in the Navy. Submitting the letter signaled my confidence that the system was basically sound and that I was willing to entrust my career to the service's strange and mysterious ways. I crafted and submitted the correspondence, then put the incident behind me.

I was able to visit Manila on several occasions and had the pleasure of meeting Zenaida's parents. They gave their permission for her to go on a date with me, and I took her to dinner at a nice restaurant, and to see a John Wayne movie. We were chaperoned by her old auntie and that was quaint. Nevertheless, we had a nice evening and she agreed to see me again whenever I came to Manila. She told me Zenaida was too formal, and asked that I call her Nida (Needa). We went out several more times, always accompanied, and our relationship blossomed and grew. When it was time for *Mount Vernon* to return to San Diego, it was with a great deal of sadness that we said our final goodbyes. We promised to write, and did, and I told her I would be back as soon as possible.

After arriving back in homeport, I went to see the captain. I told him that I was eligible for shore duty but, if he were willing, I would like to stay onboard for another year. He told me that he was delighted with that decision and would endorse my request favorably. I was jubilant, knowing that I would see Nida in the coming year when *Mount Vernon* once again deployed to the Western Pacific.

SURFACE WARFARE OFFICER QUALIFICATION

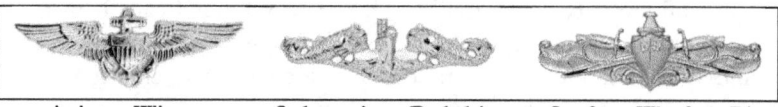

Aviator Wings **Submariner Dolphins** **Surface Warfare Pin**

Ensign Saul Klein, *Mount Vernon*'s repair officer, and I had been working on our Surface Warfare Officer's qualifications ever since a syllabus had been established and promulgated to the fleet. Aviators had long had their wings of gold and the silent service proudly sported their gold dolphins. Now at last, Surface Warfare Officers would get to wear crossed golden swords. Previously, the only evidence of shipboard officer prowess (other than a command at sea pin) was designation as a Fleet Officer of the Deck; Independent Steaming Officer of the Deck was a lesser qualification. Such qualification resided only in a letter in one's service jacket, and formerly, the surface community hadn't had a warfare pin attesting to their professionalism.

Completion of all syllabus requirements, plus a shiphandling test, and an oral board to determine our qualifications, would enable us to sport the new breast insignia created for surface officers. My fellow warrant officers aboard ship gave me a hard time for voluntarily standing watches under way, and shouldering CDO (Command Duty Officer) duties in port, striving to become qualified as a Surface Warfare Officer. Warrant officers on *Mount Vernon* stood no duty and they feared I was endangering their freedom from watches by my actions.

I didn't see it that way. I was the one standing watches and duty, not them. Nevertheless, they kibitzed endlessly about it. The syllabus was designed to take about eighteen months to complete. Saul and I had been working on our respective qualifications for about eleven months, when the Navy cancelled the old syllabus, and implemented a new one. When we learned this, we went to see the captain, to request that he "grandfather" our work to date, in order that our efforts not be wasted.

He told us that he'd really like to help us out, but that such action would not be in keeping with the spirit of the instruction. "If you want to win those golden swords, you'll just have to start over." Minutes later, two very pissed-off junior officers sat in the wardroom wondering what to do. After some venting, with no other option available to us except to give up our dream of wearing the swords, we swallowed our bile and began the lengthy qualification process anew.

Saul and I, through extraordinary application, and almost zero sleep and liberty, were able to complete the new syllabus in twelve months rather than the eighteen months allotted. Both of us also passed our shiphandling tests as observed and graded by the chief staff officer of Amphibious Squadron Five. Now, all that stood between us and official designation was an oral board.

During the SWO Program's infancy, only an O-6 (Navy captain) could officially designate a candidate as a Surface Warfare Officer. This designation was then sent to the Naval Military Personnel Command in

Washington, D.C., for official action and forwarding of a congratulatory letter to the achiever. Since *Mount Vernon*'s captain was a commander in rank, he reviewed our work and forwarded it to commander, Amphibious Squadron Five, the next senior in the chain of command.

Our commodore convened an oral board with himself as chairman, and two senior "four-stripers" (captains) in the squadron as members. Saul had his board on a day preceding mine, and was told not to discuss it with me until after we had both completed the examination. Thus, I was pretty much in the dark as to what to expect upon reporting to the amphibious assault ship *Okinawa* (LPH-3) on the appointed day and time, and being shown into the commodore's cabin.

The commodore greeted me and introduced the other members of the board. I was offered coffee and told to feel free to smoke if I desired. After the amenities were completed, the three senior officers took seats in comfortable chairs and settled back. The commodore looked at me for a moment and then said, "Lee, if you are successful here today, you will be the first warrant officer in PhibRon Five to be designated a SWO and one of only five or six in the Navy that have achieved qualification as set forth in the instruction. Some of the older warrants may have been 'grandfathered,' but you will truly have earned yours." With that, he advised me, "We'll start out with a relatively easy area. Go over to chalkboard and draw the basic steam cycle as it applies to the engineering plant on the *Mount Vernon*."

They were well aware of my seamanship expertise and so when he told me they were going to start out with something easy, I expected questions about seamanship and the like. Directed to draw the steam cycle (boilers, turbines, pumps, valves, and associated piping systems with pressures and temperatures at key locations), my heart leaped up into my throat and I thought, just for a minute, that I was going to clutch. As they looked at me quizzically, I recovered and was able to sketch it with little difficulty. After that, I felt fairly comfortable.

The exam went on for three-and-a-half hours, alternating between the chalkboard and answering questions verbally. Nothing was spared. Their questions ran the gamut from engineering to supply; from administration to the Russian matrix, regarding weapons match-ups against U.S. Naval forces; from operational doctrine to wartime rules of engagement; from navigation to seamanship; and from nautical rules of the road to command duty officer procedures in various situations.

When the commodore finally told me that they'd heard enough, I was completely drained and at that moment did not care what the final outcome might be. He asked me to leave the room, suggesting that I go to the wardroom and get some coffee, and that he would send a messenger to get me when the board had completed their deliberations. Rising slowly to my feet, I thanked the commodore and two captains for a grueling but fair and impartial board, took my leave, and went down to the wardroom to await my fate.

I hadn't been down there fifteen minutes when the commodore's cook came down and told me the board members were ready to see me. When I walked back into the commodore's cabin, I saw three ominous countenances and thought to myself, "Fuck, I guess I blew it." The three officers broke into wide grins and the commodore stepped over and shook my hand. "Congratulations, Bos'n. I think I speak for the entire board when I say we were unanimous in feeling that you really knew what you were talking about and it was obvious that you prepared well for this. Let me pin this device on you."

As I stood there, sort of dumbfounded, he adorned my uniform while the other two shook my hand. I don't remember much about my walk back to the *Mount Vernon*, other than spending much of it staring down at my new SWO device. That particularly proud moment helped to alleviate the heartache of the previous deployment.

OPERATION FREQUENT WIND

> *This action closes a chapter in the American experience. I ask all Americans to close ranks, to avoid recrimination about the past, to look ahead to the many goals we share, and to work together on the great tasks that remain to be accomplished.*
>
> —Statement by American President Gerald Ford on 29 April 1975 as Operation Frequent Wind commenced—the evacuation by airlift of American and "at risk" South Vietnamese personnel from Saigon, ending over twenty years of U.S. involvement in Vietnam.

Photo 15-9

South Vietnamese refugees arrive by helicopter aboard a U.S. Navy aircraft carrier or amphibious ship as part of Operation Frequent Wind, the final evacuation of Saigon, South Vietnam, 29-30 April 1975.
Official U.S. Marine Corps photograph

On 28 March 1975, *Mount Vernon* left San Diego on a seven and a half-month deployment. This WestPac would be radically different from her maiden one in 1973. Following a couple of days in Pearl Harbor, we began transit to the Philippines in company with the *Duluth* (LPD-6). En route, we received orders to proceed at high speed in order to join other ships for the evacuation of Saigon, South Vietnam. *Duluth* detached and proceeded to Okinawa to pick up needed equipment while we proceeded independently to the Philippines.

After a brief stopover in Subic Bay to transfer cargo and pick up supplies, we sortied to support Operation FREQUENT WIND, the evacuation of Saigon on 29-30 April. All available ships had been dispatched on very short notice to a holding area off Vung Tau, South Vietnam. As a result, almost 150 sailors and Marines were stranded ashore in Subic. We embarked them, as well as Surgical Team Thirteen to provide medical care for the evacuees, and sailed at flank speed for Vung Tau. We estimated that *Mount Vernon* could possibly receive as many as 5,000 refugees.

Photo 15-10

U.S. Navy ships of Task Force 76 staged off Vung Tau, Vietnam, for the start of Operation FREQUENT WIND, 29 April 1975. Official U.S. Marine Corps photograph A7718475

Preparations were made to feed and berth, and provide sanitary facilities and security for large numbers of Vietnamese. In addition to transforming our dock landing ship into a floating refugee center, we practiced self-defense and conducted drills and exercises. Weapons and small arms were tested and retested and additional weapons were mounted on the ship and in our small boats. Seventy-seven U.S. Navy ships took part in the massive refugee/evacuee effort; forty-eight were surface combatant ships, including *Mount Vernon*.

On the morning of 29 April, North Vietnamese forces attacked the remaining operable airfields in South Vietnam. Those aircraft that were able to get airborne found that they had no place to land. Some flew to Thailand and other countries. Many others, especially the helicopters, came out to the U.S. fleet sitting just off shore. As helicopters arrived overhead *Mount Vernon*, the code word "Hound Dog" was passed over all circuits and loudspeakers to ensure all hands were aware that landings were imminent. Being the closest ship to shore, we received the first South Vietnamese Air Force UH-1s.

There wasn't room to store the Vietnamese helicopters on our flight deck, because we needed a "green deck" (open deck) to support much larger USMC CH-53 helicopters when they went into Saigon later in the day. After the decision was made to jettison the helos, my leading petty officer, BM1 (later BMC) Eugene Martin, liberated piles of plywood sheets from the hull technicians. Once these were in place on the flight deck, as soon as aircraft had been searched and stripped of as much useable equipment as possible, a forklift slid the plywood sheets with helos on them to the edge of the flight deck where they were pushed over the side and allowed to sink.

Photo 15-11

South Vietnamese Air Force UH-1 Huey helicopters landing aboard the carrier USS *Midway* (CV-41) during Operation FREQUENT WIND.
USS *Midway* 1975-76 cruise book

Photo 15-12

Taking a break from Flight Quarters duties aboard the dock landing ship USS *Mount Vernon* (LSD-39), September 1973.
Author's collection

Photo 15-13

A South Vietnamese helicopter is pushed over the side of the amphibious assault ship USS *Okinawa* (LPH-3) during Operation Frequent Wind, April 1975.
Official U.S. Marine Corps photograph

My flight deck crew filled two 50-gallon trash cans with confiscated personal small arms. These were individually tagged, logged, and taken by armed guard to the Armory, and the process repeated to ensure that no weapons disappeared. We also searched each evacuee as they got off the helicopters. Fortunately, there was a Vietnamese woman, on the first one to land, who spoke fluent English. We asked her to assist us in searching any other women coming aboard and she readily agreed.

Chapter 15

A South Vietnamese colonel landed his Huey and exited it with a holstered gun on each hip and a leather briefcase in each hand. After being divested of his guns, he agreed to open his briefcases. Each was packed with American currency, mostly one hundred-dollar bills. I had the disbursing officer called to the flight deck and he and two armed guards escorted the colonel to the disbursing office. I then called the bridge and told the skipper about the disposition of the colonel. We "deep sixed" all of the helos, save one. It had belonged to South Vietnam Vice President Ky, and it boasted a richly appointed cabin. We took it back to Subic.

Near sunset on 30 April, hundreds of small craft, fishing vessels and anything else that would float, loaded with refugees, began coming out to the ships to seek safety. I got the CO's permission to ballast down and launch our craft to assist in getting these people to the ships that could hold them. Most were placed aboard merchant ships for transfer to Guam or other safe havens. To facilitate the loading process and security checks, causeway sections were floated and placed under the accommodation ladders of the ships. *Mount Vernon*'s craft, and those of Assault Craft Unit One, handled the bulk of this assistance by sea.

Photo 15-14

Former South Vietnamese and Cambodian Navy ships at Subic Bay, 31 May 1975. They are (l-r): Vietnamese ships: *HQ-471*, *Dong Da II* (07), *Chi Lang II* (08), *Chi Linh* (11); Cambodian Ships: *P-112*, *E-312*.
National Archives photograph #K-109092

PORT VISIT TO MANILA

After disembarking our refugees, *Mount Vernon* proceeded to Manila for a port visit. With Nida, it was wonderful time, until cut short by an emergency recall to Subic Bay to take on Marines and combat supplies. We were to load and then proceed to Koh Tang Island, off Cambodia, to support operations to recapture the merchant ship, SS *Mayaguez*.

She had been seized on 12 May by boarding parties brought alongside her by Khmer Rouge patrol gunboats. This incident occurred less than a month after the Khmer Rouge took control of the capital Phnom Penh and ousted the U.S. backed Khmer Republic. The two-pronged rescue operation involved a Marine helicopter assault on Koh Tang, and boarding of the ship. Fifteen U.S. servicemen were killed (including three Marines inadvertently left behind on Koh Tang and executed by the Khmer Rouge), and their names are the last ones inscribed on the Vietnam Veteran's Memorial.

Unbeknown to mission planners, the ship's crew had been released and thus, when the Marines boarded and recaptured the ship anchored offshore, they found it empty. On the morning of 16 May, as *Mount Vernon* was proceeding at flank speed to Koh Tang Island, I had the 0400-0800 watch on the bridge. Encountering the *Ranger* and her two escorts headed in the opposite direction at about 0515, we, as the junior ship, requested permission to proceed on duties assigned. When *Ranger* inquired about the nature of our duties, I replied that we were en route to Koh Tang to support the reclaiming of *Mayaguez*. The carrier then informed us that the merchant vessel had been liberated, her crew was safe, and the operation a complete success.

Following direction to fall in astern of her formation for return to Subic, I called the captain and informed him of this turn of events as well as *Ranger* ordering us to accompany the other ships back to Subic. "Okay, Bos'n, call *Ranger* back and have them verify the conclusion of the operation and the directive to follow them to Subic. If they do so in the affirmative, go ahead and reverse course and fall in astern of her and the destroyers. Call me before you get relieved." I replied, "Aye, aye, sir." When flashing light confirmation came, I ordered left standard rudder, and we came about smartly. The *Ranger* formation was now a carrier, two destroyers, and a "fast attack" LSD steaming together. After making the obligatory report to the CO, I went below for some breakfast, extremely happy to be returning to Nida.

Time spent in the Philippines was short, before tasking came to deliver Marines and equipment to Okinawa, and pick up fresh Marines and equipment for the rest of the deployment. I had spent some time with Nida, but not nearly as much as I would have liked. As soon as the Marine exchange was completed at Okinawa on 2 June, we sailed in company with *Duluth* for a liberty visit to Hong Kong. While there, I was able to get Mary Soo and her assistants to paint the ship from top to bottom, paying her in old brass and a worn mooring line we had saved for just this purpose. Their labor allowed my sailors to enjoy liberty without a need to preserve and paint the ship themselves.

Photo 15-15

Mary Soo and assistants, renowned for painting the sides of ships.
USS *Du Pont* (DD-941) cruise book

Photo 15-16

Mary Soo, a legend in Hong Kong for over fifty years.
USS *Rowan* (DD-782) Western Pacific 1971-1972 cruise book

Leaving Hong Kong, we called at Ilo Ilo, Panay, in the Philippines. Our visit was short but enjoyable, but I, for one, was glad when we returned to Subic Bay. Two wonderful weeks followed with as much time as possible spent in Manila with Nida. *Mount Vernon* then departed Subic once again, this time for liberty visits to Kaohsiung, Taiwan, and Kagoshima, Japan. No American warship had called at the latter port for some fifteen years or more. We were welcomed with open arms. Our money was literally no good. We would go into a restaurant to eat or bar to drink, and the townspeople refused to accept our money.

Kagoshima (a seaside city on the southwestern tip of the island of Kyushu) is a popular honeymoon spot, and best known for Sakurajima, an active volcano that faces Kinko Bay. Once sited on an isolated island, the volcano had become connected to the Osumi Peninsula following an eruption in 1914. I enjoyed Kagoshima for its spectacular beauty and gracious hospitality, and because it was a new experience. Upon our departure, *Mount Vernon* proceeded slowly out of port and set a course for Subic Bay, arriving on 28 July.

REMAINING TIME ABOARD *MOUNT VERNON*

On 1 August, as we lay moored starboard side to Alava Pier in Subic, preparing to ballast down to load craft, a 150psi air line ruptured inside a sealed ballast tank. Over pressurized, the bulging tank burst at its seams, resulting in severe damage to a number of structural members, and misalignment of the port shaft. Correction of this derangement necessitated docking the ship and, while Ship Repair Facility personnel were hard at work, I was able to take leave. Two weeks of uninterrupted time with Nida in Manila followed. I knew, by now, that I wanted to be with her always and she felt the same about me.

When I returned to the ship from leave on 3 September, I learned that we would be coming out of drydock the next day, and that my orders had come in. I would be going to shore duty at Recruit Training Command, San Diego as a battalion commander. In the interim, we made another trip to Okinawa to transfer Marines, then called at Manila. Forced to sortie for typhoon evasion, we proceeded to Keelung, on the opposite end of Taiwan from Kaohsiung. There, I loaded up on souvenirs for Nida and girded myself for detachment.

FINAL DAYS ABOARD *MOUNT VERNON*

We returned to Subic on 10 October, and began preparations to take part in a combined amphibious landing on Mindoro with Philippine naval units and Marines. *Mount Vernon* celebrated the 200th anniversary of the birth of the United States Navy on 13 October 1775. As part of the festivities, our officers donned period garb, as evidenced by my photograph in the cruise book.

Photo 15-17

The following day, 14 October, the Wardroom (ship's officers) and Deck Department held a farewell party for me at the Cherry Club in Olongapo. Unbeknown to me, BMC Eugene Martin and some of my men had gone to Manila and escorted Nida back for the occasion. When I walked into the club that night, I was overjoyed to see her sitting there. The party was a great success and I hated to see it end. I sadly said my goodbyes to Nida, promised her I would return, and told her I wanted to marry her and would write every day. With heavy heart, I watched as she boarded the Victory Liner for the return trip to Manila. Long after the bus was out of sight, I stood watching the road, wondering when I might see her again.

I left *Mount Vernon* for the last time, around noon on 15 October 1975. An hour later as my plane lifted off the tarmac at Cubi Point Naval Air Station, I watched out the window as she, *Barbour County*, *Duluth*, and *Okinawa* stood out of Subic Bay, bound for Mindoro, PI.

16

Naval Training Center, San Diego

Photo 16-1

Panoramic view of U.S. Naval Training Station, San Diego, California, circa 1926. The city of San Diego is in the left and center background, with San Diego Bay in the center and right, and Naval Air Station, North Island in the right distance.
Naval History and Heritage Command photograph #NH 105330

Photo 16-2

Aerial view of Naval Training Center, San Diego, looking north.
Naval History and Heritage Command photograph #USN 1133113

Arriving at Recruit Training Command, San Diego, my first assignment was as commander of Battalion 13, the same battalion to which I had been assigned as a recruit. It was one of the main battalions on Nimitz Island where primary training took place. We occupied one of the oldest buildings, but I was pleased with the assignment and my staff. RTC was organized such that the battalions on the primary side of training came under the control of Regiment One, while the battalions for advanced training, located on the main side at the Naval Training Center, reported to Regiment Two. Recruit Training Command, San Diego, was one of three Navy Boot Camps at the time. The other two were at Great Lakes, Illinois; and Orlando, Florida. While RTC San Diego and Great Lakes only trained male recruits, RTC Orlando trained females as well.

One day, while touring our spaces, I noticed my initials scratched into the wood of one of the banisters, where I had made my mark while a recruit in Company 118 so long ago.

Recruit Training Command had at least fifteen warrant officers and several LDOs assigned, so I felt right at home. Our skipper was Captain Robair Morhardt, a fighter pilot. He had entered the Naval Service as an apprentice seaman in World War II. After graduating from the Naval Academy in 1949, he had served in fighter squadrons in both the Atlantic and Pacific, and had flown over 200 combat missions in Korea and Vietnam. Highly decorated, he was entitled to wear the Legion of Merit, two Distinguished Flying Crosses, two Bronze Stars, twenty-five Air Medals, two Navy Commendation Medals, and the Purple Heart. (Service members only wear one of each type medal or ribbon, with stars affixed denoting subsequent awards.)

Our executive officer was equally impressive. Commander (later Captain) Bob McCullough was the epitome of a "Mustang" officer. He had been a chief radarman (now called operations specialists) when commissioned as an ensign in the unrestricted line. As an officer, he had commanded seven different ships, and Beachmaster Unit One, and would eventually command the Naval Amphibious Base at Coronado. He had been awarded the Silver Star in Vietnam, for carrying a wounded Marine on his back to safety out of the Rung Sat Special Zone, and several lesser medals for heroism. I was in awe of Captain Mac then, and I remain so today.

The Rung Sat, through which the Long Tau and Soirap rivers passed, had been known, from before the French colonization of Vietnam, as a refuge for pirates and bandits that preyed upon river and coastal traffic. The area later became one of the strongholds of the Binh Xuyen gangsters (sometimes referred to as the "Vietnamese Mafia"). American servicemen commonly referred to the Rung Sat as the Forest of Assassins, because the Vietnamese word *rung* can be translated as "forest, jungle or woods" and *sat* as "assassin, killer or murderer."

Map 16-1

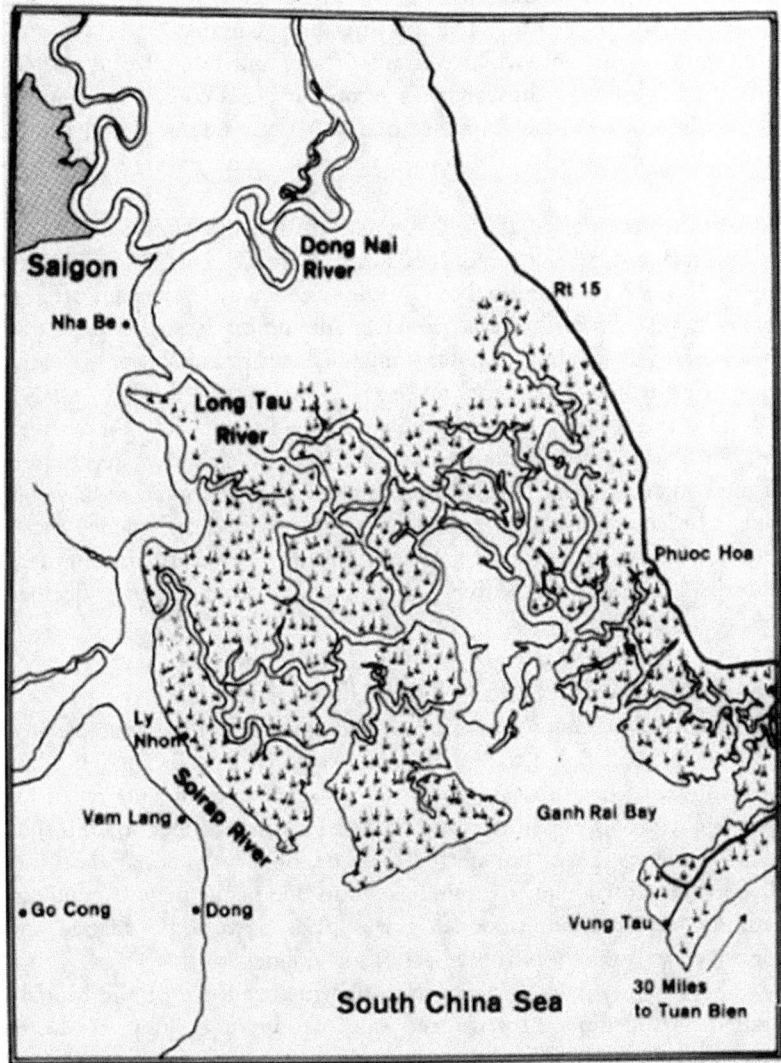

Rung Sat Special Zone
Naval History and Heritage Command photograph #NH 96343

Almost immediately after reporting aboard, I found myself at an awards ceremony where I was presented a Navy Achievement Medal for my efforts during Operation FREQUENT WIND. I was also advanced to master chief signalman. (I had made senior chief through an earlier competitive Navy-wide examination cycle while assigned to *Mount Vernon*.) In those days, warrant officer rank was only temporary and you still took examinations for advancement to senior chief and master chief in your rating. The top three enlisted ranks (E-7, E-8, and E-9) were permanent, while warrant officer and limited duty officer ranks through lieutenant were only temporary, and could be rescinded at the discretion of the Secretary of the Navy. Warrants and LDOs could also voluntarily revert to their permanent enlisted rank if they so desired.

In the summer of 1976, the results of the Chief Warrant Officer Selection Boards were posted. Not surprisingly, I did not find my name among those to be promoted to CWO-3. Several other warrant officers found themselves in the same predicament and expressed surprise that they weren't selected. I didn't say much, because I knew why my name wasn't on the list. The medal I'd received for my role in FREQUENT WIND was not going to offset the letter of admonition I had received in 1974. I seriously considered reverting to master chief, a step several of my contemporaries elected after failing to be promoted to CWO-3. Nida advised against this, conveying to me via correspondence that I should not revert, should not go back, but instead keep working hard and trust in the system. With her support and encouragement, I decided to stay the course.

SELECTION FOR LIMITED DUTY OFFICER

While aboard *Mount Vernon*, I had twice applied for Limited Duty Officer, but had failed to be chosen. At RTC, I again applied while knowing that I had almost no chance, especially after having failed for selection to CWO-3. Shortly after the chief warrant officer board results became known, I was transferred to Battalion 15. This battalion was also on the primary side of training, but in one of the newest buildings with the nicest appointments. I was pleased with the change and continued to do my job to the best of my abilities.

On 1 September 1976, I was sitting in the office of the Military Training Officer on the advanced side of training, talking to Master Chief Davidson, the MTO's adjutant, when the secretary came in and said I had a phone call from Regiment One headquarters. The master chief told me I could take the call at his desk, so I picked up the phone and said, "Bos'n Foley." The words that came through the phone were, "Lee, you fucking asshole, you and I made LDO."

"Who the fuck is this?" I asked, rather peevishly since it wasn't a joking matter to me, having already been passed over for CWO-3. "This is L. C. Mills, and you and I are on the list. I'm over here at Reg One. Come on over and you can see the list for yourself." I said, "On my way," and hung up the phone.

I streaked out of the office and jumped into my car. I definitely broke the speed limit getting back across the bridge to primary and Regiment One headquarters. I parked my car and ran in the door. Finding Mills, I almost ripped the paper copy out of his hands in my excitement. My hands were shaking as I read the names of the selectees, but L. C. hadn't lied to me. Six Warrant Boatswain's had been selected as Deck Limited Duty Officers and I was number three on the list. I just couldn't believe it! I had that damn letter in my record and had just been passed over for CWO-3. However, bigger than life, there was my name attesting that I was a selectee for LDO as a lieutenant junior grade. Shit, I even got to skip being an ensign.

I found out much later, after some research in Washington, D.C. at the Naval Military Personnel Command, that I was the first and only Warrant to be passed over for promotion and still be selected for LDO. Still later, I learned that, when the results of my Board of Inquiry had reached commander, Seventh Fleet, he had disagreed with the outcome and expressed this, emphatically, in his endorsement forwarded to commander in chief, Pacific Fleet. Both admirals viewed favorably the fact that I had not cast aspersions on my seniors and merely submitted a letter of rebuttal that stuck to facts ignored by the Board. Whatever transpired in the flag ranks was not officially conveyed to me, but I was now an LDO selectee.

I felt vindicated, knowing the system had worked as it should. Nida's assessment and advice had been correct, even though she only had a vague idea of how the Navy worked. I was glad I had listened to her rather than reverting to SMCM. My naval career was back on track, and the pie was sweetened considerably when the next promotion cycle for CWO-3 listed me, and backdated my date of rank to when I would have made it initially if not passed over. Subsequently, I was selected for CWO-4 one year early.

NEW DUTIES AND CHALLENGES

Ten days later, Captain Morhardt "frocked" L. C. and me to LTJG in a big ceremony at the headquarters building. (This term refers to the practice of pinning on a new rank without an associated pay increase before the actual date of promotion.) Following this action, we both got new jobs. L. C. became the assistant commander of Regiment One, and I was given the position of assistant military training officer. I only had this new assignment for a month and a half when Captain

McCullough (he was still the XO) drafted me for legal officer duties at Recruit Training Command. I will skip over subsequent cases I was involved with at the command, and close out this chapter with an incident representative of some of the non-legal challenges we faced.

Girls were always a problem at RTC. During my time there, other than a very few civilians like my secretary Anna, there were no females assigned. It was like a monastery. With women excluded for the most part, it became incumbent upon the sailors to find ways to introduce women to this environment. During graduation ceremonies and after working hours until 2200, women moved freely, for the most part, around the base. However, strict accountability was always in force, and circumventing the system required a great deal of ingenuity. American "Bluejackets" (enlisted sailors) were more than up to the challenge, as were some women seeking to spend time with them.

On one occasion, I happened to be walking through a barracks rather late at night. As I passed one of the recruits, he came to attention and saluted and I saluted back and kept walking. However, my mind was questioning what I thought I saw. Turning around, I ordered, "Halt, Recruit," and he did so. He was facing away from me, as I approached, it appeared to me that the seat of his dungaree trousers was filled out significantly. Becoming more suspicious, I ordered, "About Face."

As the recruit turned around in compliance, I noticed that she more than adequately filled out the front of her dungaree shirt as well. I now confirmed that he was a she, and that a large amount of non-regulation blonde-hair resided under a ball cap. Stepping over to her, I removed the cap and watched thick blond hair cascade down to below her shoulders. By this time, she was sobbing, which racked her body, and threatened to bust the buttons on her shirt at any minute. "Quiet down, girl," I said, and then walked her out of the barracks and over to Regiment Two. I had the duty officer get hold of the company commanders who had recruits in that barracks, and direct the battalion commander to return to base.

It turned out that the girl's name was Sherry and she was from Tennessee. Her husband was in one of the companies and she hadn't heard from him since he left home for Boot Camp. Only sixteen and very scared, she nevertheless hitchhiked to San Diego and somehow snuck onto the base. Looking at a posted Plan of the Day, she was able to figure out which barracks her husband was in. She then stole a dungaree uniform from a clothesline and went to his barracks by an indirect route. She almost made it to his company bay.

I had her husband brought over to Regiment Two, and allowed them a short reunion. While they held and talked to each other, I called the Greyhound Bus Terminal and reserved a seat on the next bus to Memphis. After she had changed back into her own clothes and surrendered the stolen dungarees, the duty driver took her to the terminal and stayed with her until that Grey Dog pulled out and was on its way. The recruit was sent back to his company with no disciplinary action taken, and told he had better start writing.

ORDERS TO *SAMUEL GOMPERS*

Nida and I still wrote each other almost every day. I had been able to call her twice, though the PI phone system was barely functional, and had asked her to marry me. She had agreed. Now I needed to get to Manila to make it happen. As 1977 drew slowly to a close, I contacted my detailer to see what he had in store for me. I knew I would be going back to sea duty, but not where or aboard what type of ship. When I learned I was to go to the destroyer tender USS *Samuel Gompers* (AD-37) as the first lieutenant, I was floored.

"I really don't want a tender," I told him, but my protest fell on deaf ears. "I'm putting you there for eighteen months as first lieutenant. It's a department head billet (job), so if you make full lieutenant, you'll be frocked. At the end of the eighteen months, I'll split-tour you to a "big deck" ship, probably a fast replenishment oiler." He went on to tell me the incumbent on *Gompers* was an unrestricted line officer and the CO intended to fire him. My rotation fit in perfectly, and would allow the Limited Duty Officer community to reclaim what had traditionally been an LDO billet. "Your orders will read to transfer in January 1978 and I need you to report then also. Can you forego a full thirty days leave en route?" "No sweat, Bill," I answered, "Just remember your promise to move me after eighteen months."

I hadn't wasted my time at RTC. I had been attending night school at National University and had just received my associate's degree in Business Administration a week before talking to my detailer. It was the last week of November and I would be transferring in a little over a month. In the first week of December, I got a call from a chief yeoman on the *Gompers*. When I answered, he asked, "Lieutenant Foley, can you hold for Captain Hoffman?" Answering affirmatively, I sat there wondering just what the fuck was going on. Presently, this booming voice came through the earpiece. "Lieutenant Foley? This is Captain Hoffman, CO of *Samuel Gompers*."

"Yes, Sir, what can I do for you?" I said. "I understand you've been nominated to be my new first lieutenant and I'm a little concerned. You're only a LTJG, even if you are an LDO, and the present first lieutenant is going to be fired the day his relief walks aboard. How about telling me about yourself." I responded, "Yes, sir," and went on to recount my background and what I had accomplished to date. I purposely omitted mentioning the letter of admonition. I figured, that had happened when I was a Warrant, and I deserved to start with a clean slate as an LDO.

When I finished, Captain Hoffman told me, "Okay, Lee, based on our discussion, I'm going to take a chance on you. I hope you won't let me down. When you report, be ready to start work immediately." With that, the line went dead. I sat for a while, wondering about the ramifications of that phone call. Then I shrugged it off. I knew myself and I knew I would do my best for him and the ship.

I took ten days leave, while still attached to RTC, and flew to Virginia Beach to spend Christmas with my mom. I brought her up to date on my adventures, told her about Nida, and that I was really looking forward to going back to sea. It was an exciting time in my life and I was extremely happy. Returning from leave, I got my affairs in order, and departed RTC on 6 January 1978, to embark on a whole new adventure.

17

Destroyer Tender *Samuel Gompers*

Photo 17-1

Destroyer tender USS *Samuel Gompers* (AD-37) under way, 24 November 1968. Naval History and Heritage Command photograph #NH 96875

As I walked down the pier to report aboard, I sighted the *Samuel Gompers* and was amazed at the sheer size of the ship. Almost all the weather decks and certainly the sides, anchors, cranes, and boats belonged to Deck Department. The magnitude of what was in store for me seemed awesome, but I felt confident and up to the task. Captain Hoffman had told me to be ready to go to work immediately, as soon as I reported. With that in mind, I was wearing "wash khaki's" (heavy cotton work uniform) with Boatswain's knife on my belt, instead of Dress Blues.

I found the first lieutenant having coffee in the wardroom. He welcomed me aboard, got me some coffee, and introduced me to several other officers present. We were then off on a whirlwind tour of Deck Department spaces. About two hours into the tour we heard the word passed, "Now LTJG Foley, your presence is requested in the captain's cabin." We stopped in a nearby office, where he phoned the CO to tell him we were touring spaces and would be up shortly. I didn't hear the conversation, but he visibly blanched, said, "Aye, aye, sir," many times, and carefully hung up the phone. "Lee, Captain Hoffman wants to see you immediately, and he wants you to come alone. Do you know something I don't?" I said, "Look," I've only been aboard a couple of hours and have spent it all with you." As I turned to go up to the captain's cabin, I caught him staring at me with a hangdog look on his face.

When I arrived at the captain's cabin, I knocked on the door and was invited in. Capt. Robert. B. Hoffman was sitting at his desk drinking coffee and the executive officer was sitting on one of the couches, also drinking coffee. They both stood up, shook my hand, and welcomed me aboard. The captain then waved me to a seat and told his cook to get me some coffee. That done, he turned to me and said, "Have you relieved that son-of-a-bitch yet?" Somewhat shocked, I kept a neutral look on my face and responded, "No sir, Captain, not yet. I've only been aboard a short time, and we just started touring the spaces." He continued, "What's the damn problem. You're a former Master Chief, a former Boatswain, and now an LDO."

"Yes, sir, I understand that. I know what's going on and I can run Deck Department for you. However, I want to see the spaces, know how much OPTAR (allocated funds) is left for the present quarter, and I want to know if any gear or equipment that I will be accountable for is missing." I glanced at the XO as I finished my response; he just sat there and continued to drink his coffee. When I turned back to the CO, he was writing away furiously. After several minutes he handed me a sheet of paper and said, "Read this." I took it and was shocked. I read the damn thing twice because I couldn't believe it.

The paper said in essence:

> To whom it may concern: As commanding officer of USS *Samuel Gompers* (AD-37), I hereby direct LTJG Lee M. Foley to relieve … as First Lieutenant forthwith. If anything is found to be wrong in any spaces, or with any equipment, LTJG Foley will not be held accountable. Likewise, he will not be held accountable if while taking inventory, accountable equipment or gear is missing or broken. If there is insufficient OPTAR to cover expenses for Deck Department for the remainder of the present quarter, I will direct the Supply Officer to supplement Deck Department's quarterly

grant in such a manner that the department will not be required to receive less OPTAR next quarter.

Signed: Robert F. Hoffman, Captain, U.S. Navy, Commanding."

There was a space for the XO to sign as a witness and a place for me to sign acknowledging the captain's directive. I guess I took too long looking it over, because the Old Man finally said, "Well, dammit, are you going to relieve that SOB or not?" I looked at the captain directly and said, "Right away, Captain. He'll be relieved in less than 15 minutes," then added, "Sir, before I go, would you and the XO sign that document along with me? I'll have copies made for us." Big smiles appeared on both men's faces. "Welcome to FAT SAM, Lee, you're going to love it here," the XO stated. They shook my hand again, and dismissed me.

Out in the passageway, I stood scratching my head for a minute and then thought to myself, it's his ship, we'll do it whatever way he wants to. With that, I promptly dismissed the conference from my mind and went down to the Deck Office to relieve the first lieutenant forthwith. He wasn't too happy with this turn of events, but he was scared of the captain, and little was said. After a few necessary pieces of business, I told him to write up the relieving letter, date it today, and I would sign it later. I then saluted and told him, "You had it, now I've got it."

With that accomplished, I called the quarterdeck, told them who I was and that I was officially the First Lieutenant, and told them to pass the word to have all Deck Department petty officers and chief petty officers assemble in the Bos'n locker with LTJG Foley. When I got there, it was chock-a-block with BMs with skeptical/resigned looks on their faces. I told the man nearest the coffee mess to get me a cup of coffee, black; and then I sat down on a large coil of line.

"I'm Lee Foley and as of about twenty minutes ago, I am now the First Lieutenant. For years I have heard 'They this,' and 'They that,' but now I'm 'They,' so let me tell you how I do business." I outlined what I expected from them and what they could expect from me in return. This one-way conversation ended with me telling them my two inviolate rules: "One, I expect and require absolute loyalty 100-percent of the time. In turn I will back you to the limit, whether good or bad. Two, never ever fucking lie to me. Whoever else you choose to lie to, don't do it to me or you'll be history. In turn I will be above board and honest with each one of you. Take me at face value for now and I'll do the same with you." I waited for questions, but none were forthcoming, so I told them to go to work and dismissed them.

As I stood up to leave, someone called "Attention on Deck," a convention extended to flag officers and CO's and XOs, not some "boot camp JG." Maybe it was a portent of things to come. They sure hadn't called "Attention on Deck" when I entered the Bos'n locker. Responding with, "Carry On," I left the space and went down to the Deck Office to take charge.

At the end of my first two months aboard, things were looking up and going great. Deck Department had been reorganized into five separate divisions which were responsible to customer ships and to the internal organization of *Gompers*. Trust and loyalty were starting to build up and down the chain of command and I was thankful for that. Then came a real test of "can do" spirit in the department.

Around 1000 on a Friday morning, I was trying to catch up on paperwork, when the word was passed, "First Lieutenant, your presence is requested in the captain's cabin." As soon as I heard the word, I went loping up to see what the skipper wanted. I knocked on his door and was told to enter. Once more, I found the XO on one of the couches drinking coffee. "You wanted to see me, Captain?" I said upon entering the room. "Yeah, Lee, come in and take a seat. I have a job for you." Not having the foggiest idea of what he might have in mind, I merely sat down and waited for him to spell it out for me. I didn't have to wait very long.

"Lee, on Monday at 1330, commander, Naval Surface Force Pacific Fleet wants to host a luncheon for high level Naval officials and local civilian dignitaries onboard *Samuel Gompers*. I want the exterior of the ship painted out by Monday morning, no later than 1000." Without hesitation, I said, "Can do, Captain. We'll get on it right away." The CO and XO looked at each other, then the CO said, "I just told you I wanted the ship painted out by Monday morning and you tell me Can Do?" Again, I answered him positively, "Yes, Sir. We can get it done no sweat." Like the day I reported aboard, smiles appeared, and they stood up, shook my hand and ushered me out.

HERCULEAN TASK

I called the quarterdeck and had the BMOW pass the word for all Deck Department chiefs and first class petty officers to assemble in the Deck Office. This would be a test of how much trust and loyalty had been built up in a short two months. I explained the task, emphasizing that it had to be completed by late Monday morning and all of our gear stowed away. I told them that the guests would be touring the ship after the luncheon, and it was imperative that our spaces shined. I was too old to "swing on a stage" (assist with painting over the side), but I would be aboard all weekend to offer my support. When asked by BMC Bob Matson, "Can we tell the men that you're giving up your liberty to be here with us?" I replied, "You bet, Chief. I might go on the pier to see how we're doing, but that's as far as I'll go." (Matson, my youngest chief, had worked for me aboard *Mount Vernon* as a BM2 and later as a BM1.) When I had finished, there was unanimous consent that we could do the job and would show everyone how Deck operated.

Matson asked, "If these guys are going to bust balls all weekend to make this happen, is there any way we can compensate them, Lieutenant?" I had thought about this beforehand, so I was ready with an answer. "I would like to give each of the men, and you supervisors, 5 days of "basket leave." (This refers to time off granted by a ship's captain, which does not count against the 2.5 days of leave that sailors accrue each month.) "The leave would have to be staggered, so if something came up, we could handle the load." They would have to keep meticulous records, so no one got left out, and schedule the leave wisely. "The most important thing is keeping our mouths shut. If word gets out of this reward, they'll keelhaul us all—you guys for taking Basket Leave, and me for authorizing it."

As my leaders filed out of the Deck Office to get things going, I thought about what the job entailed. I told the supervisors to ask for volunteers and not order guys to stay aboard to undertake this herculean task. The entire department volunteered to stay aboard to complete the job. I knew then, that the *Gompers* Deck Department was unique and that I was blessed to be working with them.

We used brows for painting, which we attached to our travelling cranes. More sturdy and stable than stages, this method allowed us to paint both sides of the ship simultaneously without needing to raise, lower, and move stages by hand. Additionally, using the crane method reduced the number of sailors needed for line-handling stages. Freed-up sailors were employed painting the bow and stern at the same time that the sides were being done. We started painting early Friday afternoon and by late Sunday night, the entire exterior of the ship had been painted out neatly. There were no "holidays" (small missed areas) or "leave periods" (large areas where paint had not been applied). Shit, they had even painted the overhangs of the weather decks white and repainted all the fancywork on the quarterdeck.

As we sat in the Deck Office drinking coffee, I remarked that all we really had left to do was sweep, swab the decks, shine the brightwork and scrub the quarterdeck awning and brow skirts before 0800. With a lazy smile, Nick (BM1 Robert G. Nichols) looked at me and said, "Boss, the brow skirts and awning were done two hours ago, and they are being lashed in place as we speak. I have twenty guys assigned, each with his own can of Neverdull and two clean rags. They'll start on the brightwork (brass metal) at first light. Steve (BM2 Young) will be the boatswain's mate in charge of that evolution. Dutch has the duty section geared up to sweep and swab all topside spaces prior to quarters in the morning, so I think we're set. (Putting BM1 Dutch "Buddha" Menke in charge of anything guaranteed success.)

Monday dawned bright and early. Most of us in Deck hadn't been to bed yet, but FAT SAM shined like a new baby's ass. The CO and XO were absolutely ecstatic and very liberal in their praise. The senior naval officers and civilian dignitaries were duly impressed and made many kind comments to the CO. It took almost eight weeks to reward everyone with five days "basket leave," but I had kept my word and no one was slighted. My men and I were now humming on identical tracks. Damn, we'd become a fucking mutual admiration society.

PREPARATION FOR DEPLOYMENT AND MARRIAGE

Samuel Gompers was soon to leave on WestPac, and Nida and I were to be married in the Philippines. While ensuring that all pre-deployment requirements were being carried out, I found time to visit a friend of mine, a chief legalman at the Naval Training Center. I knew there were a lot of hoops to jump through if I was going to marry a Filipina, and bring her to the United States. He had just been through the same thing and advised me on what Nida and I would have to do.

The most valuable nugget came last, "Oh, by the way, Lee. I'm being transferred to the staff of commander U.S. Naval Forces Philippines in May, and I should be able to grease the skids for you if you have all your documents in order." When he said that, I shook his hand so vigorously I thought I might sprain it and thanked him profusely. He said once he got there and was settled in, he and his wife would go to Manila and help Nida with her paperwork.

In late February, the guys and I started preparing *Gompers* for the forthcoming change of command. Captain Hoffman was leaving to command a destroyer squadron. His relief, Captain Robert J O'Malia, had started his career as a Surface Warrior, before Adm. Hyman Rickover (father of the nuclear navy and head of the civilian Nuclear Regulatory Commission) plucked him off his destroyer, and placed him in the Nuclear Power Program. After training in nuclear power and submarine school, O'Malia had served a tour as operations officer and navigator of a "fast attack boat" (SSN), and then as XO on a "boomer" (SSBN). He went on to command the USS *George Bancroft* (SSBN-643) on several "Polaris patrols," led her through an overhaul/conversion and refueling, and several more patrols. Bob was the most unflappable individual, I ever had the pleasure to know, and he was also the fairest.

Photo 17-2

Hand drawn portrait of Capt. Robert J. O'Malia, USN.
USS *Samuel Gompers* (AD-37) Western Pacific 1978 cruise book

WESTWARD BOUND

In May 1978, *Samuel Gompers* cast off her lines and, aided by harbor tugs, slipped sideways away from the pier. For the seventh time in ten years, FAT SAM was deploying to WestPac. Most of the crew were sad to leave their loved ones. I was ecstatic that I would soon see Nida again and that we would be getting married. Prior to sailing, she wrote me that all her documents had been turned in, and I responded that mine had been submitted as well. When a serviceman wishes to marry a foreign national, the red tape is absolutely unbelievable. Having been around the block a time or two, I sent my documents to my chief legalman friend who was now in the staff job in the Philippines. I also called the head of the Naval Investigative Service (NIS, precursor to NCIS) in Subic. We had met while he was at NTC and I, RTC in San Diego). He would ensure that Nida was treated courteously and with respect during her interview.

All too often, the powers that be assumed that any girl a serviceman wanted to marry was a hooker, or a bar girl. Sometimes the prospective spouse was subject to unwanted sexual advances, slander, and a way of being interviewed that is not taught by personnel management consultants. I've heard stories of girls being fondled, and told that their request to marry an American serviceman would be approved if they were friendly and so on.

My excitement grew as we neared the Philippines, and I made final plans for the wedding. In the U.S., the bride's parents plan and prepare everything; in PI it is exactly the opposite. Fellow officers had agreed to serve as Best Man and as Sword Archway men and escorts for the various bridesmaids. Aboard *Gompers* was Chief Mess Specialist Ageaolili, who had studied at some of the finest civilian baking schools in the world. He agreed to make me a cake fit for a king and queen.

ARRIVAL IN THE PHILIPPINES

I had gotten approval to go on thirty days' leave when we arrived in Subic. As soon as we were moored alongside Alava Pier at the naval station, and the Special Sea and Anchor Detail had been secured, I took a shower and changed into some light weight clothes suitable for the endless summer of the Philippines. On the pier I caught a cab to the main gate, changed 200 American dollars into pesos, passed through the bag inspection, and emerged into the Philippine world. Hailing a jeepney, I made good time getting to the Victory Liner Terminal, and within the hour I was on my way to Manila.

When the bus arrived, I caught a cab to the Bank of America in Makati expecting to find Nida there. However, the branch manager told me that she was at home. Catching another cab, I went to her house and was welcomed by her nanay (mother). Seconds later, Nida was holding and kissing me. She adored the rings I had picked out for her and, after showing them to her family she, put on the engagement ring and we sat down to plan the wedding.

Her relatives were in Manila, and in her province of Nueva Ecija in the town of Cuyapo. My guests were all down in Subic Bay. We wanted a large church wedding, but most of the large churches in Manila were already reserved for events. We finally decided to get married in the Philippine Independent Church in Olongapo, rent the Hotel Royale (the entire place) for the reception, and rent cars to chauffer Nida's relatives from Manila and her province to Olongapo. We would put them up at the Hotel Royale and then furnish cars to take them back to Manila and Cuyapo when they were ready.

The Foley wedding on 8 July was the biggest event that happened in Olongapo in 1978. The Philippine Independent Church was located halfway down Rizal Boulevard which, along with Magsaysay Drive, made up the two main thoroughfares in Olongapo. The Philippine Constabulary completely cordoned off Rizal Boulevard to traffic from mid-afternoon until midnight. Over 700 persons attended our wedding. This group included Nida's co-workers from the Bank of America, her relatives from Manila and the province, and almost the entire crew of the *Gompers*, except for those in the Duty Section. Rear Admiral Floyd Miller, commander, Cruiser Destroyer Group One embarked in *Samuel Gompers*, was in attendance, as well as Captain O'Malia and Commander Richard Vallin, our executive officer.

The church was decorated with yellow-green bunting, Nida's favorite color, and was very festive. The officers participating in the wedding were wearing "choker whites" (full dress white uniforms) with swords. At the conclusion of our traditional Philippine wedding ceremony, Nida and I, Captain O'Malia, Ms. Sally De Jesus, Maximiano Bait, and Ms. Josefina N. Sansano signed the marriage contract and it was official. Nida and I were now husband and wife.

Thanking our priest for conducting the ceremony and blessing our union, I gave him an envelope with a donation, and everyone traipsed across the street to the Hotel Royale. There was enough food for 1,000 people. Two roast pigs (lechon), complete with apples in their mouths; five separate Philippine entrées, plus American choices; all the side dishes you can imagine; endless bottles of champagne; and two extremely large wedding cakes. The festivities included the release skyward of white doves with silver bells; two six-piece bands, complete with Filipina singers; a candlelit archway; and gifts galore.

Two civilian photographers recorded the event, and people from the ship took twice as many pictures as the two official photographers. Nida and I left the reception around 0100, and there was no sign of it winding down. We were told later that the last of the guests went off to their rooms around 0545.

Photo 17-3

The Foley's Wedding Day, 8 July 1978.
Author's collection

Photo 17-4

Passing under the traditional sword arch at the conclusion of the wedding. Author's collection

Samuel Gompers' mission as a repair ship for destroyers kept her mostly at Subic to tend ships arriving there. Nida and I rented a house in Olongapo to live in while FAT SAM was in port. We decided that Nida would go home to the province when we went to sea and stay there until it was time to fly to the United States at deployment's end. Returning to normal shipboard routine after my leave, Command Duty Officers were in 6-section duty (involving remaining aboard every sixth day), so I could go home most every night. We ate out, generally at the officer's club at the naval station or the one at Cubi Point Naval Air Station. We spent weekends at White Rock Beach, a tourist resort about twenty miles from the base. Whenever I had the duty, Nida would have dinner with me aboard ship, watch the evening movie, and then depart.

DEPARTURE FROM THE PHILIPPINES

Unfortunately, our time in Subic drew to a close. Although we had been in port more than triple the time of other type ships, it wasn't enough for me. Hell, I was newly married and the stardust was still in my eyes. However, when the sea calls, a sailor must answer, so I said my goodbyes to Nida and put her on a bus to her province.

Our first port after leaving the Philippines was Taiwan. The island's real name is Ilha Formosa which literally means "island beautiful." A new port had been opened within the last two months, and we went there rather than the more traditional Kaohsiung or Keelung. Tai Chung (a city on the western side of Taiwan) was known for its fine teak furniture and, when we sailed, we had a whole storeroom full.

Photo 17-5

Tai Chung, Taiwan.
USS *Samuel Gompers* (AD-37) Western Pacific 1978 cruise book

We next called at Hong Kong. For a few cents, you could ride the Star Ferry across the bay to Kowloon, and there, buy merchandise from all over the world. When you tired of Kowloon, you could catch the ferry back across the bay and visit a Hong Kong tailor who could handle any clothing need from scratch. There were floating homes, floating villages, floating markets, and even floating restaurants in Hong Kong. If you looked hard enough you could find and buy anything.

As always, we were warned not to shop in any places that were communist, and try to keep a low profile while ashore. I had heard how forbidding the Bank of China looked, so I took a walk down Wu Pak Street in Aberdeen to see for myself. The building was massive with large doors that were closed. Next to the doors stood two Chinese Army soldiers with rifles and decidedly unfriendly faces. It was indeed forbidding and, if truth be told, kind of scary. My time ashore was spent buying gifts for Nida, and enjoying the fine cuisine and bar offerings at the Hong Kong Hilton.

TYPHOON SEASON

Our visit to Hong Kong, and all of WestPac coincided with the typhoon season. These cyclonic storms form over the warm ocean and develop spiraling winds that can reach 150-200 mph. The relatively calm center, or eye may be 4 to 30 miles across, depending on the intensity of the typhoon. For the most part, these type storms conform to known tracks, but they frequently defy predictions and do their own thing for no apparent reason. During the last few days of our port call, the weather had been slowly deteriorating.

On the day before we were scheduled to sail, I had the duty as CDO while most of the crew including the CO and XO were ashore. In early afternoon, Hong Kong went on full typhoon alert and all ships were advised to leave the harbor before the full fury of the storm broke. In winds of 40-50 knots that continued to build, the duty section and I prepared the ship for sea. We recovered our accommodation ladders and lashed them down, then rigged Jacob's ladders at several locations in order that we could get our liberty party back on board. Boats were brought up and stowed under almost impossible conditions, and men scurried about, lashing everything down.

While awaiting the return of the captain and executive officer, I set Sea and Anchor Detail and made all preparations to slip the mooring buoy and proceed to sea. Hong Kong Harbor Control was getting increasingly irritated and kept asking me how long it would be before we got under way. I kept stalling them, and then a large Royal Navy boat approached, containing the CO and XO and some of our liberty party. With them on board and briefed as to what steps had been taken, I went to the fo'c'sle and directed recovery of our anchor chain and shackle. FAT SAM then turned fair, and proceeded to sea and safety.

We rode out the storm quite well, all things considered, and suffered no broken or damaged equipment. On the third day, the skies dawned bright and clear, and we headed back to Hong Kong to collect the one hundred sixty-odd sailors who had missed the typhoon alert and our sailing. After doing so, we set a course for Sasebo, Japan.

PORT HOPPING

The "Land of the Rising Sun" is a place of splendid and startling variety. Wherever you go, from the majesty of the mountains to the bustle of Tokyo, from industrial centers to quiet villages, you will find ancient traditions and contemporary ideas in peaceful co-existence. It is at once a land of serenity, yet possessed of a fierce Samurai code. I did some sightseeing, and ran into an old shipmate at Fleet Activities on the Navy base and we had dinner together and a few beers. I bought some things for Nida, and went to the "O" Club with Dan Winter (a Chief Warrant and Repair Division Officer aboard *Gompers*) a few times. On several occasions, I went ashore with Captain O'Malia for dinner. These were pleasant occasions, which offered opportunity to learn something new in the course of the evening.

After Sasebo, we visited Yokosuka (called Yahkooska by the fleet). Several days before departing Japan and starting the long transit home, I was having drinks with the captain at the "O" Club and mentioned that I missed Nida. "Lee, why don't you take leave from here, go straight to PI, and then both of you can fly back to the U.S. together. It would be scary for her by herself, and this way she will have you to lean on during her first trip abroad." He told me the trip home would likely be uneventful, and that Bos'n Waddell could handle whatever came up, particularly since Deck Department was rock solid with some of the best chiefs on the ship. Continuing, he explained that he would prefer that I did it this way, vice taking leave in San Diego, when he would need me close at hand to help in preparing *Gompers* to be the first platform for the Women in Navy Ships (WINS) Program. He concluded by cautioning me, "However, be sure you're standing on the pier when we tie up."

I took a "Space A" hop back to the Philippines, and I departed a MAC (Military Air Command) terminal in Japan aboard a Medevac flight. The plane was mostly empty, save for one patient, a doctor, a nurse, and an aviator captain en route to Cubi Point. ("Space A" refers to military flights which servicemen can utilize for free, providing their priority is high enough among those present and wanting to board.) We went to Guam first, but by morning had landed at Clark AFB. In no time at all, I cleared Customs and was on a bus to the province of Nueva Ecija and the town of Cuyapo to be with Nida.

A province in the Philippines is often like a scene right out of the movie South Pacific. Many families in rural areas live in Nipa huts that are considered a national symbol. The most popular name for this type of house is Bahay Kubo (pronounced Baa Hi Koo Boo). Even today, many families live in these type houses, and cook using wood stoves, with candles and lanterns for light. Indoor plumbing becomes less prevalent the farther you travel into remote rural areas. It was into this world that I travelled to be with Nida. While there, Super Typhoon KADING, with winds in excess of 180 knots, passed directly over Cuyapo leaving large-scale destruction throughout the province of Nueva Ecija.

The day after the storm passed, we rented a van and driver and went to Manila, where we spent the night. The next day, we boarded our KLM Flight to San Francisco. Arriving in Frisco, it was pretty chilly for Nida as it was her first experience with cold weather. We hustled into the terminal and connected with our flight to San Diego.

Samuel Gompers returned to San Diego on 12 November 1978. I caught duty the first night the ship was in port, and that was only right. The ship enjoyed a 30-day stand-down period following deployment. This meant that for the first two weeks, you only came to work if you had the duty. During the second two weeks, half-work days were in effect for the entire crew. At the end of the stand-down, everyone went to work in earnest. As a destroyer tender, we made our living by repairing ships and, as the only tender dedicated to the nuclear surface fleet, we were much in demand. In between this tending business, we were preparing to be the first ship to receive women as crewmembers.

WOMEN IN NAVY SHIPS (WINS) PROGRAM

Yours truly was selected by his beloved captain to honcho the program. When I protested vehemently that I was an LDO, the counter argument was, "I thought LDOs could do anything, Lee." The clincher was the Old Man told me that with so many LDOs and Warrant Officers in the wardroom, no unrestricted line officer would get the backing and support they would need to get the job done. Putting an LDO in charge of the program would practically guarantee that the other LDOs and Warrants would have to go along since the fraternal ties of the "Mustang brotherhood" were so strong. Unfortunately, no one told them how strong the ties were and that we should all stick together.

Just prior to the WINS reporting for duty, I requested to extend my tour onboard to a full three years. I had been promised an 18-month split-tour when I was first assigned, and told that, at its completion, I would probably go to a fast replenishment oiler, likely the USS *Kansas City* (AOR-3). Now that I had all these irons in the fire, I wanted to see the fruits of my labors, and I was also enrolled full time at National University in San Diego, working on my bachelor's degree. The captain approved my request as did the Washington bureaucracy, after some arm twisting; the LDO community had wanted to utilize me elsewhere.

I was less than enthusiastic about being the WINS Coordinator and in having women assigned to the ship. When I left *Gompers* at the end of my tour, excluding the captain, I was the strongest proponent on board of the program and having a coed crew. I had also come to believe that the program should be widened to allow the assignment of women to every class of ship possible. They have, since then, proved their worth and salt at sea, one hundred-fold. All this came to pass, and I am very proud that I helped launch the WINS Program so many years ago.

The Repair Department was the largest department on the ship and Deck was second. Nevertheless, we ended up with the majority of women assigned. Deck Department on any ship in the Navy is not a pristine, 9-5 work environment. It is long, never ending, and sometimes, mind-numbing work in all conditions of weather. Boatswain's mates are rarely fully appreciated for their skills and abilities, and I tried my damnedest to make sure they knew I appreciated their hard work and dedication. When the women reported, I split them up into the five deck divisions, and assigned two to the deck office, one as the assistant departmental supply petty officer, and one as the yeoman.

Two of the women were rated boatswain's mates, BM3 Sassy Spencer and BM3 Sheila Tuttle. Spencer stood 5'10" in her bare feet, sported numerous tattoos, rode a Harley motorcycle, and could cuss with the best of them. Despite all the macho trappings, I still had misgivings. However, those vanished when I walked out on the main deck one afternoon and found a young, mouthy sailor jacked up against the bulkhead by Sassy who had a death grip on the front of his dungaree shirt. I arrived on the scene just as the seaman was saying "Yes, ma'am, Boats, you won't get no more shit from me."

When she was finished instructing the kid and saw that he understood and would comply with the job she had assigned him, she turned around, saluted me, wished me a nice afternoon, and went on about her business. I stopped worrying about Sassy after that. Sheila Tuttle was a qualified tugboat craftmaster and small boat coxswain long before she came to *Gompers*. She eventually changed her rating to hull technician, which I considered a huge loss to the deck community.

The day the women reported for duty, the media, as is their wont, made the event a three-ring circus and the Navy did little, if anything, to insulate the women and let the story unfold as it happened. The first few weeks of coed bliss were chaotic and hectic, to say the least. Since girls have a natural tendency to fill out clothing more so than a guy, it was nothing to see four or five males casually stand around and stare at a WINS as she stretched in the normal course of whatever job she happened to be engaged in.

One morning after Officer's Call (daily executive officer meeting with department heads), I went up on the fo'c'sle to "put out the word" to department personnel, as was my normal routine. However, nothing in my experience prepared me to find 115 female sailors crying in ranks. I was flustered, confused, and just plain didn't know "what the fuck to do." I retreated behind my rank and turning to the Bos'n, told him to take charge of this situation and "get those women to stop bawling."

With that, I spun on my heel, went down to the Deck Office, and poured myself a cup of coffee.

I guess Tom got it squared away. He came down to the office in a little while and told me that one of the girls who had been with our WINS prior to their reporting to *Gompers*, had been killed the night before in an auto accident. Since all of the women had been together as a group for several months, close friendships and attachments had been formed. The girl who had died had been everyone's friend, so that explained the crying. I did not handle the situation like I should have. Perhaps I could have been more compassionate? Hell, I don't know. Besides, I knew the Bos'n could handle it and he needed the practice if he was going to become an LDO.

The first "all hands" personnel inspection highlighted how squared away the WINS were. They all looked sharp in uniform, but presented some challenges. At such uniform inspections, a commanding officer scrutinizes every inch of a sailor's attire, and comments favorably and assigns them high marks if they are "squared away." Our captain was not exceptionally tall. Thus, as he made his way through the ranks of sailors with the XO and me in tow, he was eye-level with, in some cases, parts of their anatomy he wasn't accustomed to inspecting closely.

My newly installed assistant departmental supply petty officer was exceptionally pretty. She had been a runner-up in the Miss Texas Beauty Contest, and was both extremely well endowed and incredibly naïve. In any case, when the captain got to her, she was standing as erect as possible with her shoulders back and braced. This posture, although taught in Boot Camp and technically correct, threatened to blow all the buttons off her immaculate white shirt. The captain, having never encountered someone so formidable in a Navy uniform, turned a deep red on his face and neck. Recovering quickly, he moved on to the next sailor without saying anything.

All of a sudden, the girl who had caused him to become flustered, burst out crying, left her position in ranks and went to the Deck Office. I found the young lady there crying her heart out, and gave her a white handkerchief to wipe her tears. When asked what the problem was, she replied, "I'm so embarrassed, Mr. Foley. The captain didn't like my uniform and got all upset. I just don't know what's wrong with it. I worked so hard to make it perfect. After several seconds of contemplating that remark, I stated, "Damn, girl, there is nothing wrong with your uniform. In fact, it's perfect. What flustered the captain is that the front of your shirt is filled out so much."

She looked at me after I gave her the explanation and then started to smile a little. "I can't help how I fill out the shirt, sir. I've been like this since I was fourteen." Telling her that she would not have to stand any more personnel inspections, her smile blossomed and she asked to be excused. She would prove to be very sharp administratively, and almost single-handedly reorganized and streamlined my supply system, which eventually became a model for the other departments.

The women in the Deck divisions likewise proved their mettle. They chipped and painted, washed and scrubbed, buffed and shined, operated cranes and drove boats, slushed wire rigging, and learned marlinspike seamanship. In all these endeavors, they pulled their share of the load, and a little more. After several months had elapsed, and everyone started congratulating themselves on how well we were all coming together as a team, *Playboy* magazine came out with a "Girls in the Military" issue.

Several of our WINS were featured, and the incident received extensive national press coverage. The CO—anticipating that there would be a backlash, and retribution would be demanded far exceeding what the girls had done—convened an immediate Captain's Mast and fined each woman involved $50.00. When higher authority decided, in their righteous indignation to smite these ladies who had embarrassed the Navy, they encountered a fait acompli. Captain O'Malia had already punished them, so the Navy couldn't do so again. Having no legal way to get at the women, they took out their frustrations and anger on him.

EOOW QUALIFICATION

During my last year aboard *Gompers*, I requested the CO's permission to try and qualify as an EOOW (Engineering Officer of the Watch). Captain O'Malia, himself a nuclear engineer, wondered why I, a Deck LDO, wanted to undertake such an effort. It wasn't so much a matter of wanting to be an EOOW as it was having to be qualified as one in order to be considered for command at sea. When he saw I was serious, he had the chief engineer put me on the watchbill, but I still had to stand my own bridge watches.

Bill Woods was an LDO Engineer and really sharp. He and Engineman Senior Chief Bruce drove me relentlessly. Even with that, it took me nearly seven months to get to a point where I felt sufficiently confident to ask for an EOOW Oral Qualification board. The board was held in the skipper's conference room and was chaired by him. Members of the board included the chief engineer and Senior Chief Bruce, along with CWO-4 Pierce (a former enlisted chief machinist mate and our main propulsion assistant), and CWO-2 Zink (a former enlisted chief hull technician and our damage control assistant).

Following a grueling four hours of non-stop questions and answers, the board judged me qualified and offered their congratulations. I thought I was home free. However, the captain said, "Lee, now that you've passed your oral board, I want you to stand EOOW watches for a while. It's one thing to regurgitate answers while sitting here. It's quite another thing to have to act, or react, to a given situation as the actual EOOW." I stood these watches for about the next two-and-a-half months, whenever the ship was under way. I sweated each and every one, because of the enormity and complexity of overseeing the operation of propulsion, electrical generation, auxiliary equipment, and interrelated systems. Fortunately, I didn't ruin anything, while gaining the utmost respect for the chief engineer and his people.

Photo 17-6

Promotion to lieutenant, Captain O'Malia and Nida do the honors, 1980. Author's collection

WANING DAYS

In late October 1980, we started preparing for Captain O'Malia's change of command in early November. He had orders to be the chief of staff for commander, Task Force 73, the Seventh Fleet Logistics Czar based in Subic. The new CO was Capt. Fred Bailey, who'd had numerous commands at sea, and who was an exceptional ship handler, organizer, and leader. *Gompers* would be in good hands. On the day of the change of command, I had two weeks left on my tour. I had been accepted for the Navy's Degree Completion Program and would spend the next year attending classes at National University, where I would earn my Bachelor's Degree in Public Administration (Magna Cum Laude). As I walked down the officer's gangway for the last time, I felt a pang of sadness. I had become very close to my sailors and to the ship we affectionately called FAT SAM.

Photo 17-7

Forty-two crewmembers ship over on USS *Samuel Gompers*' birthday.
USS *Samuel Gompers* (AD-37) Western Pacific 1978 cruise book

18

Degree Completion and Shore Duty

Being absent from the Navy for an entire year took some adjustment. While attending college full-time, I did not have to wear a uniform, or check into a base, or get a haircut, or do anything Navy at all, until I completed my degree requirements and graduated. After that, I would be assigned to a normal tour of shore duty. During this period, while Nida and I were no longer part of the *Gompers* family, we continued to see our officer and enlisted friends socially.

Schooling went very well. I graduated from National University in October 1981, and reported to Naval Station, San Diego. Assigned as the Service Craft Officer, I was responsible for ten Navy harbor tugs and eight civilian pilots (all retired Navy, mostly LDOs). Related duties included oversight of the oil spill recovery team, pier berthing assignments, the naval station boat pool, and a full-scale tugboat repair and supply support facility. Bob Hagenbruch, an older lieutenant commander LDO, turned over a superb organization to me, for which I was very grateful. Bob had orders to be the first lieutenant aboard the *Witchita* (AOR-1), a fleet replenishment ship.

My boss was Commander Ed "Hoot" Gibson, a nod to his last name being the same as the legendary "Silver Screen cowboy, Hoot Gibson." Ed had previously commanded a minesweeper and, upon leaving his current assignment, would take over a frigate. The second in command of the naval station was a Mustang's mustang. Commander Tony Coulipides was a former boatswain's mate who went the Warrant and LDO route, then shifted to the unrestricted line. He'd had several commands and, along with Commander Sy Manning (a Navy legend), SEAL officer Richard Marcinko, and one other Mustang commander, had been selected for promotion to captain.

The names of these men were removed from the Captain's List by the Secretary of the Navy. Penalized for their age and non-traditional careers, their slots were given to younger commanders who'd followed standard paths. This shortsighted action probably did more to harm morale and discourage enlisted sailors from applying for a commission, than any other single act. It was a terrible and devastating mistake that hopefully will never be repeated.

I settled into my new job quite easily. Commander Gibson was a super boss, and I had the pleasure of regularly having a beer or two with the executive officer. I had my own parking space outside my office, and was allowed to run the Service Craft Division as I saw fit. When BM2 Jim Leatherman left *Gompers* and came to the naval station, I scooped him up and put him in charge of the boat pool. I had two outstanding young sailors, Kelly Houlihan and Valerie Hadlock, running the Bos'n locker and waterfront supply system, respectively. Clint Davis, a Warrant, who'd been stationed with me at Recruit Training Command, was now maintenance officer for the tugs and yard craft. Lt. Betsy Weems was in charge of the oil recovery team. They made a really good team, and I enjoyed working with them, immensely.

In January 1983, my detailer called me and said that he wanted to move me in February, instead of July at the end of my tour. I was to be going to *Roanoke* (AOR-7) as first lieutenant to relieve an unrestricted line officer. By this means, the AOR billet would once more be filled by an LDO. The only hitch was *Roanoke* was homeported five hundred miles up the California coast in Alameda. Nida and I had just bought a home in San Diego, and she had a good job as a junior accountant at Insurance Company of North America.

Roanoke was undergoing a shipyard overhaul in the Bay Area and would not be deploying for a while. Therefore, we talked about it and decided that I would live aboard the ship as a geographical bachelor and commute to San Diego on weekends. When the XO gave me my detaching Fitrep (officer evaluation), he told me that I was getting a great assignment and was a shoe-in to make LCDR later in the year, since I was in the zone for promotion. I thanked him for everything, wished him well, and took my leave. It had been a great tour, but I was anxious to return to sea in an operational environment.

During my shore duty at the naval station, I had voluntarily attended a Mine Warfare course exported to San Diego by commander, Mine Warfare Command, based in Charleston, South Carolina. When I took the course, I had no idea that I would someday command *Excel*. I just wanted to keep my knowledge of mine warfare (which was then admittedly very scant) current.

19

First Lieutenant aboard *Roanoke*

Underway replenishment was the U.S. Navy's secret weapon of World War II.

—Fleet Adm. Chester Nimitz, U.S. Navy.

Photo 19-1

Fleet replenishment ship USS *Roanoke* (AOR-7) off San Diego, 24 July 1976.
National Archives photograph #USN 1168327

Roanoke turned out to be one of the best assignments I ever had. When I reported, she was almost two-thirds of the way through overhaul in Todd Shipyard in San Francisco. I arrived in the Bay Area on a Saturday, and after getting settled, went immediately to the ship to look around. I had purposely planned my arrival this way in order to see what I was inheriting. The senior boatswain's mate aboard that day was Chief Steve Glissman. He gave me the grand tour, leaving nothing out and not trying to sugar-coat anything. After four hours of crawling up, over, around and through spaces and equipment, I felt that I had a fair handle on what kind of shape Deck Department was in, and what I had to work with in the way of people. I thanked the chief for his unvarnished assessment, and went up to the wardroom to grab a quick cup of coffee.

Photo 19-2

Chief Engineer LTJG Ben Lindsey, USN.
USS *Roanoke* (AOR-7) Western Pacific 1981-1982 cruise

While there, I met "Gentle Ben" Lindsey, the chief engineer. A former machinist's mate and now an LDO, Ben was an ace, and he and I would work well together. Satisfied with my visit, I left the ship and went back to the BOQ (bachelor officer quarters) to shower and change clothes before heading down the coast to the Naval Surface Warfare Center at Port Hueneme (a small beach city surrounded by the city of

Oxnard and Santa Barbara Channel), for a week of UNREP (under way replenishment) training.

The week started with classroom instruction in standard operating procedures for UNREP maneuvers. We first learned about rig team organization, safety procedures, and communications. From there, we progressed to hands-on training, involving operating and rigging both the delivery side and receiving stations. The week went by in a whirl. When it was finished, I was confident I would be able to lead UNREP evolutions aboard *Roanoke*. The following Monday, I reported aboard the replenishment ship for duty.

The skipper, Capt. Bill Reed, an aviator, had me up to his cabin. After the amenities were over, which included him telling me how happy he was to have an LDO as first lieutenant, he gave me an assignment I tried desperately to decline. "Being in the yards, the job of First Lieutenant is not as pressing as it will become once we become operational, so I want you to assume the duties of Overhaul Coordinator for the remainder of the overhaul."

Photo 19-3

Capt. William H. Reed, USN.
USS *Roanoke* (AOR-7) Western Pacific 1981-1982 cruise book

"I really think you need to keep me as the First Lieutenant, Captain," I replied, trying to dodge this additional duty. Reed smiled at me and said, "I thought LDOs could do anything. Are you saying you can't do the job, Lee?" The old fox had me boxed, with no way out. "LDOs can certainly do anything, Captain, and I'm sure I could do the job in an outstanding manner, but…" That was as far as I got before he interrupted, "I knew I was right about LDOs and you, Lee. I'm glad you decided to take the job." With that he shook my hand, and I found myself walking aft on the main deck after departing his cabin, wondering just "how the hell" I had "volunteered" myself into this situation.

Later, while having coffee with the chief engineer in the wardroom, I mentioned what had transpired. Gentle Ben burst out laughing and told me, "When Bill Reed sets his mind on something the person involved might as well capitulate, because he's going to do what the Old Man wants regardless of his own desires." I relieved LCDR Jim Loadwick as first lieutenant on 4 March 1983, and a week later, assumed duties as Regular Overhaul Coordinator.

Photo 19-4

LTJG Mike Cameron wearing a few of his many ribbons.
USS *Roanoke* (AOR-7) Western Pacific 1984-1985 cruise book

Six officers worked for me in Deck. In addition to my extremely competent Bos'n, Tom Adair, I had five "stars" in Dwight Beltz, Al Hensley, Mike Cameron, Joe Murphy, and Jim Sass. Mike Cameron was our resident "Hit Man." If you had a problem you wanted squared away asap, you sent for Mike. He had been an enlisted soldier in Special Forces, a true "Green beret" and the Army's Soldier of the Year, before later accepting a commission as an ensign in the Navy. He was so heavily decorated with U.S. and foreign awards, he looked like a walking advertisement for a John Wayne movie. Mike, whether in action with women or in karate demonstrations, was simply awesome.

Near the end of overhaul, almost continuous testing, adjusting, re-testing and certifying of equipment was ongoing as we prepared to leave the shipyard. Finally, early one foggy San Francisco morning, *Roanoke* slowly slid away from the pier and glided out into the main channel. Once headed fair, our course carried us underneath the Oakland Bay Bridge and the Golden Gate Bridge as we threaded our way through the ubiquitous sailboats to open ocean and the commencement of sea trials. Our trials went so well, we returned to the Bay three days later, and tied up at Alameda Naval Air Station, rather than returning to the shipyard. There were still numerous small glitches requiring correction, however, by and large, *Roanoke* was ready to operate.

Photo 19-5

Being promoted to lieutenant commander by Captain William Reed, with the executive officer, Commander Kevin Cummings, standing behind the commanding officer. Author's collection

NEW COMMANDING OFFICER

Photo 19-6

Rear Adm. Robert Toney aboard the ammunition ship USS *Flint*, circa 1986-1987. He is accompanied by CDR Kenneth Slaght, her commanding officer.
USS *Flint* (AE-32) Western Pacific 1986-1987 cruise book

Captain Reed left *Roanoke* to become commander, Service Group Two, and into my life came a man who was to have a profound impact both professionally and personally. Captain (later RADM) Robert Lee Toney was the ultimate UNREPPER. He served with distinction as the executive officer of the *Wichita* (AOR-1), successfully commanded the *Kiska* (AE-35), then served as chief staff officer for commander, Service Group One. Now he would command *Roanoke*, and be one of the very first Service Force officers to achieve flag rank.

Subsequent to *Roanoke*, Toney became deputy commander, Naval Surface Force Pacific, and then dual-hatted as commander, Naval Base San Francisco, and commander, Service Group One. In the latter role, he spearheaded the effort that resulted in the people of San Francisco voting to allow the battleship *Missouri* to be homeported in the Bay Area. He went on to become the head of all Security and Logistics for the U.S. commander in chief, Pacific (USCincPac) command in Hawaii.

I learned, early on, that Captain Toney wanted positive results, officers that would solve problems on their own as they arose (keeping him informed of course), and he wanted winners. If you didn't fit that mold you didn't hang around long. Under Captain Reed, we had been skilled and professional operators. *Roanoke* now quickly became the UNREP ship to emulate. One example of this was her performance in the culminating event of Refresher Training.

Navy Refresher Training is a lengthy, grueling, comprehensive examination of a ship and her crew, required as part of pre-deployment certification and training. West Coast ships undergo this training and inspection in San Diego and adjacent waters. At that time, East Coast ships underwent the same at GTMO (Guantanamo, Cuba). Failure of key milestones could result in the officers responsible being "relieved for cause" (fired), up to and including the ship's commanding officer if identified problems were not quickly corrected.

The culminating Major Conflagration exercise was the single most important event during Refresher Training. As a result of some manner of simulated attack, the ship would suffer heavy personnel and equipment casualties. As the crew began to make headway reacting to this catastrophe, damage and casualties would continue to mount until they were either overwhelmed or, collectively, rose to the occasion.

Roanoke's exceptional success in Refresher Training drew specific praise from commander, Naval Surface Force, Pacific; subordinate commander, Training Group, Pacific; and commander, Fleet Training Group. Deck Department and aviation were noted as outstanding overall. While in transit up the coast back to Alameda, I decided to request augmentation to the unrestricted line. Transiting from the Limited Duty Officer community to being an unrestricted line officer was a necessary prerequisite to any possibility that I might gain selection to command a Navy ship.

ADDITIONAL PREDEPLOYMENT EVOLUTIONS

After catching our breath, *Roanoke* began operating in earnest, while still preparing to deploy to WestPac and the Indian Ocean. We rearmed and reprovisioned the carriers *Enterprise* (CVN-65), *Carl Vinson* (CVN-70), and *Constellation* (CV-64)—transferring in excess of 2,000 tons of ordnance, 1,000 tons of stores, and over 18 million gallons of fuel without any missteps. Deck Department passed an Aviation Readiness evaluation with zero discrepancies, achieved a score of 99.2 percent in the 3-M Inspection (related to maintenance performance, management and reporting), and completed Nuclear Weapons Refresher Training with no errors. The Personnel Reliability Program (associated with the handling team) was judged especially worthy of note.

Amid this hard work, reenlistment of 75 percent of eligible first-term sailors, and 100 percent of second term personnel and careerists, evidenced high department morale. With everything else going on during this hectic period, I was able to qualify as a Tactical Action Officer (TAO) and fulfill those duties, among others, during four major fleet exercises including RIMPAC-84.

Photo 19-7

Photograph at left depicts a Phalanx Close-in Weapon System (Vulcan 20mm gun) aboard the guided missile destroyer USS *King* (DLG-13).
National Archives photograph #K-102265
At right, a Sea Sparrow missile launched from the carrier USS *Nimitz* (CVN-68) to destroy an incoming target drone, during pre-deployment training.
Naval History and Heritage Command photograph #L55-17.02.07

A tactical action officer is responsible for the weapons, sensors, and propulsion of a ship or group of ships in the absence of the captain. The TAO has the same authority to maneuver and defend against an enemy threat as the captain, if the captain is unavailable to assess the situation and take action. Qualification/designation as a TAO by one's commanding officer is a prerequisite for selection for command. Of the three principal requirements—OOD, EOOW, and TAO—Tactical Action Officer is normally achieved last, and signifies great trust in an officer's judgement, and knowledge of weapons employment and rules of engagement.

Being a Service Force ship (and not a cruiser, destroyer, or frigate), we did not have 5-inch gun mounts or long-range missiles. We did have a NATO Sea Sparrow missile system and two Phalanx Close-In-Weapons-Systems (CIWS). In addition to my duty, when on watch, to order "batteries released" if necessary, the day-to-day maintenance and upkeep of these weapon systems was also my responsibility. I thought they should be assigned to the Operations Department rather than Deck, and this convention eventually occurred.

CHANGE OF COMMAND
When we finally returned to Alameda, we plunged into preparations for a change of command. Captain Toney had been selected for rear admiral and would be relieved by Captain Rick Holly. As we worked at rigging the ship and dressing her out for the big event, I was ecstatic to learn that, not only had my request for augmentation been approved, I had also successfully screened for Executive Officer Afloat, a major hurdle for an unrestricted line surface warfare officer.

The change of command went flawlessly. The usually fickle Bay Area weather came through with an absolutely gorgeous day with hardly any wind, and *Roanoke* sparkled and shone as though she had just been commissioned. Captain Ralph Brown, commander, Service Group One, and the former CO of the *Kansas City* (AOR-3), was the guest speaker. Near the end of the ceremony, Captain Brown, until that moment Captain Toney's superior, removed the skipper's shoulder boards and replaced them with those of a one-star commodore.

The Navy had eliminated the rank of commodore (1-star admiral) after World War II, and promoted captains were jumped up to rear admiral (2-stars). The rank of commodore admiral (1-star) was enacted in 1982, but short lived, replaced by rear admiral (lower half). Two-star admirals were then rear admiral (upper half). Commodore is the title of a Navy captain commanding a squadron of ships.

Captain Brown then stepped back and saluted Rear Admiral Toney, signifying that the position of boss had irrevocably changed.

WANING TIME ABOARD
With Rick Holley in the captain's chair, *Roanoke* continued to charge aggressively. Under Captain Toney's leadership and direction, *Roanoke* earned every departmental excellence award and the Battle Efficiency Award. The latter signified that *Roanoke* was judged by our commodore to be the most "battle ready" ship in Service Group One. Our high level continued, as the ship completed all required training and inspections with high marks.

After participation in READIEX 84-4 and FLEETEX 85, Phase I, exercises in which the ship was lauded by the flag officers in charge, *Roanoke* returned to the San Francisco Bay. At Anchorage 12, we loaded ammunition for deployment. *Roanoke* then proceeded to Alameda for one final weekend in port. I drove to San Diego to spend time with Nida, our infant son Bo, and my mom, before returning to Alameda. Just before leaving the ship to drive home, I received news that I had been selected for command at sea and was now the prospective commanding Officer of USS *Excel* (MSO-439). I was so excited and worked up, I could not sleep while in San Diego.

Photo 19-8

Liberty ship SS *Henry Bergh* wrecked in the rugged Farallon Islands, 1 June 1944. National Archives photograph #80-G-236262

When I got back to the ship late Sunday night, orders were waiting for me, detaching me in October 1984. On Monday, we sailed on schedule, rendezvousing with the rest of the *Carl Vinson* Battle Group shortly after clearing the Farallon Islands, off the coast of San Francisco. Formed up, we headed west, and worked on perfecting our group operations. By the time the battle group reached Hawaii, the ships were a closely integrated team and humming to perfection. I left the ship there and flew home, having been relieved of my duties by LT Rick Golden, an old time LDO unrepper.

20

Pre-Command Training

Photo 20-1

Navy Surface Warfare Officers School building in Newport, Rhode Island.
Naval History and Heritage Command photograph #NH 65561-KN

When I got back to California after detaching from *Roanoke*, I took a lengthy leave in San Diego to spend overdue time with family. Then, I kissed them goodbye once again, and drove across country to Newport, Rhode Island—home of the "Surface Fleet's schoolhouse." I was there to attend the Prospective Commanding Officer's Course conducted at the Surface Warfare Officers School Command.

There were twelve of us; three captains, eight commanders, and one lone lieutenant commander, me. I arrived to snow on Thursday, 17 January 1985, and left in snow on 23 February 1985. I don't mind the cold, so snow was fine with me. The senior officers providing our instruction were the "cream of the crop" and I found the curriculum exciting and challenging.

Captain Phil Coady was the director of both the Prospective Commanding Officer and Executive Officer courses. Ordered to command of an "Aegis" (*Ticonderoga*-class) cruiser, he later achieved Flag Rank. His assistant, Capt. Don Dyer, had previously commanded several ships, including the destroyer *Mooseburger* (DD-980) during the invasion of Grenada in 1983. Dryer succeeded Coady, and went on to command a destroyer squadron. Captain Bud Weeks replaced Dyer, and he commanded a destroyer tender. Commander Tom Danaher, one of our instructors, skippered a *Cimarron*-class oiler after leaving the training command. They were all standouts who knew the subject matter cold. They gave freely of their time, vast knowledge, and experiences, and I did my best to take it all in.

No matter what type of ship we'd been ordered to, a staff member had served in one as either an XO or CO. This intimate knowledge was quite beneficial to us. In addition to classroom work, we went aboard ships to correlate the classroom instruction with the way fleet units were doing business. We were also required to demonstrate our seamanship and shiphandling skills, as well as night navigation prowess aboard Yard Patrol Craft (YP).

Photo 20-2

Setting sun silhouettes the masts of yard patrol craft moored at piers near Luce Hall, Naval War College, Newport, Rhode Island, September 1971.
National Archives photograph #K-90661

Driving the YP was a piece of cake for me as was the navigational check. These two events were the fun part of the course. As for visiting the fleet units, I thought that portion of the curriculum was well worth the effort. Overall, the school was outstanding, and I know what I learned in the PCO Course stood me in good stead in my command tour. When it ended on a cold, blustery, and snowy Friday, I packed my truck, left Newport in my rearview mirror, and headed south down the coast. Two days later, I arriving in Charleston, South Carolina. The naval station hosted the commander, Mine Warfare Command and associated facilities, including the U.S. Minewarfare training command.

I was there to attend a high-level mine warfare course. However, I quickly came to believe that the curriculum was more applicable to mine planners than "MSO ship drivers." Some parts were pertinent to my needs, at least half was not. For those en route to a Mine Division or Mine Group staff job, the curriculum was likely of great importance. At the invitation of the officer in charge of the course, I spent considerable time outside of class designing a course I thought would be more beneficial to a CO of a minesweeper. I never learned if my ideas were adopted, but they seemed to be well received. While I paid attention in class and did all work assigned, I was eager to get to *Excel*.

Hanging out with a chief boatswain's mate from *Samuel Gompers* helped the time pass more quickly. After learning that my shipmate had retired and settled down near Charleston, Manuel Gomez and I spent weekends talking Navy and drinking beer. (His wife graciously allowed this.) These interludes did wonders for me. I woke up one Thursday morning, and realized we only had a half-day of school left, and then I could be on my way. Upon completion, I wasted little time. By late evening, I was well into Texas and headed west. Mid-afternoon Saturday, I rolled into our driveway in San Diego. It was great to be home again. No more school. Now it was time to perform.

U.S. Mine Force Motto
(Pride in opening the seas for the Fleet)
Where the fleet goes, we've been

USS *Excel* (MSO-439) memorabilia: older and newer version jacket patches, above, and a commemorative letter envelope, below.

21

Command of *Excel*

Photo 21-1

U.S. Atlantic Fleet Change of Command Ceremony aboard the battleship USS *Wyoming*, circa 16 September 1914, probably at the New York Navy Yard. Rear Admiral Charles J. Badger is at right, reading his orders as he turns command over to Rear Admiral Frank Friday Fletcher (right center). Looking on (in left center) is Rear Admiral Bradley A. Fiske, aide for operations to the Secretary of the Navy.
Naval History and Heritage Command photograph #NH 95153

Every Surface Warfare Officer aspires to command at sea. It is the ultimate achievement and nothing eclipses it. When I was selected for early command as a Lieutenant Commander, I was one of only twenty-two such officers (and the only Mustang) Navy-wide. Rarefied atmosphere to be sure, and I was grateful for being included in that exclusive group.

I reported to *Excel* on 17 April 1985 and she almost immediately stood out of San Francisco Bay. We proceeded southward to take part in a mine exercise off the Monterey Peninsula with several other minesweepers (MSOs). CDR John Scott, who I was scheduled to relieve as commanding officer, welcomed me, and told his crew to assist me in learning the ship. For six days, I was into everything, trying to absorb as much as I could about the minesweeper, and her officers and crew, before taking over from John.

Photo 21-2

Ocean minesweeper USS *Excel* (MSO-439) under way in San Francisco Bay, mid-1980s. Author's collection

It was rougher than a cob while we were under way, but I was happy to be at sea. It felt wonderful to have a deck rolling under my feet once again, while seeing the ship operate and perform her unique mission. We returned to Naval Supply Center, Oakland, where *Excel* and sister ship *Gallant* (MSO-489) berthed. A grand "Hail and Farewell" party was held on the Friday night preceding the Saturday morning, 27 April 1985, change of command. This event honors those departing from a ship and thanks them for their service. At the same time, it welcomes those who are joining, and helps to build camaraderie and esprit de corps.

Saturday dawned bright and beautiful. It was an absolutely glorious sunny day, with azure blue sky and no wind to speak of. I was very proud as I looked out over the audience, confident in my own abilities, but awed by the responsibilities I was about to assume. Admiral Toney was among the guests seated on the pier, and I was gratified that he had found time to attend. My wife Nida, son Bo, and mother Dorothy were also there, of course, smiling and taking it all in. As music from the San Francisco Navy Band filled the air, the dignitaries involved in the formal ceremony filed onto the fo'c'sle of *Excel*, which served as a raised platform above the guests and crew on the pier below.

Chaplain Schuster preceded Commodore Tom York (commander, Mine Group One), followed by CDR Peter Milcovich (commander, Mine Division Five Two), CDR John Scott (commanding officer, USS *Excel*), and myself. Navy Regulations stipulate certain formalities that must be adhered to during a change in command ceremony—in which total responsibility, authority, and accountability for a Navy ship passes from one officer to another.

Photo 21-3

LCDR Foley reading an award prior to presentation to a member of the crew of the ocean minesweeper *Excel* (MSO-439). Author's collection

Such events begin when all hands are called to quarters. When the executive officer reports that the crew is assembled, the commanding officer and his relief proceed to the ceremonial area. If the departing officer wishes to say a few words, this is the proper time. After a brief speech, he or she then faces forward and reads the orders of detachment to the officers and crew, then steps back. The new commanding officer steps forward and reads his or her orders, then faces about, and salutes their predecessor and states, "I relieve you, sir" or "I relieve you, ma'am." If the commodore of the squadron or group of which the ship is a part is present, applicable verbal reports are then made to him or her.

The new commanding officer may or may not give a short talk to the assembled officers and crew, but is required to state that all standing orders will remain in effect. The new captain then turns and orders the executive officer to continue with ship's routine. This ends the ceremony.

Our ceremony followed this order. After parading of the Colors and the National Anthem, Chaplain Schuster gave the invocation. Commodore York, as guest speaker, then made his prepared remarks, followed by Commander Milcovich. The latter individual, as commander, Mine Division 52, was responsible to York for both *Excel* and *Gallant*. Next, John Scott gave his farewell speech then reluctantly, I'm sure, read his orders detaching him from command of *Excel*, and ordering him to the *Kansas City* (AOR-3) as executive officer. At conclusion, he turned to me and said, "I'm ready to be relieved." I read my orders, also made a few remarks, faced John, saluted, and said, "I relieve you, sir." We then both turned, faced Commodore York, saluted, and reported our relief and assumption of command, respectively. I was now the commanding officer.

As is tradition, *Excel*'s commissioning pennant was presented to Commander Scott, the chaplain gave the benediction, the Colors were retired, and we, the official party, repaired to the captain's cabin to rid ourselves of our swords. We then signed the appropriate logs and papers, had some pictures taken, and got ready for a reception at the Navy and Marine Corps Museum on the Treasure Island Naval Station. With my chest bursting with pride, I affixed the Command at Sea pin on the right front of my uniform, and watched from the corner of my eye as John sadly shifted his to the left. The relative position signifies whether the wearer is currently in command, or was previously so.

On Monday morning, I walked up *Excel*'s brow and was "rung aboard" for the first time. Two strikes of the ship's bell (Bong, Bong) preceded the announcement "*EXCEL* arriving," followed by a single strike (Bong), as I stepped onto the quarterdeck. By this means, the officers and crew of a ship know when their captain has arrived. Bong, Bong, "*EXCEL* departing," Bong, would occur each time I left the ship. An Absentee pennant fluttering from the mast informs all within eyesight when a ship's captain is not on board. Such hauled down, means the captain is present.

OFFICERS AND CREW

Shortly after I was settled in my cabin with fresh coffee, the executive officer showed up. Lieutenant Davis Bourne was a tall, slender South Carolinian who had matriculated at the Citadel (the Military College of South Carolina). He thoroughly understood the intricacies of MCM operations, was well thought of by the squadron staff, knew *Excel* thoroughly, and was a superior shiphandler. I told him how pleased I was to have a hard-charging young officer as my XO, then asked him to gather the officers in the wardroom for a "meet and greet session." I followed this up with a similar meeting with the Chiefs. After lunch I met with the enlisted men on the fantail. During this process, I concluded there was a wealth of talent on board.

As is common in the Fleet, during my tour aboard *Excel* old hands periodically departed, replaced by fresh new faces. I hope that readers will indulge an old officer citing some of my crew who were there at the start or later joined the ship. "The Wardroom" (collective term for the officers assigned to a ship) was comprised of members from a variety of commissioning sources. I've already mentioned Davis. Ensign Ken James, the Operations Officer, was a Naval Academy graduate; LTJG Tony Meadors, Chief Engineer, came from the NROTC unit at the University of Illinois; while Ensigns Walt Steele and Dave Bruhn (the First Lieutenant/MCM Officer, and the Damage Control Assistant/Supply Officer, respectively) received their commissions via Officer Candidate School. Dave, like myself, was a Mustang officer. Interestingly, before completing his enlistment and returning to college, he'd served with Chief Litton (discussed shortly) aboard the destroyer *Leftwich* (DD-984).

In addition to this group of fairly young, but enthusiastic officers, we also had a small group of seasoned "weekend warriors." *Excel* was a Reserve Training ship, and the officers who drilled aboard her were all winners, and well they should be. A decade or so earlier, the officer in charge of the Reserve Center in Sacramento had created a Mine Force Support Group, which existed for only one year. This officer then took command of the Inactive Ship's Maintenance Facility at Treasure Island. He recruited reservists from Sacramento who began providing services to MSOs and, then still existing, MCSs (smaller coastal minesweepers). Some of these reservists were later "handpicked" a second time to drill aboard the "sweeps."

LCDR Jim "Crusher" Crossen was the SelRes (Selective Reserve) unit coordinator, LCDR Kirk Levendahl (a nuclear submariner working on his PhD in physics at U.C. Berkeley) carried out engineering duties, and CWO4 Gil Houston was the Combat Information Center officer. For a Chief Warrant Machinist (and former enlisted submariner), such duty might appear incongruent, but Houston was a broadcast engineer for various radio stations, and he could fix anything. Houston would drill aboard *Excel* for nearly twenty years. Commander Milcovich was the Reserve commodore, and CDR Spencer Hipps, his chief of staff.

In the "Goat Locker" (Chiefs Quarters), Senior Chief Electrician's Mate Glenn Berglund was both the senior enlisted engineer and the Command Senior Chief. My peerless Chief Hull Technician Rodney Litton was a superior leader, firefighter extraordinaire, and carpenter (an indispensable person on a wooden ship). Litton was a true "old salt." His first ship in the Navy had been the USS *Hewell* (AG-145), depicted as USS *Reluctant* (AK-601), "the Bucket," in the 1955 film *Mr. Roberts*. *Hewell*, the former unnamed Army freight ship *FS-391*, had been commissioned in the Navy after World War II, and it offered interesting duty. Litton recalled her cargo hold having served as crew berthing, with no interior passageways leading to or from it. On occasions when the seas were too dangerous to be on deck, sailors in berthing remained there. Those wanting to sleep, found rest elsewhere.

Photo 21-4

Light cargo ship USS *Hewell* (AKL-14) at anchor, circa 1951-1953. Naval History and Heritage Command photograph #NH 105033-KN

And we had still more Chiefs. Small ship duty, which offers great responsibility, can provide associated advancement opportunities. Bob Buenavista, in concert with Stan Howard (his Reserve counterpart), kept our vintage Packard engines humming. "Doc" Aguinaga provided superb medical care, and carried out myriad collateral assignments. Riefke was our Reserve Personnelman. Chief Storekeeper Black probably lost a lot of hair trying to keep me out of trouble regarding usage of ship's funds. His wife Dianne was our ombudsman, the link between myself and the wives of crewmembers. "Guns," Ralph Henney, an extremely young chief gunner's mate, also served as the ship's Chief Master at Arms ("policeman").

On a small ship, every crewmember, regular and reserve, served a critical purpose. Without those mentioned below and many others (which space doesn't allow naming), *EXCEL* would not have lived up to her name. They were all magnificent. QM1 Richard Husted was the best quartermaster I ever saw during my career. In fact, his navigational skills far surpassed those of some commissioned officers serving primarily as navigators. YN1 Chip Featheringham was as "big and bad" as a boatswain's mate, and could type faster than any yeoman I had ever seen, error-free at that. He was extremely versatile and absolutely dependable.

ET1 Gene Legler was as strong a leader as he was an outstanding electronics technician. MS1 Jun Miranda was perfection personified, a superb cook and mess management specialist. EN1 Leo Baclig, a quiet individual and great engineman, achieved the distinction of becoming a certified Pacific Fleet diesel inspector while aboard *Excel*. Few Chiefs ever achieve this level of expertise, and almost never a First Class Petty Officer. EN1 Craig Wendt was also a notable "wrench" (engineer) and *Excel's* answer to John Rambo. HT1 Brent Choate was an excellent hull technician, and a strong second to Chief Litton. BM1 (SW) Brooks advanced from seaman to chief boatswain's mate in the Mine Warfare Community. He forgot more about "Sweeps" than any of us will ever know, and was absolutely committed to the job at hand. Who else would hand their 5-year old child some rags, while aboard the ship in port, and have them wipe up an otherwise inaccessible puddle of oil, beneath the sweep winch reel?

Talent was just as deep in the lower ranks. BM2 David Garrigus was an exceptional boatswain's mate and leader. His marlinspike and deck seamanship skills were absolutely superior. SM2 Hansen was a master of many trades in addition to those of a signalman. QM2 Pat Conkright was the Reserve counterpart to Dick Husted. STG3 Clint Roney kept our sonar "up on step." MS2 Revives was a cook's cook, who elevated his rating to an art. SKSN John Mantey managed supply parts, and was (along with Husted and Hansen) a Quartermaster of the Watch on the bridge. EN2 Greg Hopkins was indispensable in the main engine room. EN3 Eric Leary was a hard-charging engineman who could always be counted on to do his best. IC3 Allen was a highly knowledgeable interior communication electrician whose gear was "always up." FN Joe Hernandez was a special sailor and a tremendous asset to the ship.

RMSN Levesque was courteous and exceedingly professional as a radioman and in everything else. He was also one of the strongest, if not the strongest man aboard, having been a competitive weightlifter before entering the Navy. Formerly a member of Deck Force, when told that aboard sailing ships of old, with very tough crews, one of the principal qualifications to becoming Chief Mate (second in command) was the ability to beat up every other man aboard, he quipped "in that case, I should be in charge, not BM1 Brooks."

RETURN TO MONTEREY

Photo 21-5

Aerial view of the town of Monterey and harbor, 11 September 1942.
National Archives #80-G-10969

I spent the rest of my first week as CO roaming the ship and talking to the men. You sure as hell can't learn what's going on if you sequester yourself in your cabin, and are not out and about. I tried not to bother the crew as they went about their duties, but made it a point to say a few words here and there. When you take care of your people, and they know you really care, they'll take care of you.

Our first time back at sea was the return to Monterey, to participate with two other ships in festivities for Armed Forces Day. I had the XO get us under way so I could observe how to use the pitch and propellers and rudders to conn the ship. We got under way smoothly and proceeded out of the Bay and south down the coast, arriving at Monterey without incident. The Monterey Peninsula is a beautiful place to visit and the residents are very friendly. The ships' crews were feted and shown a great time. I visited Carmel on a Sunday morning, and had brunch at the Hog's Breath Inn; owned by Clint Eastwood. The commanding officers called on the president of the Naval Postgraduate school, as well as local dignitaries, while our respective crews enjoyed liberty. At the conclusion of this visit, *Excel* returned to the Bay Area to prepare for a sixty-day cruise to Alaska.

Photo 21-6

Drawing of Astoria on the Columbia River by Alfred T. Agate, circa 1840. Naval History and Heritage Command accession #98-089-GK

Our schedule called for participating in a MINEX (Mine Exercise) with *Enhance* and *Gallant* off Astoria, Oregon. At completion, we were to proceed up the coast to Seattle, the headquarters of commander,

Mine Group One. Following necessary briefings, we would set out across the Gulf of Alaska to Ketchikan, and then visit Juneau, Anchorage, and Kodiak. At the conclusion of our Alaskan adventure, we were to return to Oakland with a short stop in Seattle on the way. I should explain that *Enhance* was a Seattle minesweeper. Of the nine Pacific Fleet MSOs, two were based in San Diego (*Pluck* and *Constant*), two in the San Francisco Bay area (*Gallant* and *Excel*), and the other five (*Pledge*, *Implicit*, *Esteem*, *Enhance* and *Conquest*) in the Seattle/Tacoma area.

When we joined the other MSOs off Astoria, I had no thought that we might become involved in a Search and Rescue (SAR) mission. The waters off the mouth of the Columbia River are always rough and crossing the bar to tie up in Astoria is an experience in itself. In any event, a large fishing boat capsized while plying its trade off the Oregon coast and the Coast Guard asked the MSOs to assist in SAR efforts. Eventually, we sadly recovered the body of one victim, which we turned over to the Coast Guard. My crew, unsolicited, "adopted" this man's two sons as honorary crew members and took up a collection, which (along with a letter I penned to his wife and a picture of *Excel* signed by everyone) was sent to the family in an attempt to express our sympathy and compassion. The wife and sons eventually visited *Excel*, an event that was very emotional for all concerned.

Photo 21-7

Commander, Mine Group One, conference at Seattle Washington, 2-3 May 1985. Author's collection

Our SAR mission completed, we proceeded to Seattle where a most enjoyable weekend was spent. Commodore York hosted a party at his home for the commanding officers and we had a great time. Tom and his gracious wife, Luci, were the consummate hosts and guests were made to feel at home. They lived in large quarters at Sand Point that had a breathtaking view of Puget Sound.

ALASKAN WATERS

Our brief visit over, seven minesweepers sailed from Seattle bound for the great Alaskan wilderness. In company were *Excel, Enhance, Gallant, Pledge, Implicit, Conquest,* and *Esteem*. Commander, Mine Division Five One was initially embarked in *Implicit*, but spent time aboard *Conquest* and *Esteem* as well. Commander Mine Division Five Two was in *Excel* for most of the cruise, but also rode *Gallant*.

While transiting the Gulf of Alaska bound for Ketchikan, we encountered conditions so bad, rigid protocols for ship-to-ship communications were abandoned. In the height of this gale, as *Excel* lost hull-sheathing to wind and wave, a P-250 firefighting pump was torn from the fo'c'sle of another MSO, and a third MSO ingested sea water, "Fuck it, just fuck this shit, let's turn around," came over the bridge radio. "If we try to turn around, we'll broach," quickly followed. The worst possible case in heavy seas is to turn beam to the waves. This is called broaching, which can capsize a vessel if the waves are large enough. As succeeding waves strike, and a ship rolls back a shorter arc each time, eventually, if nothing changes, it may roll completely over and sink. We lost electrical power and steering.

It's important to emphasize here, that the engineering team which I praised earlier, did not yet exist. After the Vietnam War (in which minesweepers cleared mines from Haiphong Harbor, North Vietnam, as a condition for the release of American prisoners of war), the Navy had transferred MSOs returning to the West Coast to the Reserve Force. Crew size was halved, and funding for operations and maintenance dramatically cut. As the years passed, the ships fell into disrepair. This degradation was made worse by the exemption of MSOs from such things as Refresher Training. Why find problems for which there was no budgeted funding to address?

Things began to improve, a year or so before I reported to *Excel*. Hot spots in the world had increased Navy awareness of the importance of mine warfare, but not by much. More importantly, commander, Mine Squadron Five (later re-designated Mine Group One), successfully lobbied the Navy to deploy eight of the nine Pacific Fleet MSOs for the first time since the Vietnam War. The ships met in San Francisco, and sailed together to Hawaii to participate in RIMPAC (Rim of the Pacific), an exercise involving ships from Allied countries.

At completion, five of the MSOs returned home. *Excel*, *Esteem*, and *Enhance* proceeded north to Adak, Alaska, and then hopped home, visiting other Alaskan ports. *Excel* was the only MSO of the group to still have Packard engines. The others had Waukashas, necessitated by Packard going out of business decades earlier, and the associated challenges in obtaining necessary parts. These wants resulted in the squadron diesel inspector riding *Excel*, should she break down and need on-the-spot expertise and assistance.

Returning to the present, I took the conn and attempted to keep *Excel* from sinking as she went "beam to" into the gale-force winds and seas. For almost an hour, we fought the ship and the elements before electrical power was finally restored and we were able to get headed fair. While we were in this situation, the other Sweeps circled *Excel* like wolves around a dying stag, except in this case they were standing by to render assistance or initiate rescue operations if necessary. Everything I did was sort of automatic, based on many years of sea duty experience. When I finally turned over the conn, I noticed the bridge watch team going through their motions with stunned looks on their faces. I told them they had done a magnificent job, then left the bridge and went down to my cabin, locked the door, and heaved my guts out.

The other "close call" took place late at night with all of the MSOs operating in close proximity to each other. I had just left the bridge to use the head, after telling the XO to keep a close eye on things and I would be right back. Wouldn't you know, that during my brief absence, we again lost all electrical power, this time in pitch-black darkness. With all our lights out, and having to steer by engines while trying to avoid the other ships, it was dicey at best. I ran to the bridge with my heart in my throat, and found Davis backing full to avoid colliding with *Implicit*, while simultaneously directing sailors with bullhorns on each bridge wing to tell other ships to stand clear. We got power back within twenty minutes and resumed normal operations. I had absolutely no doubt that Davis' quick actions and presence of mind saved *Excel*. I awarded him the Navy Achievement Medal, which was upheld by higher authority.

There were no more major incidents, and *Excel* went about her mission of visiting ports, conducting MCM operations and training, and preparing for a Supply Management Inspection (SMI). The SMI is difficult to pass for Supply Corps officers, let alone an ensign who was also the Damage Control Assistance. Dave Bruhn was up to the task. Aggressive, meticulous, and people-oriented, his efforts and those of his sailors resulted in *Excel* qualifying for the Blue "E" Departmental Award signifying Supply Excellence. We later became commander, Naval Surface Force Pacific Fleet's sole nominee for the Alfred Ney Award for Best Small Mess Afloat. We were a "good feeder."

Photo 21-8

Heavy cruiser USS *Louisville* (CA-28) at Ketchikan, Alaska, in 1938.
Naval History and Heritage Command photograph #NH 92600

Not to be outdone, Deck Department got into the act. *Excel* had never been able to find the opportunity, or make time, to successfully moor to a buoy, an annual required exercise that all ships must complete. Now in a calm, back-water cove where we had ostensibly gone to do some serious fishing, Walt Steele and his boatswain's mates fabricated a buoy that we could use to conduct the exercise. The entire evolution was executed flawlessly, and we were able to capture each sequence on film. These pictures were later forwarded to the Group, which not only gave us credit for completion, but also commended Deck Department for its ingenuity in fabricating a working buoy.

JUNEAU, ALASKA

Every port we visited boasted something unique. Kodiak has the largest grizzly bears in the world, Anchorage displays its cosmopolitan demeanor side by side with Alaska of the Gold Rush days, Ketchikan shares its remote wilderness appearance, and Juneau is the Capital of Alaska. If wondering what Alaska of yore looked like, Juneau serves as a good example. Surrounded by high mountains, wooden cabins dotting their sides, and with ubiquitous seaplanes taking off and landing in the mirror-like bay, the city offers a quaint downtown area with the world-famous Red Dog Saloon. Here, practically in the center of the Land of the Midnight Sun, I would gaze at Juneau in the early morning.

Alaska captured my mind and soul, and I vowed to return some day. Many years later, my family and I did just that, and lived in Alaska for close to ten years.

Photo 21-9

Destroyer USS *Dallas* (DD-199) noses her bow toward Juneau, 1937.
Naval History and Heritage Command photograph #NH 109568

KODIAK, ALASKA

While the minesweepers were in Kodiak, Commodore York flew up to visit his little wooden armada. He would ride one of us to Anchorage and then fly back to Seattle. *Excel* was chosen for the first leg. In transit, the commodore made it a practice to retire to the XO's stateroom after lunch to let his meal settle. As we plied our way to Anchorage, the weather deteriorated. York was an old salt from way back and had been riding Sweeps since he was a LTJG, so he thought nothing of the weather and went to the XO's stateroom (employed as Commodore quarters), after lunch, as usual. When he hadn't made an appearance on the bridge by early-afternoon, I sent the BMOW below to check on him.

When the BMOW arrived at the stateroom, he could hear the commodore yelling, "Get this fucking desk off me." However, the door was jammed and wouldn't open. The hull technicians were called and they succeeded in breaking down the door and entering the stateroom. During some heavy rolls, the bunk in which the commodore was resting had ripped loose from the bulkhead, and overturned. This wouldn't have presented any particular difficulties, except for the fact that a desk had similarly escaped and lodged between the bunk and the door. Of the two apparent options: hope the ship started pitching, to propel the desk forward; or break down the door, the latter seemed most prudent.

Wooden MSOs were sufficiently light they rolled alongside a pier, let alone in a heavy sea. Once liberated, the commodore somewhat regained his sense of humor and helped the HTs put everything back in place. However, I've always harbored the thought that he figured I had somehow planned that little show.

Photo 21-10

Painting *Kodiak Quarters* by William F. Draper, 1942.
Naval History and Heritage Command accession #88-189-C

COMMAND RESPONSIBILITIES

The two most difficult things I had to do while in command were hold Captain's Mast, and replace an officer. Captain's Mast, or just "Mast," is the forum by which a CO dispenses disciplinary action for infractions of Navy Rules and Regulations. I had been the guest of honor at several such as an enlisted sailor, and I did not like holding Mast on a young sailor for the same type of mistakes I had made. When forced to do so, I had the XO schedule Mast late in the afternoon, in order that I could go home immediately after. I emphasized to shipboard leaders that I preferred they handle everything they possibly could. The rest could be adjudicated at Executive Officer's Inquiry or, if a serious offense, then the case could be brought to Mast.

When *Excel* returned from Alaska, we spent about a month in port, during which there was a casualty to a Packard diesel propulsion engine. Packard went out of business in the late 1950s. It was now in the late 1980s and *Excel*, along with some of her sisters, was limping along as best they could. The engine had been out of commission for more than a week and nothing seemed to be happening. The rules say you must submit a Casualty Report within three days if ship's force is unable to fix a piece of broken machinery or equipment in house. I hadn't done this based on advisement the engine would be repaired promptly.

Time passed and finally, at 2200 one night while sitting at home, I'd had enough. I told Nida I needed to go back to the ship. She said she would accompany me, so we seat-belted our sleeping son in the back seat of the car, and drove to Naval Supply Center, Oakland. Nida and Bo remained in the car, while I went aboard. My annoyance turned to anger when I found the quarterdeck completely unmanned. There was no one on watch to ensure security at the ship's access point. A meeting that may have been unpleasant for the chief engineer, would now be worse, because as the Command Duty Officer, he was solely responsible for *Excel* in my absence.

Walking into the wardroom, I found him with his feet up on the table watching television. Following heated preliminaries about the absent quarterdeck watch, I said, "Tell me what the status is on our Number One Main Engine." He was overly casual in response. "Well you know, Captain, we're having trouble finding out the problem, but I'm sure we'll figure it out in a few more days." I then asked him, "Why aren't there any enginemen working on the engine?" He said, "Well, Captain, it's kind of late." By this time, I was ready to explode. I picked up the phone in the wardroom, called Dave Bruhn at home and said, "Dave, this is the captain. I'd like to see you on the ship as soon as possible."

"Aye aye, Captain, I'll be right there," was Dave's response, like it was a normal occurrence to be called back to the ship at almost midnight by the CO. While I waited, I had the chief engineer go find out what was going on with the quarterdeck watch. I sat with a cup of coffee to try to calm down and get my temper under control. As he returned to the wardroom to tell me the quarterdeck watch was reestablished, Dave followed him in, and said, "You wanted to see me, Captain?"

The soon to be ex-chief engineer stood there subdued and pale, as I replied, "Dave, you are now the chief engineer. Number One Main Engine has been down too damn long, and I want it fixed ASAP. Get fucking hot." Without fanfare, he replied, "Aye, aye, sir," turned around, and got on the phone. I got some more coffee, poured a cup for Nida and took it out to the car. Gratified to see that the watch was back on station where they belonged, I returned to the wardroom to see what was happening.

In my short absence, Dave had called most of the enginemen and directed them to report back to the ship forthwith. He had also gotten hold of Chief Sandoval, the Mine Group diesel inspector, at his home, and received some starting pointers. With that much accomplished, I told the former chief engineer that his being relieved of those duties did not negate his responsibilities as the command duty officer. When he acknowledged that directive, I went home for a few hours' sleep.

When I arrived aboard later that morning, I got myself some coffee and went to the engine room. Ten rather grimy enginemen were up to their elbows inside the propulsion engine with smiles on their faces. A radio was playing, there was hot coffee and some pastries nearby, and they were engrossed in their work. Dave was right there with them, and had been so all night since they trooped aboard, leading by example and not relaxing in the wardroom.

When I talked to the XO a little later, he indicated surprise that I would replace one of the department heads without consulting with him first. I merely looked at him and said it was my ship and my call. Three days later, the engine was up, tested satisfactory, and fully operational. I knew, right then, I had hired a winner to head the engineering department. Subsequent events have underscored that belief, over, and over, and over again.

Normally when an officer is removed, or relieved, for cause, he is transferred off the ship. However, I didn't feel that would be in either the former engineer's or *Excel*'s best interests. Instead, I reassigned him as communications officer/supply officer, providing opportunity to redeem himself. Dave's only duty going forward was Chief Engineer; a newly reported officer, Ensign Guy Boney, now being the DCA.

Excel's officers, with the exception of the XO and myself, were all "first tour division officers." At that time, the standard career path for a shipboard officer began was a 24-month division officer tour aboard a ship, followed by an 18-month assignment on a different one. Most officers were then ordered to a couple of years of shore duty, before attending Department Head School. Two department head tours on different ships followed. Davis, my XO, was a second tour division officer, having previously served aboard the *Kalamazoo* (AOR-6).

Shortly after we returned from Alaska, Davis detached and went to recruiting duty in Charleston, South Carolina. His relief was LCDR Jim Taplett, a Naval Academy graduate and the first officer to complete Department Head School prior to reporting to an MSO as XO. Every once in a while, a commanding officer and executive officer's talents, personalities, and abilities blend so perfectly that everything they touch turns to gold. Such a relationship existed between Jim and myself. I was volatile and impetuous, he was steady and serene, I tended to hurry administrative documentation, he crafted and submitted it well before existing deadlines. I had little patience with incompetence, he counseled patience and understanding. Jim Taplett was a Class Act. I owe a debt of gratitude to whatever detailer at the Navy Military Personnel Command assigned him to *Excel*.

Photo 21-11

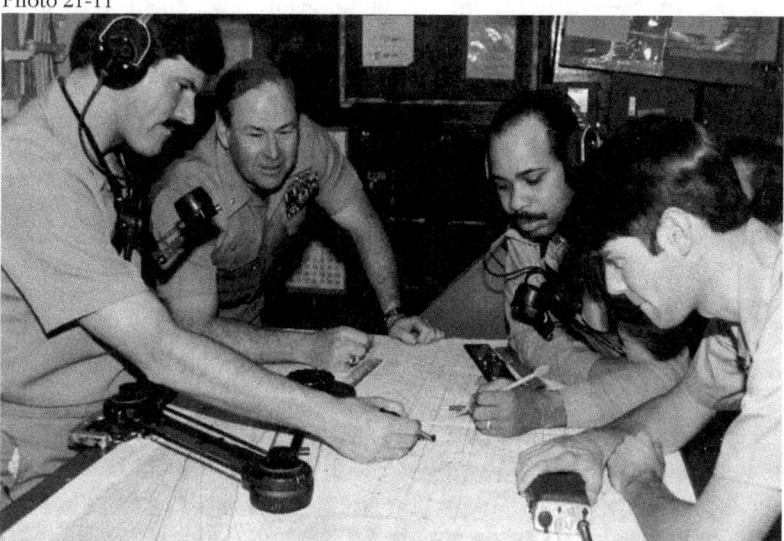

Action in *Excel*'s Combat Information Center during a mine exercise. Jim Taplett (far left) and OS1 Brown (second from right) are plotting, while Chris Trombetta (far right) observes, ready to provide bearing and range information updates to a Zodiac boat carrying a mock explosive slung beneath it for simulated drill mine destruction.
Courtesy of QM1 Richard Husted

DRIVING THE SHIP

The most exciting and fun part of my command tour was driving *Excel*. She could pivot on a dime, was very forgiving of error, and responded like a thoroughbred to every demand. I probably conned (maneuvered the ship via helm and rudder orders) more than I should have, because I reveled in handling her. I conned from the bridge, wings, forward of the pilot house (below the bridge), fo'c'sle, and fantail. These activities were not "larks." I'd found that standing centerline forward of the pilot house was the best location from which to "point buoys." This term refers to making an approach on a Dan buoy (used to mark channels swept clear of mines), while retrieving it. Bridge wings provide the best vantage point when making an approach to or getting under way from a pier. Conning from the fantail is sometimes useful when streaming or recovering sweep gear in particularly challenging seas.

Photo 21-12

Dan buoy being brought aboard *Excel*. After the ship's bow had been brought close enough alongside a buoy for a boatswain's mate to ensnare it with a grappling hook affixed to a heaving line, the buoy would be walked aft along the main deck, until in position to be lifted aboard by a quarter-crane.
Courtesy of QM1 Richard Husted

I backed into tight places, took *Excel* through locks, spun her around in a space that offered only twenty feet of room at either end, and raced her against another minesweeper. I towed a tug and was, in turn, towed. Finally, I refueled using the conventional astern-method as well as taking her alongside the fleet oiler *Kawishiwi* (AO-146) for UNREPPING via light line.

Photo 21-13

USS *Excel* (MSO-439) en route to Vancouver, British Columbia, Canada, 6 June 1990. Courtesy of NavSource, photograph by Rick Garcia

Prudence, or regulations, sometimes dictated that I take a pilot aboard for a transit, or to enter or leave a port. However, on the one occasion that I allowed a pilot to have the conn, he banged the ship into the pier while trying to clear it at Astoria, Oregon. Strong currents were setting *Excel* on the pier. Our convention was to take in lines 1, 3, and 4, and "spring on line 2," while backing the inboard screw and going ahead on the outboard one. By this means, we could get as far as possible sideways off the pier, before taking in line 2 and backing both engines full. The pilot, reportedly the youngest on the Columbia River, saw no reason to use the mooring line in this manner. His order, "Bring in all lines," preceded our impact with the pier.

After this incident, either I or one of my men drove *Excel* when we had a pilot on board. I qualified the officers, of course, and also some enlisted men, as under way OODs. YN1 Chip Featheringham became the first enlisted sailor in the Mine Group to achieve this honor.

ADOPT A TOWN PROGRAM

While he was commander, Naval Station Treasure Island/commander, Service Group One, Admiral Toney began a program whereby ships and towns in the Bay Area "adopted" each other. He felt this would foster better understanding between the Navy and locals, and provide a means to give back to the communities for their support. He asked that

I "adopt" Antioch, a town of around 110,000 people located along the San Joaquin-Sacramento River Delta in the East Bay.

Jim Taplett contacted local officials in Antioch and arranged for us to sail up the Sacramento River and moor there for a day and night of activities. LT Chris Trombetta, an "Ivy League school" graduate (University of Pennsylvania) and Ken James' replacement as operations officer, assisted Jim with scheduling and planning. We encouraged the crew to bring dependents on our trip upriver, and many did so. Nida and Bo joined me, and greatly enjoyed the experience. As I maneuvered *Excel* alongside the pier in Antioch, Bo watched me closely and listened to my orders. After we were tied up, and I was through with such, he looked at his mom and me, and said, "I want to be a captain, like Dad, so I can stand around and say Very Well."

Photo 21-14

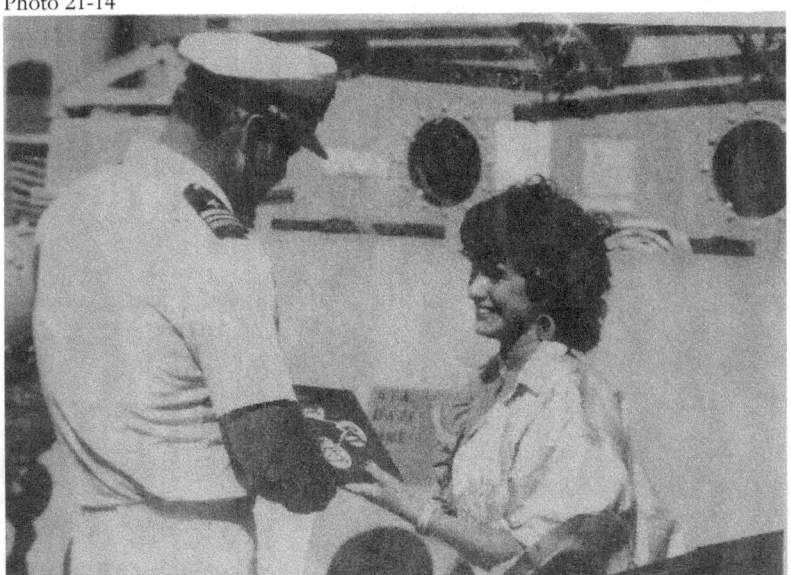

Presentation of an *Excel* plaque to Antioch High School student body president Jennifer Marchetti, during a ship's visit to the San Francisco Bay delta city.
Author's collection

Our trip was a huge success. Congressman George Miller was gracious and other local politicians and dignitaries made us feel very welcome. We exchanged plaques and gifts with Antioch High School and the city, and made many new friends for the Navy. A highlight for Nida was meeting her Uncle Juan. He had retired as president of the Philippine Stock Exchange in Manila and was visiting family members in Antioch. It made for a nice reunion, and allowed for the introduction of some of Nida's family to Bo.

The following day, we thanked everyone for their hospitality, said our goodbyes, then returned down river to the bay, and on to Naval Supply Center, Oakland. I sent a message to Admiral Toney describing the highlights of our visit, and expressing my belief that the program was an outstanding way to integrate the Navy and residents in the Bay Area.

LOCAL OPERATIONS AND VISITS TO FESTIVALS

Photo 21-15

Member of the Navy's Marine Mammal Program.
Eugene H. Buck and Kori Calvert, "Active Military Sonar and Marine Mammals: Events and References," CRS Report for Congress

After returning from Antioch, we spent a couple of weeks conducting local operations and serving briefly as a training support platform for the Navy's Marine Mammal Program. The program was based in San Diego, but worked in different locales, training dolphins and sea lions to locate mines and enemy swimmers in the water. We employed our sonar to track the animals and ensure they were doing what they had been trained to do. It was a change from our normal activities, and a chance for us to become familiar with another type of countermeasures.

PORTLAND ROSE FESTIVAL

Photo 21-16

Heavy cruiser USS *Augusta* (CA-31) at Portland, Oregon, July 1933.
Naval History and Heritage Command photograph #NH 57458

In June 1986, we went to Portland, Oregon for its famous Rose Festival. This annual event is coveted by Navy ships; everyone wants to partake of, arguably, the best liberty on the West Coast. MSOs were ideal candidates for visits to localities involving narrow channels or limited pier space at which to berth. Also, they were economical to operate and had more flexible schedules than ships regularly deployed.

To reach Portland, it was necessary to make a twelve-hour scenic cruise up the winding Columbia River to the city. Separating the states of Washington and Oregon, the river is the chief inland tributary in the Pacific Northwest, with banks so steep in places that ships have in years past taken shelter from storms by mooring to trees. Upon arrival in Portland, Navy ships moor along the river wall in the heart of the city, and their crews set out to enjoy liberty.

Sailors have the opportunity to enjoy a meal in the home of a congenial host or date a local girl, through a program designed to match the interests of sponsors and guests. Many crewmembers, believing they are more likely to win a quiet evening than a hot date, head straight for town. A daytime carnival atmosphere is replaced at night by parties. Much anticipated throughout the year, these social events draw comely attendees from adjacent states as well as local areas.

SEATTLE SEAFAIR

Mid-Summer found us in Seattle, enjoying SEAFAIR, an eight-week celebration of community and all things sea farin'. The festive affair offered a marathon run, as well as various races and competition on the water, and many attractions during the Fleet Week portion. Boat races, community parades, shows, and the magnificent Blue Angels helped make our visit truly memorable.

WORLD EXPOSITION AT VANCOUVER

Photo 21-17

Hospital ship USS *Mercy* (AH-4) entering Vancouver Harbor, 5 August 1931. Naval History and Heritage Command photograph #NH 49831

In August 1986, *Excel* visited Vancouver, British Columbia, as part of the U.S. Navy's representation for the 1986 World EXPO. My wife and son flew up for the gala event and we had a grand time. Dignitaries and Royalty were in attendance, including Prince Charles and Princess Diana, Prime Minister Margaret Thatcher, Vice President George H. W. Bush, and many others. The U.S. Pavilion (one of sixty-five total) was NASA-oriented, highlighting the space race between the United States and the Soviet Union. Also featured were ancient Egyptian artifacts in one pavilion, dinosaur bones in another, and a prototype of a high-speed train that floated on a magnetic track in the Japanese Pavilion. There were plans for building a tunnel to link the U.K. with the rest of Europe (something that is now in place), and famed French oceanographer Jacques Cousteau offered rides aboard his expedition vessel *Alcone*.

Joan Rivers and Liberace were in attendance, as were other international stars. Carte du jour offerings included Czechoslovakian beef goulash, Moravian omelets, a Japanese sushi robot churning out sushi rolls, and Canadian caribou steaks and musk ox burgers. Fast-food lovers could avail themselves of McBarge (McDonald's floating restaurant), and elsewhere, hot dogs, French fries, and cotton candy. Every conceivable type of drink—including beer, wine, hard liquor, water, and milk—was available; musical acts abounded; and rides were everywhere. EXPO had its own monorail that circled the site. If you weren't squeamish you could ride the Scream Machine, a roller coaster with two 360-degree loops and a corkscrew turn. There was so much to see and do, it was easy to quickly become overwhelmed.

RECEIPT OF ORDERS

That autumn, *Excel* began a four-month overhaul at Lake Union in Seattle, for replacement of her Packard engines and wooden mast, and receipt of other upgrades and needed work. One day I received a call from my detailer, asking if I would consider ending my command tour early in the shipyard. I would again be relieving John Scott, this time as Executive Officer of the *Kansas City* (AOR-3). I was not keen to give up the best job in the Navy, but was enticed by *Kansas City*'s operating schedule. She was scheduled to deploy with the *Missouri* Battle Group to the North Arabian Sea and the Persian Gulf in early summer in 1987. Her skipper, Captain Phillip Anselmo (later RADM), was an aviator and associated with the Tomcat (F-14 fighter) Program. I weighed the pros and cons, discussed the situation with Nida, and then decided to accept, which set the stage for a change of command in late October 1986.

As my command tour came to a close, I reflected on everything that *Excel*'s crew had accomplished. We had received every excellence award for which we were eligible. These included the White "M" for minesweeping, Blue "E" for supply management, Green "E" for command and control, White "E" for gunnery, Red "DC" for damage control, and Red "E" for engineering.

Excel was runner-up for the Alfred Ney Award (for Best Small Mess Afloat in the Pacific Fleet), and recipient of the commander in chief, Pacific Fleet, Golden Anchor Award for fiscal year 1986. This award serves as visible recognition to commands for achieving excellence in career motivation programs. Perhaps more importantly, it demonstrates that superior retention is based on genuine concern for meeting the personal and professional needs of the men and women entrusted to your care. Winning this award allows a ship to paint its anchors gold as a symbol and inspiration to other ships. My crew represented the very best the Navy had to offer.

Photo 21-18

Large Capital Letters proudly displayed on *Excel*'s deckhouse signify receipt of Excellence Awards for minesweeping, damage control, supply management, gunnery, and command and control.
Courtesy of QM1 Richard Husted

Photo 21-19

The "Red E" on *Excel*'s stack signifies excellence in engineering.
Courtesy of QM1 Richard Husted

A contributor to the multiple awards was *Excel*'s receipt of grades of excellent and outstanding in all areas during REFTRA (refresher training). During this several-day comprehensive inspection, a horde of examiners descend upon a ship to scrutinize every aspect of operations and associated material condition of machinery and equipment. The culminating event is the "major conflagration," in which graders initiate overlapping simulated emergencies, including battle damage. *Excel* was the first Pacific Fleet wooden-hulled minesweeper to pass this difficult challenge, which requires great collective effort and prowess by a crew.

Excel also later received another unexpected award, earned while I was in command. One day a package arrived in the mail aboard ship, containing a rectangular white flag, with gold sun and border, and blue waves adorning it. When Chris Trombetta was queried by my successor about how the ship had come to receive a rare, Secretary of the Navy Energy Conservation Award, he replied, "The last chief engineer wouldn't let me use any engines."

Photo 21-20

Recipients of the annual Secretary of the Navy Energy Conservation Award (created in the wake of the oil shortages of the 1970s) are entitled to display the associated flag for a period of one year. Ships thus honored flew the flag from their mast.

Dave Bruhn had left *Excel* to attend Department Head School, and then report to the guided missile frigate *Thach* (FFG-43) as chief engineer. While *Excel*'s CHENG, he'd sought to preserve remaining life left in our old Packard propulsion engines by minimizing their usage. Allowing the operations officer use of only two of the four engines, while twisting about practicing mine hunting, was one means of doing so. In his zeal, Dave had tried to convince me to adopt one-engine operations in open waters. Using a single propulsion engine, on the port or starboard side, causes a ship to veer slightly in the opposite direction, requiring opposing left or right rudder to compensate. I nixed the idea. Helmsmen had enough to worry about adjusting for wind and wave. Regarding the award, minimal engine use meant less fuel consumption, thus the SecNav recognition.

CHANGE OF COMMAND

I'll dispense with many details related to the change of command, since sufficient information about these affairs was presented at the chapter's head. Suffice to say, it took place at the Naval Reserve Center in Seattle with music by the Fort Lewis Army Band. Commodore York was again the principal speaker. When I was finished making my remarks and reading my orders, LCDR William Weronko said a few words, and read his orders. When he was through, he turned to me and formally stated, "I relieve you, sir." We then both turned, saluted the commodore, and informed him of same.

I smiled and acted jovial, but I was empty inside. My crew was my extended family and I would miss them all horribly. The reception after the ceremony was absolutely amazing. I received a large painting of *Excel*, several plaques, the brass nameplate (with the names of preceding commanding officers and myself) from the door of the CO's cabin, and a cross-section cut from *Excel*'s wooden mast that was being replaced. The food spread was phenomenal, as was a very detailed cake in the shape of an MSO made by the ship's cooks. It was all done up so wonderfully. We eventually took our leave, and Nida, Bo, and I settled in for the long drive home to San Diego. This highlight of my career was over and would never be experienced again.

22

Replenishment Ship *Kansas City*

Photo 22-1

Battleship Battle Group Sierra; L-R: *Leftwich* (DD-984), *Bunker Hill* (CG-52), *Long Beach* (CGN-9), *Missouri* (BB-63), *Kansas City* (AOR-3), *Curts* (FFG-38), and *Hoel* (DDG-13). Author's collection

After arriving in San Diego and enjoying some leave for a few days, I was off to Newport, Rhode Island, once again. This time I would be attending the Prospective Executive Officers Course. Like the PCO Course, it was conducted by excellent instructors, and I learned a hell of a lot. There were thirty-five of us in the course, mostly LCDRs, with a sprinkling of LTs, and two CDRs, as I recall. In addition to lecture material, we learned a lot sharing experiences with one another.

While at Newport, I found out that Captain Philip Anselmo, the commanding officer of the *Kansas City*, was scheduled to be relieved in April 1987 by Captain Ernie Christensen. Christensen was the stuff of legend. The son and grandson of admirals, Naval Academy graduate and Navy pilot, he had flown "the slot" for the Blue Angels. This term refers to the center position of a (Blue Angels Flight Demonstration Team) formation, from which there are few, or no escape options in the event of a mechanical failure or mistake made at the flight controls of an adjacent aircraft only feet away.

Christensen had previously commanded Fighter Squadron VF-114 (F14 Tomcats), before taking command of "Top Gun," the Navy's elite Fighter Weapons School, and then Carrier Air Wing Two. Now he would be my boss on board *Kansas City* and I was in awe of what he had accomplished. We talked on the phone and met once, I believe. I couldn't remember ever meeting a "four-striper" who was so "down to earth." He was self-confident, humble, and cool, rolled into one. With my training completed, I packed my car and headed back cross-country to San Diego for the holidays.

Photo 22-2

1970 Public Relations photograph of LT Ernie Christensen, as #4 Slot Pilot on the Blue Angels Demonstration Team. Courtesy of Rear Admiral Christensen.

Photo 22-3

CDR Christensen, commanding officer, Navy Fighter Weapons School ("Top Gun").
Courtesy of Rear Admiral Christensen

As the New Year was ushered in, I reported aboard *Kansas City* in January 1987. Captain Anselmo gave me a warm welcome and made me comfortable almost immediately. Knowing that I had commanded an MSO, he used to kid me about its size and the fact it was made of wood, but it was all in jest, and it wasn't meant sarcastically. Sometimes I used to tease him back, very respectfully of course, about our command at sea pins being the same size so it didn't matter the ship size. He would just laugh and we'd move on to other things.

Photo 22-4

Capt. Philip S. Anselmo, USN.
USS *Constellation* (CV-64) Western Pacific 1987 cruise book

After things had settled down and I had relieved John Scott as executive officer, I didn't spend much time in my office. John was headed to the battleship *Missouri* (BB-63) as her weapons officer, an absolutely plum assignment, and I was happy for him.

Photo 22-5

CDR John Scott, USN.
USS *Missouri* Western Pacific 1987-1988 cruise book

I was familiar with an AOR, having been the first lieutenant on *Roanoke*, but even ships of the same class have subtle differences, and I wanted to learn them, so I could better serve Captain Anselmo while he was in command, and Captain Christensen after he assumed command. I also wanted to better serve the officers and crew. I had some definite thoughts on how an XO should conduct business and I started to implement them. I inspected crew berthing daily, but not just for cleanliness. I wanted our sailors to have the best berthing possible and sought ways to improve our compartments.

I spent considerable time with BMCM Post, the command master chief, learning about the sailors themselves. He definitely knew what was happening on *Kansas City*, and really cared about the welfare and well-being of the crew. Even though there was a huge age difference between the master chief and most of the crew, he related to them very well and they readily shared with him their problems and concerns.

Photo 22-6

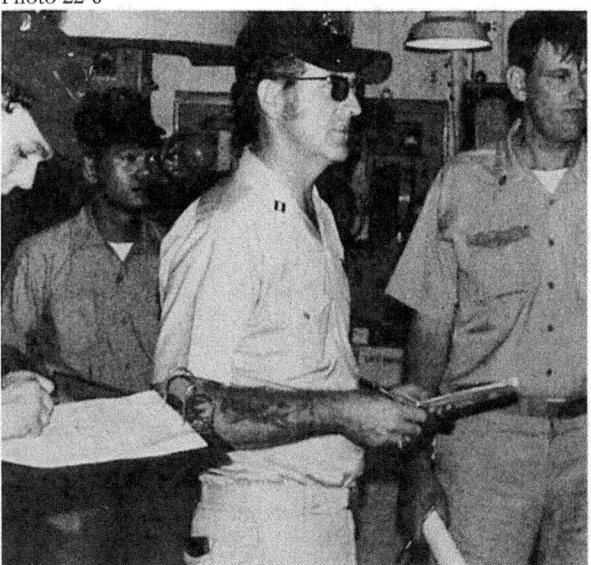

LT Jerry Spillers, conducting an inspection several years earlier, while first lieutenant aboard the ammunition ship USS *Pyro*.
USS *Pyro* (AE-24) Western Pacific 1980 cruise book

Most XOs that I had worked for and observed, usually had an officer aboard who was their confidant and "sounding board." This practice allowed the second in command to vet their thoughts and ideas in private with someone they trusted. I had a special affinity with LCDR Jerry Spillers, a Deck LDO, the senior department head, and someone who was close to me in age. Jerry and I were in boot camp at the same time, although we never knew each other. We had made chief, senior chief, and master chief at the same time, he as a boatswain's mate and me as a signalman. We had a lot in common. Jerry was an exceptional officer in all respects, and a true friend.

One day Captain Anselmo called me up to his cabin and said, "You know, Lee, we're going to sea tomorrow for UNREP exercises and I'd like you to get the ship under way." I answered, "I'd be honored to do that, Captain." He got up and shook my hand as a sign of dismissal, but as I was walking toward his door, he called after me, "perhaps your command at sea pin might expand driving an AOR." This was said with a smile, and I replied, "You never know, Captain, it just might." I did consider it an honor that he would allow me to get KC under way, and it gave me a warm feeling inside.

The next morning, we set the Sea Detail; the ship cleared the pier and stood out of the bay, like I had been doing it all my life. It was really a thrill to conn her, although I had butterflies in my stomach during the whole affair. Until then, the biggest ship I had driven was *Samuel Gompers*. It worked out well, though. From the line handlers to the engineers, everyone involved in ship propulsion, movement, and safe navigation were terrific. I had the good fortune to be a part of it.

In addition to Jerry, we had other "hard charging" department heads. Chaplain (Commander) Wayne Bouck saw to the spiritual needs of the crew, LCDR Tusing was a supply officer without peer, and LCDR Weyrick led our air detachment. Lieutenant Kelly and LCDR Hawkins saw to our medical and dental needs, respectively. Lieutenant Sipple was our LDO Engineer, LT Daily our administrative officer and navigator, and LT Izenburg the operations officer.

Our First Division officer was LTJG Bob Loken, a Deck LDO who would ultimately achieve the rank of captain, a rare accomplishment for a limited duty officer. The other junior officers were solid, enthusiastic, and reliable. We had a wealth of talent in the Chiefs Quarters, for which I was grateful. Chiefs are the backbone, the glue that holds it all together and makes it run smoothly. When you have a strong CPO Corps, your ship can do anything. The rest of our sailors, from seaman recruit to first class petty officer, worked hard and were team players. Team play was the key to *Kansas City*'s success.

CHANGE OF COMMAND

We went through a series of inspections and exercises in preparation for a deployment to WestPac that summer. In the interim, April arrived, bringing with it the change of command. The officers and crew made the ceremony come off flawlessly, and I couldn't have been more pleased. I gave Captain Christensen some time to catch his breath and then met with him to learn how he wanted me to run the ship for him as executive officer.

We sat in his cabin, over coffee, in a relaxed atmosphere that put me immediately at ease. We discussed a whole range of topics: administrative matters, personnel, and his command philosophy. He was very pleased with how clean and shipshape *Kansas City* was. He wanted me to maintain same, and to start thinking about where we could locate a gym for the crew. I needn't meet him at the quarterdeck in the mornings when he came aboard, but was to come by his cabin as soon as practical to discuss planned activities that day. He also wanted me to review the previous evening's message traffic before he arrived, and brief him if necessary, to avoid any surprises. Following these and other matters, he asked for current status on preparations for deployment.

I came away from the meeting really looking forward to going to sea with him as the skipper. After I got my normal day off and running, I had coffee with Jerry and conveyed my impressions. The captain had told me that he would be holding informal weekly meetings with the department heads. As such, I didn't feel I needed to do the same. It was easier for them, and for me, to catch them individually if the boss or I needed something. Meetings, just for the sake of meetings, always seemed superfluous to me, and I did not want to waste their time.

DEPARTURE ON DEPLOYMENT

Photo 22-7

Heavy cruiser USS *San Francisco* (CA-38) passes under the Golden Gate Bridge to enter San Francisco Bay, California, on a foggy day in December 1942. National Archives photograph #80-G-40093

All too quickly 25 July arrived, and *Kansas City* eased away from her berth, sailed under the Golden Gate Bridge, to become an integral unit of BBBG (battleship battle group) SIERRA. The battle group was comprised of USS *Missouri* (BB-63), *Bunker Hill* (CG-52), *Leftwich* (DD-984), *Long Beach* (CGN-9), USS *Hoel* (DDG-13), and USS *Curts* (FFG-38). Captain James Carney, USN, commanding *Missouri*, was intimately familiar with at least one of the battleship's escorts; having previously been CO of *Leftwich*. The Navy was then experimenting with deploying battle groups formed around battleships, in an effort to prove the viability of four WWII-era "battle wagons" brought back into service.

Secretary of the Navy, John Lehman, in his quest to increase the size of the Navy to 600 ships, had brought the *Iowa* (BB-61), *New Jersey* (BB-62), *Missouri* (BB-63), and *Wisconsin* (BB-64) out of "mothballs" amid skepticism of the value of this action. No matter, the Marines loved the battleships' naval gunfire support capabilities, and installing Tomahawk missile launchers helped quell arguments that the ships were obsolete in an era of sophisticated *Ticonderoga*-class cruisers with long-range missiles. An explosion in the No. Two 16-inch gun turret of the *Iowa* on 19 April 1989, killed forty-seven of the turret's crewmen and severely damaged the turret itself. Following an investigation into the cause, all four battleships were placed back out of service.

Photo 22-8

Battlegroups Echo and Sierra sailing together
as a demonstration of American Sea Power.
Author's collection

At one point during our cruise, Battle Group Sierra joined forces with Battle Group Echo led by the carrier *Ranger* (CV-61). While UNREPPING, we began playing songs from the movie "Top Gun" over topside loudspeakers during breakaways to honor the Old Man.

The whole battle group loved it. Complementing this arrangement, *Kansas City*'s band, Six Pac, performed when ships were alongside.

Photo 22-9

Kansas City or *Wichita* (AOR-1) refuels *Missouri*, as the cruiser *Gridley* slides into position, to replenish on the starboard side of the AOR. USS *Missouri* Western Pacific 1987-1988 cruise book

As on most UNREP ships, the captain controlled the port side while I manned the starboard side. Each bridge wing sported a white canvas sun screen. While the captain had his taken down so he could enjoy the rays, I loved mine, as my skin only burns redder and redder. Our days were long, but I absolutely loved UNREPPING. There was nothing better than "haze gray and under way" (being at sea).

Photo 22-10

Kansas City replenishing *Ranger* and *Long Beach* in the Gulf of Oman. Author's collection

SUPPORT FOR OPERATION EARNEST WILL

Our operations, following arrival in the Gulf of Oman, included support of protecting the shipping lanes in the Strait of Hormuz. As part of the Iraq-Iran War, which lasted from 1980 to 1988, Iranian naval and Revolutionary Guard forces attacked shipping making passage through the Straits of Hormuz into the Persian Gulf. The purpose of this action was to deny Iraq the sale of oil and associated revenue supporting its war efforts. Iraq, in turn, sent F-1 Mirage fighter aircraft to attack shipping headed toward Iranian ports in the Gulf to deliver cargo or load oil.

The pilots did not visually identify targets before launching missiles. Any radar contact on a vessel inside an Iraq-established "line of death," located off the Iranian coastline, was fair game. A mistaken Exocet missile attack on the frigate USS *Stark* (FFG-31) on 17 May 1987 had caused the death of thirty-seven crewmembers, the wounding of five more, and much damage to the ship.

Photo 22-11

An *Oliver Hazard Perry*-class frigate escorting one of a number of oil tankers in convoy. Two frigates accompanied each convoy into and out of the Persian Gulf via the straits. USS *Missouri* Western Pacific 1987-1988 cruise book

Map 22-1

Persian Gulf, Gulf of Oman, and surrounding countries.
University of Texas Library CIA map

Because Iranian shore-based Silkworm missile batteries covered the Straits of Hormuz, *Missouri* or a carrier, or both, on station in the Gulf of Oman, served as a "clenched fist." Iranian and Revolutionary Guard forces were attacking ships not sailing under protection of the American flag. Attack aircraft were poised to launch off the carrier, and strike Iranian naval forces should they attack a convoy.

At least four former *Excel* officers were in the Gulf at that time. I was aboard *Kansas City*, and of course, John Scott on *Missouri*. My former XO, Jim Taplett, was now first lieutenant aboard the tank landing ship *Barbour County* (LST-1195), which had towed MSOs *Enhance*, *Esteem*, and *Conquest* to the gulf to sweep ahead of the convoys. (Iran was also illegally mining international waters in an attempt to close the straits to shipping.) Finally, Dave Bruhn, my former chief engineer, was aboard the frigate *Thach* (FFG-43) as her engineering officer.

Many years later, a former *Excel* sailor, storekeeper John Mantey, would be severely injured while serving in the region. Stationed in Saudi Arabia, he was wounded during the terrorist attack on the Khobar Towers complex in Dhahran, on the night of 25 June 1996, resulting in his involuntary medical discharge from the Navy.

REPRIEVE FROM REPLENISHMENT DUTIES

Our duty of course, was to UNREP Navy ships. To provide our sailors interludes from these repetitious activities, the captain encouraged the crew to involve themselves in athletics and had me schedule periodic Sports Days. "Bubba" Tusing (the supply officer) graciously cleared out a storeroom on the port side, which Bob Loken (first division officer) turned into a first-class gym with all types of exercise equipment. On Sports Days, the skipper and chaplain led 5K runs on the main deck. Tug of war matches were also held, as were "Smokers" (three-round boxing events wearing protective head gear.)

Separately, we found time for one swim call. Laying to in the Indian Ocean, we put out protective nets for the men to swim inside. With sultry 95-degree heat, a quick swim was a welcome relief, even in those warm waters. After ninety continuous days at sea, the boss mandated a "Steel Beach" Picnic (an affair on the main deck of a ship) combined with a beer day. Hot dogs, hamburgers, potato chips, and potato salad were the order of the day, as well as two beers apiece, and Holiday Routine—which did wonders for morale.

VISIT AT SEA BY THE SECRETARY OF THE NAVY

Kansas City was honored during this part of our deployment by a visit from the Secretary of the Navy, James Henry Webb Jr. A Naval

Academy graduate and former Marine Corps officer, Webb had served as a platoon commander with Delta Company, 1st Battalion 5th Marines. He was awarded the Navy Cross for heroism in Vietnam, as well as the Silver Star, two Bronze Stars, and two Purple Hearts.

Photo 22-12

Secretary of the Navy, James Webb, and Captain Ernie Christensen.
Author's collection

Photo 22-13

Kansas City's Executive Officer with the Secretary of the Navy.
Author's collection

Webb had come to KC via helicopter from the *Ranger*. He asked Captain Christensen how it was that *Kansas City* was a service ship, but was so clean operating in the North Arabian Sea. The captain just pointed at me and graciously said, "My XO."

SHELLBACK INITIATION

Finally, it was time to take a breather in Australia. I had sailed the seas the world over but, with twenty-six years in the Navy, was still a slimy pollywog. Never having sailed across the Equator, I hadn't had the opportunity to become a trusty Shellback. How fortunate it was then, that our course to Perth, would have us cross the Equator and hold a traditional Shellback initiation. Can you imagine the sheer joy of the Shellbacks in the crew when, following a thorough search of personnel records, they found out the XO was a pollywog?

On 28 November 1987, I was given a Subpoena and Summons Extraordinary to appear before the Royal High Court of the Raging Main, and answer to the three charges. Charge I was my being a slimy pollywog; Charge II was impersonating a Shellback for over 25 years; and Charge III was insulting our most reverent commanding officer by being a slimy pollywog, when he had been a trusty Shellback for decades. I protested, of course, but my words fell on deaf ears, and I was consigned to the Shellbacks to suffer my fate.

Photo 22-14

Kansas City's executive officer, and other "slimy pollywogs" sport donkey ("jackass") ears, as they are led, crawling on non-skid deck surface, as part of a Shellback Initiation. Author's collection

It was a very long day, especially for a 45-year old with creaky knees, but I wouldn't have missed it for the world. Finally becoming a Shellback was worth every minute of the indignities that were heaped upon us. At completion, with a smile on my face, I headed to my stateroom to take a warm shower and put on clean clothes. To this day, I still carry my Shellback Card in my wallet. For that matter, I still wear my Navy Dog Tags, so there you are, shipmates.

Photo 22-15

Proof that I was finally a trusty Shellback.
Author's collection

Perth and Sydney more than lived up to their acclaim. *Kansas City* enjoyed both port visits. We first called at Perth, then spent Christmas in Sydney. It was my first time in Australia, and I was fascinated by everything. Both cities were memorable, the Aussies were friendly, and the "tinnies" (cans of beer) were cold.

Photo 22-16

Perth, Australia, rising proudly from the banks of the Swan River.
USS *Missouri* (BB-63) Western Pacific 1987-1988 cruise book

Photo 22-17

View of Sydney's famed opera house and harbor bridge, approaching the port city.
USS *Missouri* (BB-63) Western Pacific 1987-1988 cruise book

All too soon we weighed anchor, and returned to UNREPPING. On the way to the North Arabian Sea, we again crossed the Equator, but this time at the International Date Line. Thus, on 5 January 1988, we all became Golden Shellbacks, a singular honor that only happens rarely. On this, the back leg of our deployment, we had an interesting dynamic. The commanding officer of the *Bunker Hill*, Captain Philip M. Quast, was selected for rear admiral. Up until then, the CO of *Missouri* had been in charge. The changes were worked out above my paygrade, and we retained our Battleship Battle Group Sierra designation.

Photo 22-18

Rugged landscape meets blue ocean along eastern coast of Australia.
USS *Missouri* (BB-63) Western Pacific 1987-1988 cruise book

Sailing under the Golden Gate at deployment's end, we felt much pride. *Kansas City* had performed magnificently, as evidenced by our receipt of the commander, Service Group One Battle Efficiency Award. By this action, Rear Admiral Toney signaled that he considered us the most battle-ready ship in the group. It was a perfect capstone to an outstanding deployment. It was certainly great to be back home with our loved ones. My remaining time on KC was short, and I knew orders to go ashore would be forthcoming.

I was doing paperwork in my stateroom one afternoon, when I received notification from Radio that the Commander's Selection list was out, and I was on it. I thought the RMs were pulling my leg because I wasn't even eligible yet. Sure enough though, my name was on the list. Quite frankly, I was shocked. I was early selected for promotion by a full year. Captain Christensen frocked me to commander (pinned on my new rank, without associated pay until official date of promotion) with help from Jerry Spillers. I called Nida, gave her the good news, and said we would celebrate the coming weekend when I drove home.

Our weekend was spent having fun, along with my mom. After returning to the ship, I called my detailer to discuss my forthcoming orders. I could either be enrolled as a student at the Naval Post Graduate School in Monterey, California, or attend the College of Naval Warfare (senior officer's course) at the Naval War College in Newport, Rhode Island. I opted to go to the Naval War College, a decision I never regretted. In July 1988, I turned over executive officer duties aboard *Kansas City*, and headed home to San Diego.

23

Naval War College

Photo 23-1

Luce Hall of the U.S. Naval War College, which overlooks Narragansett Bay, Newport, Rhode Island, March 1970.
National Archives photograph #K-82130

My year as a student at the United States Naval War College was a great experience, and a broadening one in which I was exposed to ideas and an expansive world outside my previous sphere. The college had been established on 6 October 1884, under the stewardship of Commodore Stephen B. Luce, its first president, and faculty members Tasker H. Bliss (a future Army chief of staff), James R. Soley (a future assistant secretary of the Navy), and Captain Alfred Thayer Mahan. In 1890, Mahan published *The Influence of Sea Power upon History, 1660–1783*, a revolutionary analysis of the importance of naval power as a factor in the rise of the British Empire.

Photo 23-2

Engraving of Alfred Thayer Mahan after a sketch by Gribayeitoff, 1894, while he commanded USS *Chicago*; and a formal portrait as a flag officer. Mahan retired in 1896, but his reputation as a historian and strategist led to further employment, including service on the Naval War Board during the Spanish-American War. NHHC photograph #NH 48058 on left, and an unnumbered one on the right

The Naval War College, one of four service colleges (the others being its Army, Air Force, and Marine Corps counterparts), was the first of this group able to confer a master's degree upon students who successfully completed the curriculum. Prior to this, officers at the war college could take concurrent classes at Salve Regina in Newport, to earn a master's degree. The Catholic liberal arts college, founded in 1947, was sanctioned by the New England Association of Schools and Colleges—the same organization that accredited America's "Ivy League" Schools and the Naval War College.

Photo 23-3

Salve Regina College, founded by the Sisters of Mercy in 1947.
Author's collection

The academic year in which I was a student, 1988-1989, was the first time that the War College conferred a master's degree. The MS in National Security and Strategic Studies that I received, was augmented by a second master's degree in International Relations from Salve Regina University, obtained by attending night classes. (This was quite a step up from a kid who had hated junior and senior high school.) There was a lot of writing at NWC and that is something I prided myself on. Yet try as I may, and believe me I worked hard, the best grade I was able to achieve was a B+. That's not shabby, but such grades do not "a distinguished graduate make," let alone Highest Distinction. My grades at Salve Regina sort of mirrored those at the war college.

Photo 23-4

Admiral William J. Crowe, Jr., USN.
Naval History and Heritage photograph #NH 105120-KN

Professional development accompanied our academic work at the Naval War College, which included distinguished speakers. By far the most impressive and unassuming of these was Admiral William J. Crowe. As chairman of the Joint Chiefs of Staff, he articulated a brilliant, clear view of world affairs without resorting to notes of any kind. Rather than stand behind the podium, he unbuttoned his dress blue blouse and sat on the edge of the stage floor, above our seating in the auditorium, with his legs dangling. He talked to us about the Navy and its place in the world order—simply, clearly, and directly.

Those familiar with the admiral's extraordinary career, may know that his first command was of the Navy's then newest diesel submarine, the USS *Trout* (SS-566). This followed much experience in submarines, advanced education, and assignments to very important duties ashore. These included George Washington University Law School and Stanford University; flag lieutenant and aide to the commander of the U.S. Atlantic Fleet Submarine Force at New London, Connecticut; assistant to the Naval Aide to President Dwight D. Eisenhower; and personal aide to the Deputy Chief of Naval Operations for Plans, Policy and Operations. I could go on, but you get the point. Of particular interest to me was that his initial sea duty had been aboard the destroyer minesweeper USS *Carmick* (DMS-33).

JOINT DUTY ASSIGNMENT

In May 1989, with graduation less than a month away, I and other students were working on our follow-on assignments. For "Navy types" it was mandated that we have a "Joint Service tour," assignment to another service or organization outside the Navy. I was first proposed by my detailer for NATO staff duty in Brussels, Belgium, as a nuclear weapons coordinator. This prospect was quite exciting, but the officer I would have relieved, extended his tour. Next, NORAD in Colorado Springs, Colorado, but the incumbent there also remained in place. Finally, I was proposed assignment to the Defense Nuclear Agency in Alexandria, Virginia. If selected, I would be stationed in Hawaii, serving as the director's personal liaison to commander in chief, Pacific.

I was requested to travel to Washington, D.C. for an interview with the director, Vice Adm. John T. Parker, USN. At the appointed time and place I presented myself to the admiral's aide, also a full commander, and stated I had an appointment. He looked at me with some disdain, and remarked off handedly that the admiral didn't need a former Master Chief representing him to a 4-star Admiral in Hawaii. I replied that I was an early selectee for commander and had held command at sea, while he had not. As my blunt reply sort of set him "back on his heels," the admiral summoned me into his office.

The interview lasted about 45 minutes and was relaxed and cordial. I happened to notice a copy of *Surface Warfare Magazine* lying on his desk, opened to an article I had written about early command. When the interview ended, the admiral thanked me, and said he would be in touch. The next morning, the phone rang; it was my detailer. I had been accepted for the liaison to the CincPac position, and could expect my orders within the next couple of days.

24

Defense Nuclear Agency

Photo 24-1

Aerial view of Johnston Atoll and Sand Island.
Author's collection

When the Foley family got off the plane in Honolulu, we were met by a young lady named Martha Rodgers. She was yeoman second, and would be my secretary during my tour. She presented Nida, Bo, and me with the traditional leis, and told us our Navy housing would not be available for about ten days. Accordingly, the Navy had arranged a suite for us at the Hilton Hawaiian Village on Waikiki until we could move into our quarters in Pearl City. Once ensconced, we went down to view the beach, and bought Bo his first boogie board.

Living in the hotel was great. We ate out at some of the many restaurants in Waikiki or sometimes opted for room service. One night as we dined at a torch-lit restaurant open to the beach, our Filipina waitress asked Nida if she was a local. Without batting an eye, Nida looked at her with a smile and replied, "No, I'm imported." This started a friendship between the two women.

I worked in the same building at Camp H. M. Smith that housed CincPac (commander in chief, Pacific). There was an office for me, one for Martha, and a conference room, all connected. Martha was highly organized, extremely efficient, and detail oriented. She was always a step ahead of me, as we took care of the boss back in Washington, D.C., and represented DNA's interests.

Admiral Huntington Hardisty, CincPac, was a naval aviator, who had commanded the replenishment ship *Savannah* (AOR-4) and carrier *Oriskany* (CVA-34). Shortly after assuming my duties, Martha arranged for me to call on him and present myself as the new personal liaison for the director of the Defense Nuclear Agency. Martha had provided a brief biography of my career to the admiral's aide, so we spent a few minutes talking AORs. I next called on Rear Admiral Toney, who was responsible for CincPac logistics and security. I assured both admirals I was available 24/7 if I could assist the staff in any way.

My job, while not overly taxing, was multi-faceted. I was tasked with maintaining elevated levels of awareness in nuclear safety, security, and survivability as a strategic planning specialist. Part of this involved working closely with the commanding officer of Johnston Atoll (an Air Force colonel). Related duties included arranging for congressional delegations to visit CincPac and be briefed on DNA initiatives. I also occasionally briefed non-congressional visitors, and had final authority for granting classified visits to the Lawrence Livermore and Los Alamos Laboratories, as well as the Nevada Testing Site.

JOHNSTON ATOLL

Johnston Atoll consists of four small islands, Johnston, Sand, North (Akau) and East (Hikina) which, located approximately 700 miles southwest of Honolulu, was designated a Naval Defense Sea Area and Airspace Reservation. The Defense Nuclear Agency oversaw the atoll. Personnel there were employed by DNA, belonged to a tenant government service agency, worked for a military contractor, or were assigned to the atoll in a base operating support role.

The main island, Johnston (about 690 acres in size), was the base for all operations and management activities supporting host and tenant missions. The site was formerly used for the testing of nuclear weapons in the late 1950s and throughout the 1960s. In early 1971, the Army leased forty acres to store chemical weapons, formerly held in Okinawa. Stocks of "Agent Orange" (an herbicide and defoliant chemical) were also brought from Southeast Asia and stored there until the late 1970s.

In 1973, the Defense Nuclear Agency assumed control of the atoll. A dozen years later, construction of the Johnston Atoll Chemical Agent Disposal System (JACADS) began in 1985. In June 1990, chemical demilitarization operations commenced. I played a key role in this effort by coordinating the retrograde of chemical weapons from Germany and the Solomon Islands to Johnston for "demilling." As part of my duties, I usually spent one-to-two days a month on the atoll to monitor activity and keep the DNA director apprised of progress.

Photo 24-2

Johnston Atoll Chemical Agent Disposal System Plant.
Author's collection

LOS ALAMOS AND LAWRENCE LIVERMORE

After settling in to my new assignment, I asked Martha to set up an extensive itinerary that would take me back to DNA Headquarters in Washington, D.C., for three days of orientation; followed by official visits to Los Alamos and Lawrence Livermore Laboratories; and concluding with a formal visit to the Nevada Test Site. The primary mission of the sites known collectively as Sandia National Laboratories is to develop, engineer, and test non-nuclear components of nuclear weapons. The primary facility is located on Kirtland Air Force Base in Albuquerque, New Mexico, and the other in Livermore, California. My tour of the labs and the associated Nevada National Security Site was fascinating.

The 1,360-square-mile site in Nevada is located about sixty-five miles northwest of Las Vegas. Within the barren, desert site is the mysterious "Area 51" and Groom Lake, a highly classified Air Force remote detachment from Edwards Air Force Base in California. Although the official name for the facility is Homey Airport and Groom Lake, it is also known as just Area 51, Dreamland, or Paradise Ranch. The Air Force will neither confirm nor deny what really happens at this remote, top secret, base. However, it is now known that it involves "Black Projects," including the development and testing of experimental aircraft and weapons systems. The Lockheed U-2 ultra-high altitude, reconnaissance aircraft was developed and tested there.

Photo 24-3

EP-X-U-2 Experimental electronics patrol aircraft in flight.
National Archives photograph #KN-25621

I was shown the Project Sedan site where a shallow underground nuclear test was conducted as part of Operation PLOWSHARE, a program to investigate the use of nuclear weapons for mining, cratering, and other civilian applications. A 104 kiloton-device was buried 600 feet deep. The blast displaced more than 12 million tons of dirt and created a crater 100 meters deep and 390 meters in diameter, the largest man-made crater in the United States. I was also taken into a tunnel and one mile underground, where a device was situated. Standing there gave cause for serious introspection.

Not long after I returned to Hawaii, Major General Gerry Watson, U.S. Army (new director of the DNA) visited the liaison office, called on CincPac, and toured Johnston Atoll. I accompanied him to the atoll, while he methodically inspected the Demilling Plant. When he left to go back to Washington, he told me he was exceptionally pleased with my efforts and that it seemed I had breathed new life into the position.

I had been assigned to my duties for almost two years and both Nida and I were feeling somewhat hemmed in. We had toured the other islands in addition to Oahu, and feted my mom at Christmas with an old-fashioned luau. However, by this time, we were experiencing "Rock Fever" with an associated desire to return to the mainland. While I was exploring the possibility of splitting my tour and possibly being assigned to DNA's Field Command at Kirtland Air Force Base in Albuquerque, New Mexico, I received a call from Admiral Toney to come to his office.

SALVAGE OPERATIONS

When I arrived, the aide waved me in, and the admiral got right to the point. "Lee, we have a major situation at Johnston Atoll. The motor vessel M/V *Militobi* has become stranded and beached on Johnston and her presence is threatening retrograde operations. I need you to go out there and take care of the problem. You'll be designated as officer in charge of salvage and destruction." I said, "No problem, Admiral. I'll just have my yeoman notify the DNA director and I'll be on my way in thirty minutes." I went down to my office and asked Martha to contact DNA to let General Watson know what was going on, and to get hold of the Army folks to have their plane standing by to ferry me out to the island. I called home and let Nida know what was going on, and then drove out to the airfield and my waiting plane ride.

After arriving at Johnston and surveying the situation, I called Pearl Harbor and arranged for a salvage ship to come to the atoll. When the ship arrived, I went aboard and explained the situation. My direction to her commanding officer was to pull the 158-foot *Militobi* free and put her to sea. If the 486-ton cargo ship was seaworthy, he was to tow her to Pearl. If not, I gave him a written directive to sink her. All of this had to be done very expeditiously, because we could not afford to have retrograde operations interrupted for very long.

While I coordinated from ashore, *Militobi* was pulled off the island and moved away from the field of operations. When the CO reported to me that *Militobi* was too holed to tow back to Pearl, I directed him to tow her to deep water, break the tow, and let her sink. This was accomplished and the salvage ship headed back to Pearl. I sent a message to Admiral Toney and General Watson letting them know the mission was accomplished, and commended the CO of the salvage ship for his expeditious help. I further stated that retrograde operations had resumed and I was returning to Hawaii.

SPLIT-TOUR APPROVED

In discussing the possibility of a split-tour with my detailer, I learned there was, in fact, a position open for a commander at the Defense Nuclear Agency Field Command. I wanted to get Nida and Bo to Albuquerque and settled, so Bo could begin the new school year there rather than in Hawaii, and then have to start again in New Mexico. The detailer agreed to fund their move to Albuquerque in the summer of 1991, and I would follow them there in January 1992.

I had to fly to Albuquerque on business for DNA so I took that opportunity to find a suitable house, send a video to Nida to see if she approved, then went ahead with the purchase. The house was located in Rio Rancho, which at the time, was a "bedroom community" for people working in Albuquerque. With my business complete for DNA and the house purchased, I flew back to Hawaii, arranged for our personal belongings to be shipped to our new home courtesy of the Navy, and took leave to accompany Nida and Bo to New Mexico.

When our furniture arrived, Nida and Bo were settled, and Bo was enrolled in elementary school, I flew back to Hawaii and checked into a room at the BOQ where I would live until actually being transferred in January 1992. When the time came to depart, I paid my respects to Admirals Hardisty and Toney, thanked them for their hospitality to DNA, and asked Martha to take me to the airport. After I left, she continued to excel in all areas, making YN1 and YNC without difficulty. She was an absolute winner in all respects and I was so pleased for her.

25

Final Duty Station

Checking into the FCDNA (Field Command Defense Nuclear Agency) at Kirtland Air Force Base in Albuquerque, I was obviously familiar with its mission and a lot of the employees. When I reported in January 1992, Rear Admiral Mack Gaston, the previous director, had been relieved by Army Brigadier General Leonard D. Miller. Field Command was divided into several directorates, and I was in charge of the one primarily dealing with nuclear weapons. My boss was Navy Captain Lippincott, a quiet, unassuming aviator who was a pleasure to work for.

My primary tasks were to coordinate the world-wide program for control of the national nuclear stockpile, direct the collection and reporting of nuclear stockpile information, and manage nuclear weapons allocations. I had direct responsibility, reporting to the Joint Chiefs of Staff, for stockpile emergency verification tests and procedures. Another duty was oversight of the modernization of the Nuclear Management Information System. Every one of the military and civilian personnel that comprised my staff was an expert in his or her field. They were an awesome group.

My personal secretary was a middle-aged Hispanic lady named Lydia. In addition to her secretarial duties which she was very good at, she was the "keeper of the gate." No one got past her to see me unless I sanctioned it. Once my mom came to see me in an unclassified area, but separated from outsiders. When a senior civilian stopped by, I could hear Lydia through the door telling the visitor he would have to wait because I was with my mom. Lydia was a jewel.

DECISION TO RETIRE

In the summer of 1992, I had a year left on my assignment at Field Command, and was torn about what to do next. Did I want to just think of satisfying my desire to remain in the Navy and see what I might still achieve, or contribute to a more stable environment for our son Bo. He was then at an age when he needed two parents 24/7, not one at home, and the other assigned elsewhere. This might seem like an easy choice, but for me it was agonizing. If I retired it would be giving up a way of life I'd been immersed in for over three decades. The Navy fit me like a glove. In the final analysis, I knew what had to be done. I decided that I would retire when my time was up at FCDNA, and keep doing my job to the best of my ability, while making plans for life after the Navy.

At the top of my priority list was being employed in the civilian sector from the moment I took off my uniform. I started job searching for what might be available in the Albuquerque area that would provide a decent living for my family when combined with my Navy retirement. A federal government contractor based in Albuquerque needed a personnel manager with a nuclear background to manage their contract at the Department of Energy, right on Kirtland Air Force Base. Following an interview, they offered me the job.

Nida was concerned with this possibility, and I asked for terminal leave, using accumulated time on the books instead of taking cash value at the termination of Navy Service. Captain Lippincott approved this request, and was able to get concurrence from Field Command. I also submitted a request to the Navy to retire on 1 June 1993. Within a week, I had a letter back from Washington, approving this action and I was set. I called the contractor, and told them if they still wanted me, I could start work on the first of March and, just like that, I had the job.

The holidays went by in a blur. On 28 February 1993, I departed FCDNA on leave until my retirement ceremony on the 1st of June. While away, I worked for the contractor at DOE while I was technically still on active duty. On a gorgeous New Mexico day, with a cloudless azure blue sky, I arrived at FCDNA one last time.

RETIRMENT CEREMONY

The retirement ceremony was held in the Field Command courtyard with General Miller and Captain Lippincott conducting it. An Air Force major orchestrated the event and it was absolutely flawless. Hell, he could have been a naval officer because he did it so well. My mom, wife, and son were in attendance, naturally, as were close friends and shipmates from days gone by, co-workers from FCDNA, and local families and friends from Albuquerque and Rio Rancho.

I had a hard time getting through my retirement remarks, because the lump in my throat was so big I could barely swallow. When Nida and I crossed the gangplank for the final time, I kept a stiff upper lip, as the Brits say, and the rest is history. God Bless the United States Navy for allowing me to serve in its ranks.

Of the many special photographs taken on that day, my last in uniform, four, symbolizing family, service, and good shipmates, follow:

Final Duty Station 261

Photo 25-1

Bo, Nida, and I cutting the retirement cake.
Author's collection

Photo 25-2

My retirement Shadow Box, hand-made by Senior Chief Boatswain's Mate David Caro, USN, a shipmate from the USS *Samuel Gompers* (AD-37), using teak from the deck of the decommissioned battleship USS *Wisconsin* (BB-64).
Author's collection

Photo 25-3

Dave Bruhn (L) and Jim Taplett (R) traveled from Washington, D.C., for the retirement of their former commanding officer aboard *Excel*. Author's collection

Photo 25-4

BM1 Dutch "Buddha" Menke, USN, (Retired), a close friend from our time together aboard "FAT SAM," the destroyer tender *Samuel Gompers* (AD-37). Author's collection

Postscript

Photo Postscript-1

Beginning of the dream, and at the end of the journey; young Lee Foley at age eight, and forty-two years later, on retirement day, a sober, seasoned, senior Naval officer. Author's collection

For various reasons, I waited almost twenty-five years after retiring (1 June 1993) before attempting to put my experiences in some semblance of order that might make interesting reading. Shipmates that I have personally served with, on some of my ships and ashore, may not recall some of the incidents or situations described.

The years have tended to dim my memories of certain things, and explanations of some of the events in this book may not be exactly as they occurred. With respect to dates, I tried very hard to be accurate, but may have erred on occasion. For that I apologize and accept full responsibility, and would ask readers to forgive this simple old retired sailor for any perceived fallacies. Obviously, *MUSTANG* includes a few accounts that might be considered sea stories. It's not unusual, for the teller of such tales to begin with the declaration, "This Ain't No Bullshit," and all sailors know that such tend to include some embellishment. If I am guilty of this, it is unintentional; I may have gotten carried away by some events, as I relived them penning this book.

My goal was to share decades of Navy service and experience that could be enjoyed by Navy brethren, and others who want a glimpse of sea-going life. Many events along my lengthy path from Seaman Recruit to Commander have been omitted. Similarly, where appropriate, I have cited individuals by rank, or rate, or rating rather than by name. In *MUSTANG*, I allude to occasional differences with seniors. In no way did such snags lessen my respect for these individuals, or their skills and abilities as naval officers. I truly learned from each and every one.

A lot of my difficulties were caused by actions on my part and/or my Irish bullheadedness. Nevertheless, I thrived because I loved the Navy, never quit, and never abandoned my aspirations. If my story encourages even one young sailor to go for the "brass ring," *MUSTANG* will have been successful. It is all too easy to be put off by challenges or difficulties. Do not let that happen to you. To those of you who succeed in reaching your lofty goals, I offer this time-honored Navy accolade, "BRAVO ZULU" (Well Done).

Photo Postscript-2

Fancy knot board given Nida and me as a wedding present by BMC Manuel Gomez, USN (Retired), evidence that pride and tradition will live on in the ever-changing United States Navy.
Author's collection

About the Author

Commander Lee M. Foley, U.S. Navy (Retired) served thirty-two years on active duty, as both an enlisted man and an officer, between 1961 and 1993.

He was a Signalman as an enlisted sailor and advanced to Master Chief Petty Officer. As a Warrant Officer he climbed the ladder from WO-1 to CWO-4 as a Boatswain. Selected as a Deck Limited Duty Officer in the rank of LTJG, he was promoted up through LCDR when he applied for and was accepted as an unrestricted surface line officer.

Orders to command of USS *Excel* (MSO-439) followed much previous sea duty aboard ten ships, including amphibious, service force, salvage force, an aircraft carrier, and a destroyer. His last sea-going service was as the Executive Officer of USS *Kansas City* (AOR-3).

Commander Foley is a graduate of the Naval War College and Salve Regina University, with Master's Degrees in National Security and Strategic Studies, and International Relations, respectively. Assignment to important duties followed this education: Personal Liaison of the director of the Defense Nuclear Agency to commander in chief, Pacific, in Hawaii; and head of a directorate at the Defense Nuclear Agency's Field Command in Albuquerque, New Mexico.

Following military service, Foley worked for government contractors providing a variety of services. Later, he was the Head of Security for Sandia Casino and later was the General Manager and Chief Financial Officer for Silverwolf Casino in New Mexico and Montana, respectively. Most recently he retired as a City Manager in Alaska in 2014. He and Nida, his wife of 41 years, reside in the Philippines.

www.ingramcontent.com/pod-product-compliance
Lightning Source LLC
Chambersburg PA
CBHW051630230426
43669CB00013B/2250